Belonging and Becoming in a Multicultural World

Rutgers Series in Childhood Studies

The Rutgers Series in Childhood Studies is dedicated to increasing our understanding of children and childhoods throughout the world, reflecting a perspective that highlights cultural dimensions of the human experience. The books in this series are intended for students, scholars, practitioners, and those who formulate policies that affect children's everyday lives and futures.

Series Board

For a list of all the titles in the series, please see the last page of the book.

Belonging and Becoming in a Multicultural World

Refugee Youth and the Pursuit of Identity

LAURA MORAN

RUTGERS UNIVERSITY PRESS

NEW BRUNSWICK, CAMDEN, AND NEWARK, NEW JERSEY, AND LONDON

Library of Congress Cataloging-in-Publication Data

Names: Moran, Laura K., 1978– author.
Title: Belonging and becoming in a multicultural world : refugee youth and
the pursuit of identity / Laura K. Moran.
Description: New Brunswick : Rutgers University Press, 2019. |
Series: Rutgers series in childhood studies |
Includes bibliographical references and index.
Identifiers: LCCN 2018053055 (print) | LCCN 2019004671 (ebook) |
ISBN 9781978803077 (E-pub) | ISBN 9781978803091 (Web PDF) |
ISBN 9781978803053 (pbk. : alk. paper) | ISBN 9781978803060 (cloth : alk. paper)
Subjects: LCSH: Teenage refugees—Australia. | Assimilation (Sociology)—
Australia. | Multiculturalism—Australia. | Group identity—Australia.
Classification: LCC HV640.4.A78 (ebook) | LCC HV640.4.A78 M67 2019 (print) |
DDC 305.235086/9140994—dc23
LC record available at https://lccn.loc.gov/2018053055

A British Cataloging-in-Publication record for this book is
available from the British Library.

♾ The paper used in this publication meets the requirements of the American
National Standard for Information Sciences—Permanence of Paper for
Printed Library Materials, ANSI Z39.48-1992.

www.rutgersuniversitypress.org

Manufactured in the United States of America

For Georgia and William

CONTENTS

Belonging and Becoming in a
Multicultural World

Introduction

One night during the early stages of my ethnographic research, I stood outside a school auditorium before an African dance performance. Tino playfully accused Samah of "freestylin' it," in reference to her speaking Dinka and Swahili dialects merged with English. Samah was wearing what she described as "traditional African clothing" and listening to American hip hop music. A different day, same school, Vic teased Elijah that she would "hit him up African style" if he didn't get out of her seat. Elijah responded by pointing out how "annoying" it is when Vic speaks in her "West African language mixed with English." "I understand her, but it's annoying," he said, "she doesn't even know the history of her own people." Vic looked down. "If you're from different countries you're still African. That's OK, right?" she said.

In another part of town, while I sat with them in the waiting room of their doctor's office, three siblings of Karen descent discussed how best to characterize their own sense of national and cultural belonging. The eldest, Catalina, explained, "I just call myself Karen. I am not white people." Her younger brother, Thakin, answered, "I'm Australian. I wanna be Aussie!" And Jessica, the youngest, offered, "I have both. We like both foods now, we like Aussie food too, don't we?" They went back and forth in this way for some time. Each sibling was challenging one another's perspective on what establishes belonging—what elements of a person's experience or background constitute a sense of identity.

The subtle complexity expressed in these exchanges presented itself again and again throughout the course of my research among young people from refugee backgrounds in Brisbane, Australia. It was certainly apparent that a range of cultural, ethnic, and racial influences coalesced in the formulations of these young people's sense of themselves. However, they oscillated in their expressions of identity between emphasizing their ability to pick and choose from such influences—to "freestyle," as some of them described it—and downplaying this

1

flexibility in favor of presenting their racial and ethnic identity as fixed and binding. The contradiction this represented, whereby young people demonstrated both reluctance and enthusiasm in their acknowledgment of certain aspects of their background, surprised me.

I'll confess that I came to my research not devoid of the naive assumption that young people, and particularly young people of migrant and refugee backgrounds, were somehow color-blind and without national and cultural bias or allegiance. That with the frequency and intensity of their "multicultural" encounters and with the broad range of cultural influences that may be present in their peer groups alone, I mistakenly believed, racial, ethnic and national background would become increasingly less significant. It's not that I thought, exactly, that these young people were just too hip and broad-minded for race to achieve any level of significance in their mind-set, it's just that I thought something else would dominate. Other things would matter more. A "culture" among them, less clearly divided along racial and ethnic lines, would reveal itself.

To a degree, this notion played out. Young people living in contexts of heightened diversity have been shown to "work the hyphens" of their identities (Fine 1994, quoted in Harris 2013). Strict parameters around racial and ethnic lines appear to have dissipated and been redrawn as young people create networks across division and through overlapping connections to class, culture, gender, language, religion, sexuality, interests, and the list goes on (Harris 2013, 4). My informants were no exception. They identified as African-Australian, Australian-Sudanese, Karen-Australian, Karen-Karen, and a number of other ever-evolving combinations, though perhaps the most pointed example was the young Sudanese man who identified himself as "Blackanese."

As the term "Blackanese" suggests, and as I also came to understand in the time I spent with them, despite the sophistication of their refusal to fit neatly within ethnic and racial categories, "race" for these young people, was a big deal. They talked about race; they talked about skin color; they engaged with and made fun of racism; they critiqued one another's representations of racialized selves—and they did so, on a near constant basis, with humor in playful exchanges between one another. As the course of my research unfolded it became harder and harder to deny that, indeed, to these young people it kind of was about race—at least in large part.

The nature of my inquiry began to shift—if race is a dominant theme among these young people, why? And what do I do with this understanding? How does it fit within the current body of youth scholarship which seeks to demonstrate young people at the forefront of multicultural success in forging connections across ethnic and racial divides? And more critically, what does a preoccupation with race and ethnicity say about the ideas this most recent scholarship drives toward countering—ideas that posit the multicultural project is doomed to failure as evidenced by racial conflict and violence erupting the world over and often with young people placed squarely in the crux of the crisis (Thomas 2011)?

As I muddled through these questions, and in describing my research to others, people would sometimes fixate on the degree to which these young people were "integrating" into what was broadly conceived as Australian culture, or instead, preserving and honoring their ethnic heritage. I began to see how my research informants encountered this fixation, or variations of it, in small but incessant ways in their everyday environments. Also, I saw how, imbedded in this preoccupation with integration versus preservation, young people were implicitly framed by their racial and ethnic background. What I found was that not only did skin color and ethnic background matter to these young people, but that it mattered in part because they encountered it so frequently in the framing of "multiculturalism" that loomed large in the terrain of their daily lives. In their foregrounding and alternate denial of race and ethnicity as central to their own sense of identity, these refugee youths were demonstrating a degree of sociopolitical savvy. Their identity work demonstrates what I describe as a *dynamic responsiveness* to social context, through which they reformulate the expectations of those aspects of the broader culture that intimately affect their daily lives.

In the social landscape of Australian multiculturalism, young people from refugee and migrant backgrounds are exposed to a range of competing messages and expectations. On one hand, there are ongoing pressures to rapidly absorb and integrate into Australian society, and at the same time, young people perceive and experience a sometimes celebratory and overt racialization of their identities in accordance with an ethic of tolerance (Garner 2010). In response, young people's representations of identity surfaced in relationship to these messages of integration and tolerance which underlie the broad moral agenda of Australian multiculturalism. Young people from refugee backgrounds, living in the nitty-gritty of multicultural context, perceive the management of their diversity in a way that infiltrates their identity making practices. They absorb, reframe, work within, and reach beyond the sometimes binding framework of the Australian multicultural message as they forge a sense of themselves. And they do it together by bouncing off one another in exchanges, sometimes playful and teasing, and sometimes tense and heated.

Moments such as those described in the opening vignettes emerged as central, in my observations, to young people's self-representations through which a sense of cultural location and social belonging was approached. Tino and Samah, Vic and Santino, Catalina, Thakin and Jessica, through their friendly jabs, casual observations, and varied references to symbolic cultural resources and influences, revealed much about the wide-ranging social contexts in which their lives unfolded and their sense of their own place within those contexts. One of the primary aims of this book is to understand the significance of such formulations and examine how they relate to the making of identities and the broader social environments in which they transpire.

Youth in the World

This book is a youth-centered ethnography. It's about young people. It's about multiculturalism and the refugee experience. It's about race and ethnicity. But at its core, this book is about identity. Over the course of my research, it became apparent that in their framing of how they see and represent themselves, young people were in part responding to the messages with which they were most regularly confronted in their social environments. With this observation, I acknowledge also that this is what we all do. We formulate opinions, ideas, and a sense of ourselves against the backdrop of the sociopolitical context of our lives and the issues and questions that frame them.

In other words, our sense of ourselves in not formulated exclusively by our experiences, but also by our interpretation of the way those experiences are framed by others. As we filter and interpret the various ways in which our lives are framed, our sense of identity—how we conceive of and portray ourselves—ultimately allows us to cultivate and foster a sense of belonging. And not only does a particular social and political landscape impact upon the varied ways in which we develop a sense of identity, but the reciprocal effect—how our sense of who we are can affect the nature of that landscape—is also revealing. At its ultimate extension, exploring the identity-making practices of a group of people helps us to understand what is experienced as significant, prominent, or pervasive in social context. The identity-making practices of refugee youth in Australia have an important story to tell. They shed light upon barriers to inclusion in multicultural context, the impact of race and nationalism, and the significance of both the refugee experience and global networks in young people's lives.

These are inarguably issues worthy of our critical consideration in the current Western social and political landscape. With numbers of refugees and asylum seekers in the world surpassing 65 million, 28 million of whom are young people (UNHCR 2012), and a post-Trump, post-Brexit sociopolitical landscape to which issues of migration and race are central, the refugee crisis is one of grave and global consequence. We need not look far on our news and social media feeds—which abound with gut-wrenching images and audio soundtracks of children being torn from their parents at the U.S. border; children, usually boys, held in grim jail-like detention facilities; and young Syrian refuges crossing the dessert alone or left dust and blood covered on an ambulance chair—to see how central and how profoundly politicized children are to this crisis (Kelly 2018; Sherwood and Malik 2014; Tharoor 2016; Whyte 2018).

Moreover, the notion of youth agency, the circumstances in which this agency emerges, and the ways in which it is enacted, most recently highlighted in the uprising and political mobilization of youth in response to gun violence in the United States, is a demonstrated barometer of the culturally significant moments and vital social issues with which we are faced (Heim, Truong and St. George 2018). The book speaks to these two increasingly important global debates; the upswing of youth as social actors and the mass migration and resettlement of refugees.

Book Overview

In this book, I explore the everyday lives of young refugees, predominantly from North East Africa and South East Asia. I present material exploring their daily interactions in the locations where they most regularly hung out, such as at school, home, shopping centers, bus and train stops, and parties. I explore young people's exchanges with one another, as well as a range of interactions and experiences that unfolded within their broader social environments. This exploration of the dynamics of their identity making process is set against an analysis of the Australian multicultural agenda and its increasingly contested political and broad moral framework.

My ethnographic research was collected over a four-year period, during which I lived and conducted fieldwork in the metropolitan area of the northern and central suburbs of Brisbane, Australia. I first met a number of the young people with whom I conducted research through my employment as an after-school program coordinator at a nonprofit community center in the northern suburbs of Brisbane. Through this role, I gained access to a number of schools and met the core group of young people whose opinions and experiences provide the material for this book.

The observations I collected focused on the dynamics and tensions of belonging that were evident in how young people defined themselves and their sense of social place in the context of living with diversity. In particular, I explore young people's racialized and ethnic self-representations and how they are both emphasized and denied as young people seek belonging within friendship groups, through wider networks, and against the background of the pushes and pulls of Australian multiculturalism.

My principal aim in presenting this material is twofold. First, I hope to shed light upon the complex dynamics through which young people of refugee and migrant backgrounds cultivate a sense of self and belonging. I am interested in how they engage and respond to the treatment of their racial, ethnic, and cultural difference through dynamic responsiveness to a multicultural framework that purports to foster their inclusion. Second, I examine young people's identity-making practices and the tensions that emerge in their pursuit of belonging in terms of how such dynamics speak to and reflect upon cultural pluralism in the Australian context. What does it mean for the potential of inclusion in the Australian national space? And beyond this, what might such dynamics mean for the future lives of these young people, or others who must similarly build lives out of uncertainty and displacement in the context of articulations of national belonging?

The theoretical thrust of the book focuses on the ways in which youth identity is formulated through dynamic responsiveness to sociopolitical context. I demonstrate this dynamic in the ethnographic chapters of the book, which detail what I'll describe as young people's hybridized and essentialized representations of identity. Those representations emerge as a form of "symbolic capital" (Bourdieu 1986) in dialogue with the messages of integration and tolerance inherent to multicultural discourse. In particular, I explore how race and ethnicity might be mobilized by research participants in their alignments with and against one another as they seek belonging to both national and diasporic contexts.

In chapter 1 I will further detail the ethnographic context and methods that led to the book and introduce the theoretical foundations through which I interpret and analyze the research. Chapter 2 approaches the Australian context in greater depth. Here I detail Australian immigration policy and its culmination in today's modern, multicultural framework and speak to the particulars of Australian multiculturalism in comparison to other relatively new, settler societies. It is here that I locate the ethnographic setting and the Australian multicultural agenda, within the context of critical debates around immigration, race, and resettlement throughout the Western world. Through this discussion, I will detail what I refer to as key discourses of Australian multiculturalism—integration and tolerance—and how young people encounter these discourses in their everyday lives. I go on to look at the backgrounds of the majority of participants and what it might mean for them to be of refugee backgrounds in Australia. In chapter 3 I provide the theoretical framework of the book and engage with the relevant literature on youth and identity to which the analysis of my ethnographic material responds. I argue that through their engagement with the central multicultural ideals of integration and tolerance, young people draw upon their racial and ethnic identity to articulate a sense of themselves that responds to the discourses of multiculturalism they encounter in social context.

These foundational chapters provide the background to make meaning out of my research participants' everyday practices and the negotiations of belonging in which they engage. Throughout the ensuing ethnographic chapters of the book, I demonstrate how young people answer the competing calls to both integrate with the white Australian population and to enshrine their ethnic and racial heritage, through what I describe as their hybridized and essentialized representations of identity. Chapter 4 considers young people's identity work in multicultural context through their everyday practices of making and describing their social relationships. I explore the role of choice in friendship making and choosing romantic partners as a process by which young people emphasize and downplay a sense of racialized, ethnic identity in engagement with the discourses of multiculturalism they encounter in their everyday lives.

In chapter 5 I depart from the everyday practices of identity making and explore the more exceptional and explicitly self-conscious practice of performing identity. I examine how young people adapt various cultural resources, concepts, and associations, both locally and globally, in ways that are not obvious or straightforward for cultivating ethnic and racial affiliations and engaging with the complexity of multiculturalism in their own lives. Chapter 6 takes a broad view of these young people's identity practices in the political realm of national context as they engage with issues of race and citizenship. In this chapter I explore the complexities of young people's negotiation, interpretation, and adaptation of experiences with race and racism, as well as the flexibility they demonstrated and allowed one another in their engagement with citizenship. In chapter 7 I conclude by presenting the major themes of the book and their implications for both deepening our understanding of identity formation among transnational diasporas and refugee youth, and for the potential of inclusion in the context of modern, multicultural societies. My focus on what I describe as dynamic responsiveness allows for a wider lens that considers, not only what these young people are doing as they cultivate a sense of identity and belonging, but also the often overlooked reasons as to why.

If we push beyond identity, we garner understanding about both the experience of racial, ethnic and national belonging and inclusion among young people of minority backgrounds, and about the social and political backdrop of the places from which such experiences emerge. In all, and through a broader lens, I seek to explore and illuminate the varied and complex ways people, and young people especially, may engage with and respond to the contemporary world in pursuit of social belonging. This book offers one depiction of how that happens among a community of refugee young people in Brisbane, Australia.

Layered with complexity, this a story about how young refugees define themselves within their new lives in Australia. Australia endorses multiculturalism—a multiculturalism that contains a central and complex paradox. It promotes integration on one hand, while simultaneously celebrating tolerance for difference on the other. This book takes up the practices of identity making with a new theoretical emphasis on young people's dynamic responsiveness to that multicultural context, as they alternatively emphasize their fluid, open or hybridized qualities, and their fixed or essentialized ones. Dynamic responsiveness builds upon current research on young people's everyday processes of making and unmaking identities by establishing, not only that such processes occur, but how lived context and youth engagement with sociopolitical messages motivates those processes. In doing so, it helps us to understand how the mechanisms designed to foster inclusion can work in unanticipated ways as young people forge their own pathways to belonging and becoming.

1

Fieldwork and Research Foundations

Early in 2008, after having lived in Brisbane and volunteered extensively with the refugee community for approximately two years, I was hired to coordinate and run an after-school tutoring and mentoring service for high school–aged young people from refugee backgrounds. At approximately the same time I embarked on a doctoral program in which I planned to conduct research among young people from refugee backgrounds. In the not uncommonly serendipitous unfolding of ethnographic research, my work in the after-school program coincided with what were the early stages of my doctoral research. This allowed me to get to know a number of young people who would eventually act as key informants when I formally began my fieldwork one year later.

Over the course of my fieldwork, I conducted participant observation at this after-school program as well as at a local high school. After getting to know the young people in these formal settings, I began spending time with them in their homes and at the places where they regularly hung out, such as local shopping malls, the city center, parks, community halls, train and bus stations, family gatherings, and parties organized by and for young people. In Chapter 2 I detail the Australian context and its significance for conducting this research. Here, I introduce Brisbane, the key sites in which my research unfolded, and the young people I came to know in the process.

Research Setting and Methods

Brisbane, the capital city of Queensland, on the eastern coast of Australia, has a population of approximately 2 million. Like most of Australia's urban centers, Brisbane can be described as a diverse multicultural hub (Brisbane City Council 2018). According to Brisbane City Council's Multicultural Communities Program, approximately 2,000 people from refugee backgrounds arrive in Brisbane each year; the number of people from refugee backgrounds residing in Brisbane at the time of writing the report was 30,000 (Community Life Program 2002). This included people from recently arrived refugee populations in Africa, the Middle East, and Asia, as well as an aging population of people who arrived from Continental Europe as refugees following World War II and Vietnamese people who have continued to arrive in Brisbane as refugees since the Vietnam War (Community Life Program 2002). Approximately 23 percent of Brisbane's population was born overseas, and 17 percent of households speak a language other than English (Brisbane City Council 2018). The number of people from refugee backgrounds settling in Brisbane continues to increase.

Despite its increasing diversity however, in comparison to Australia's larger urban centers such as Melbourne and Sydney, Brisbane has a relatively small refugee population. For my purposes, this made Brisbane an optimal fieldwork context. Areas of lesser cultural diversity reveal the complexities of social cohesion that emerge less directly through national discourses, broad stereotypes, and media representations (Forrest and Dunn 2011, 450). When I embarked on my doctoral research, Brisbane had experienced a relatively recent influx of non-English-speaking refugees. Since 2003, Brisbane has seen a surge in Sudanese refugees entering Australia as humanitarian entrants (Shakespeare-Finch and Wickham 2010, 24). More recently, since approximately 2007 Brisbane began receiving rapidly increasing numbers of Karen refugees, from Burma, who have been settled in large numbers on the Northside of the city (Queensland Health 2012). The majority of the young people represented in this book are of Sudanese and Karen refugee backgrounds.

As in many "river cities," Brisbane is roughly broken into the "Northside" and "Southside," based upon the Brisbane River, which bisects the city. The time I spent with young people at the after-school program, the school, their homes, and various other places was spread across a range of suburbs. There was minimal variance between these suburbs in terms of the socioeconomic status in which the schools and homes of young people were located. The families of my research participants had low incomes and generally lived in government-subsidized housing with large numbers of extended family members and friends rotating in and out of the homes (see Department of Immigration and Citizenship [DIAC] 2011b, 36; see also Australian Government 2012). The after-school program was located only a few suburbs away from where I was living at the time. Many of the young people whom I met there lived close by. As a result, impromptu visits were frequent, and our families came to be close over the course of my research.

I initially came to know the majority of the young people I discuss here through an after-school program and a local high school. What I refer to throughout the book by the pseudonym "Paddington High" is a Catholic coeducational secondary school located in Brisbane city with approximately thirty students from refugee backgrounds enrolled. Paddington High offers both academic and vocational training, and it emphasizes social justice in access policy and promotion of the school. Nineteen of the young people represented here were enrolled in this school. Of these, eighteen were African—fifteen from Sudan, two from Uganda, one from Sierra Leone—and one was Anglo-Celtic Australian.

The after-school program, which I refer to as "Kedron Club," was located at a community center on the Northside of Brisbane. It was originally designed to provide homework support to students from refugee backgrounds and evolved to additionally provide mentoring and social support. It was a voluntary program that young people would regularly attend with their friends, where they sometimes made new connections. Anywhere between four and thirty young people attended during a typical session. Twenty of my research informants participated in this program; they came from Burma, Thailand, Sudan, and Papua New Guinea.

Research Methods

The primary methods I employed in my "hanging out" research (see also Ngo 2010, 13), or more formally, ethnographic fieldwork, were participant observation and semistructured individual and group interviews. The ethnographic perspective is fundamentally an attempt to understand the world from the point of view of social actors, rather than the a priori categories of the researcher. My approach to the field research was designed to provide a window into young people's lives and their interactions with one another in the *places* where they most regularly spent time together.

I designed and implemented the after-school program and was formally employed as its coordinator. Balancing my role as researcher with one of explicit authority as Kedron Club coordinator presented a unique set of ethnographic challenges (see also Back 1996, 22; Madden 2010). While Kedron Club provided entry into the lives of a number of young people in the initial stages of my research, those young people knew me and regarded me as an authority figure. I worried that this might make them more reluctant to share aspects of their lives or feel pressure to participate. Because of this, rather than targeting individuals, I explained my research to the group as a whole and assured them that their participation was voluntary and not in any way required. And then I waited. As I had coordinated the after-school club for a year before beginning fieldwork meant that time was on my side. Over the course of that year, my relationship with many of the young people became mutually familiar and comfortable.

My official role in Kedron Club also meant that I had to pay particular attention to how I constructed fieldwork so as not to traverse the boundaries between a place where students came to relax, get advice, and get assistance with their schoolwork, and a place where I was seeking to extract insights and information. Because of this, I spent the majority of my fieldwork with the young people

I knew from Kedron Club outside of this program setting. While group interactions were observed, and recorded with participant permission during program hours, the bulk of the more in-depth exploration of various themes, including asking clarifying questions and conducting interviews, was undertaken in less formal atmospheres. In other words, I had to make a concerted effort to carve out time where my only role was as a researcher and I was not also undertaking the task of imposing order.

Of course, my role in Kedron Club was not the only power dynamic at play in this research. While there is always an implicit power differential between researcher and participant, it is markedly exacerbated when the participant is a young person. While I was initially regarded as a teacher by the young people, I was regarded as a "young" teacher, which helped in building trust and rapport. I was sometimes challenged when I told young people that I was not a teacher to "prove it" by doing things that they didn't think a teacher would do, like swearing at other students or calling them derogatory names (usually based on skin color, which I will discuss later). I did not do these things. But I did consciously attempt to establish myself as a researcher rather than a teacher.

In a final note on the power dynamics that impacted upon my study, as an American, I enjoyed some privileged status among these young people—they were intrigued by America generally and they expressed some affinity toward me for also being from "somewhere else." However, my position as a Western, Anglo, female researcher inevitably established an immediate division between myself and my informants. I sought to compensate for these dynamics during fieldwork as much as I could, but my principal strategy was to maintain awareness of these reflexive concerns and how they influenced my time spent with the young people conducting fieldwork, as well as my interpretation and analysis throughout the research process (see Denzin and Lincoln 2003, 26).

Despite these challenges, which are inherent in the nature of ethnographic research, hanging out in Paddington High, in Kedron Club and in the "spaces between home and school" (Noble, Poynting, and Tabar 1999, 32) proved that these were revealing sites through which to explore the dynamics of creating belonging in the everyday lives of young people from refugee backgrounds. At Paddington High, I was present for the daily routine of the lunch hour, attended some classes, and lingered with students in both formal and informal after-school activities. Throughout much of the day, outside of the lunch hour and when not attending a class, I positioned myself at a picnic table in the middle of the courtyard. Students would come to this area to receive extra help from the ELL (English language learner) teacher, who was also positioned there for set portions of the day, or to chat with each other, possibly avoid class, and generally pass the time.

After school, I would attend the dance practice that most of the young people attended at certain times during the school year, and which was located in a back wing of the school and largely unsupervised; or wander with them into the city or to the train station, where they would linger for a time before going home. I spent time with participants in the relatively informal setting of Kedron Club as they worked on homework—and where they gossiped, teased, and hung out under the guise of doing homework. Thus, through my initial introduction to young people in these formal settings, I also came to spend time with them in more informal spaces like shopping centers, inner-city public recreation spaces, and train and bus stations, as well as in the homes and at private gatherings of the young people.

It was during these in-between spaces and times that I was able to be there as the undercurrent of conflict between Tino and Nine slowly escalated and intensely erupted; as Samah and Lauren gossiped about the boys they had crushes on; as Santino attempted to get "hugs" from girls; as Vic experienced setbacks and frustrations in the process of bringing her mother to Australia; and as Lisa experienced ongoing conflict with her father and shared her sadness over having to switch schools. Hanging out and sharing in these experiences of the young people allowed me to observe as the negotiations and tensions of belonging unfolded and as identity was constituted and represented in complex and often contradictory ways.

Twenty-seven young people participated in interviews through which I could tease out some of the issues observed in other fieldwork settings. At the start of the interviews, I urged the young people to only discuss those things that they saw as essential to their life experience and that they were comfortable discussing. I also reminded them that the research would be anonymous and confidential and gave them the opportunity, in which many took immense pleasure, to select the name they would like to use to protect their anonymity. Many of the young people carefully selected an alias, while others claimed not to mind if the name by which I knew them was used in my research. Nonetheless, all personal names are pseudonyms.

It was my methodological imperative not to delve into the life history of my informants in terms of their refugee status or journey to Australia beyond what they offered in casual conversation or in initial interview questions. This choice was based upon the vulnerabilities of my research participants as young people, the general research saturation they experienced regarding this aspect of their lives, and indeed, because I was most interested in learning how they defined themselves and created a sense of belonging with one another in the social landscape of the Australian context in which they currently lived. The things they highlighted and the things they left out were equally revealing to me in the interview process. Beyond this, I felt that allowing the young people to define for themselves what was significant in their lives helped to foster rapport.

As a result, however—and while I recognize the massive impact of the ruptures they have experienced on their sense of self and belonging—the breadth of information I provide here on their life histories and the pre-migration contexts of their lives is not extensive. For example, I do not detail many of the things generally associated with research among refugee populations, such as their socioeconomic status in their countries of origin or their experiences with war, torture, and trauma. Moreover, as it was my express purpose to explore the ways in which young people defined and presented themselves in the pursuit of belonging, it was outside the scope of this book to interview family members. The experiences of home and family life, as well as the tensions of parental expectations and familial conflicts, are engaged in my analysis insofar as they were discussed and addressed by the young people. Consequently, the perspectives of family members throughout my research findings are filtered through the interpretations of the young people themselves.

It is also worth noting at the outset that I do not interpret my ethnographic data through a gendered lens. This is primarily because gender was not a theme that emerged significantly in participants' accounts and representations of themselves during fieldwork. Gender is indeed of consequence when considering issues of race and ethnicity in young people's lives, as the hierarchical dynamics and language of race intersect with other social relations such as gender, class, and sexuality (Carroll 2017). Moreover, migration, displacement, and even multiculturalism are gendered in ways that intersect with age (Pruitt, Berents and Munro 2018). I therefore incorporate some theorizing of gender and intersectionality subsequently and in Chapter 3 and also expound on this analysis where appropriate in the ethnographic chapters.

However, I chose not to focus on gender as central to my analysis of the ethnographic data presented out of fidelity to my participants' concerns, of which race and ethnicity took precedence. While significant factors such as family life and familial roles, age, gender, and cultural background certainly influence the self-understanding and social location of these young people in significant ways, the precise focus and contribution of this study is to demonstrate the everyday ways in which young people, with one another, represent a multiplicity of identifications in the pursuit of belonging—and in the process, they may unsettle the perceived influence of these categories or draw upon them in unexpected ways.

While the whole of their lived histories no doubt affects the complex ways in which these young refugees make sense of their present social worlds, my focus is instead on the everyday practices through which they represented their identities in ways that attempted to foster a sense of place and belonging in Australia. It was this endeavor that seemed to lie at the heart of the interactions between the young people as well as their interpretations of their experiences as portrayed in interviews. And it was largely through this filter that young people evoked (or in some cases, deemphasized) other elements of their individual experiences such as aspects of life in their country of origin or their experiences as refugees.

The Participants

My key research informants comprise thirty-nine young people, thirty-seven of whom were from refugee backgrounds, who were aged nine to twenty years and residing in Brisbane.[1] It was through my relationships with those key informants that connections developed with a broader range of young people who also came to influence my research. While it was those key informants with whom I conducted interviews and was able to most directly pursue my research agenda, through this snowball effect, I also consider a wider group of siblings, family members, friends, and friends of friends as participants in my research.

Thirty-eight of my key informants had been living in Brisbane for between two and six years at the time they participated in the study (apart from the Anglo-Celtic Australian participant, who had lived in Brisbane for most of her life). The young people were aged between 9 and 20 years old, but the majority were aged between 14 and 16 years. One was 9 years of age; ten were between 10 and 13 years of age; twenty-one were between 14 and 16 years of age; six were between 17 and 19 years of age; and one was 20 years of age. The wide range in participants' age is mainly due to participation in the research by siblings. It was often the case that while spending time in the home of a young person I met through Paddington High or Kedron Club, a sibling would join in the interview or express an interest in contributing their experiences to my research. In addition, at both Paddington High and Kedron Club, young people hung out with siblings and friends of siblings, creating a wide age range within friendship groups.

Fifteen of my key informants were female and twenty-four were male. They came from the following countries: twenty-three from Sudan; two from Uganda; one from Sierra Leone; eleven from Thailand who had previously lived in Burma (eight identified as Karen, one as Chin, and two as Burmese); one from Australia; and one from Papua New Guinea. Of the twenty-three from Sudan, three participants came to Australia via Uganda, twelve came via Kenya, and eight came via Egypt. Of the eleven participants who came from Burma and Thailand, all came to Australia via the Tham Hin refugee camp in Thailand. The participant from Papua New Guinea came to Australia directly as a migrant.

The route they took to Australia proved significant for the young people. For example, the few Sudanese young people who came to Australia via Cairo would describe the others who came via Kenya and Uganda and, most likely, spent the majority of their time there living in the Kakuma and Kiryandongo refugee camps, respectively, as "a little behind us," in terms of markers of sophistication in things like taste in fashion and music. The young people from Burma and Thailand often referenced the refugee camps where they lived before coming to Australia and distinguished their current friends whom they had known from the camp before arriving in Australia from friends they had made in Australia.

Thirty-seven of the thirty-nine key informants had refugee status in Australia (one was a migrant and one was from Australia). During my research, twenty confirmed that they had Australian citizenship. Of these, twelve were from Africa, seven were from Burma, and one was born an Australian citizen. Six informants stated that they did not yet have Australian citizenship. Of these, four were from Africa and two were from Burma. Thirteen informants were not sure whether they had Australian citizenship.

My research participants were, of course, chosen in part due to access, availability, and the logistical unfolding of my fieldwork (e.g., central members of friendship groups were included regardless of ethnic background or status in the Australian context). However, I was deliberate in the decision to explore my research questions among young people from a range of backgrounds, as this approach allowed for me to explore the processes of identity making among young people with a broad lens and the aim of moving beyond constructions based on ethnicities, nationalities, or experiences as refugees.

Similarly, my deliberate focus on a small cohort of participants allows for a nuanced investigation into the lived impact of multiculturalism on young people's lives that is more broadly generalizable than a focus on a larger cohort. It enables an emphasis on everyday articulations of belonging and a multiplicity of cultural resources upon which young people may draw to assert a sense of belonging and participation in the political context of their lives outside of their explicit ethnic or national alignments. Because of the relatively small core group of research participants and the logistical, ethnographic skew toward young people of Sudanese backgrounds, it was outside of the scope of my research to take a comparative approach to the ways in which diverse groups of young people approached identity based on national or ethnic background.

While in the ethnographic chapters I make some comparative assertions between the identity practices of different friendship groups (which, in some instances, were divided along national and ethnic lines), I steer clear of broad comparisons between ethnic groups. Without a larger cohort of research participants, I felt a comparative approach would risk stereotyping. Instead, the aim of my research design allows for an exploration of the fluidity in young people's emphasis on all sorts of markers of identity.

I have provided an overview of statistical data such as age, gender, country of origin, route to Australia, refugee status, and citizenship here to provide the reader at the outset with some basic facts about these young people and the circumstances under which they arrived in Australia. In the thick of my research and as I sought to understand something of the lives and experiences of these young people, however, such facts were of value only to the extent that they were emphasized as important by the young people themselves. The ethnographic process, one of hanging out and immersing myself in the daily lives of my informants, was about being present to the emotion and routines of their lived experience, which came alive below the surface of these objective facts.

This book seeks to distil the relationship between youth processes of identity making and the multicultural context in which they unfolded in my fieldwork. In the concluding section of the chapter, I outline the core concepts and theoretical foundations of the book as they emerged in my research and are approached in the scholarly literature.

Identity and Dynamic Responsiveness in Multicultural Context

My fundamental concern is with the ways in which young people exhibit a kind of dynamic responsiveness in their engagement with an underlying ethos emerging from the broad social fabric of Australian multiculturalism. Messages emerging from the Australian multicultural context inform these young people's identities and impact upon their sense of displacement and belonging. As I demonstrate, it is not only the experience of racism or exclusion that can fuel young people's highly racialized identity work, but also their engagement with the very ideals designed to address that experience. It is here, in a kind of subconscious dialogue with the continual and abstracted messages about who they are and how they fit in, that the work of identification occurs. As such, I view young people's identity-making practices through the conceptual lens of dynamic responsiveness.

Their dynamic responsiveness, made apparent in these young people's interactive exchanges with one another, informs a core of agency through which they engage with the expectations and demands imposed upon them. The conceptual architecture of dynamic responsiveness allows for a nuanced elaboration of young people's agency as they grapple with sometimes conflicting social phenomena such as peer cultures, family, multiculturalism, and national discourses concerning citizenship. The identity work of young people from refugee and migrant backgrounds is certainly self-conscious, and it is sometimes fueled by underlying perceptions and motivations, but it is always responding to some level of awareness of the larger sociopolitical context that frames their lives. I hope to illuminate such dynamic responsiveness by demonstrating young people's engagement with the rhetoric surrounding multiculturalism that they encounter in their everyday environments. From this perspective, I critically analyze the notion of the modern "hybrid" or "plural" youth identity.

Responsiveness, in the making and unmaking of identities, is ultimately about the cultivation of belonging. I am interested in those moments when participants negotiated and asserted notions of nationality, race, and ethnicity in the pursuit of social place and belonging. Belonging, as a scholarly concept related to identity politics, is often associated with nationalism and nationalist movements (Skrbis, Baldassar, and Poynting 2007, 261). In a given social context, it may be fiercely asserted by some while it is simultaneously denied to others. In practical terms this means that the ways in which people cultivate and assert a sense of belonging is constantly shifting. The fluid nature of cultivating belonging is particularly evident in the lives of young people who are immersed in complex relations of power and for whom a sense of self and belonging are deeply significant pursuits.

I argue that these young people's negotiations of identity and belonging are undertaken at the interface of experiences and perceptions of racism and in response to the discourses that emerge to confront it. By critically exploring their identity-making processes, I hope to reveal both how young people pursue a sense of belonging in a dynamic, responsive relationship to social context, and the extent to which such being, or belonging, is made available to them. Pierre Bourdieu's theories (1977, 1984, 1986, 1990) relating to the reproduction of social power and its effect on social agents, which I explore in greater depth in Chapter 3, underpin this central concern and have informed my understandings of the social context in which I recorded and interpreted ethnographic data.

The theoretical foundations that I take as a starting point from which to explore refugee youth identity in response to the Australian multicultural context rest upon the following scholarly positions: (1) that the making of identities is a continually evolving process of asserting sameness and difference in relation to others in dynamic interaction with existing power structures; and (2) that the dominant Australian Anglo-Celtic identity may constitute a form of capital through which the terrain of Australian multiculturalism is overdetermined. Fundamentally, I seek to demonstrate how young refugees in Australia intuitively sense and respond to the racialized power dynamics of Australian multiculturalism in their formulations of identity.

Let me further unpack the theoretical underpinnings of my research and locate them within the scholarly literature on youth, identity, and multiculturalism. First, in order to anchor my approach within the context of similar research and outline key theoretical concepts, I will provide a brief historical overview of the scholarly literature on youth and the emergence of a focus on the broad concept of identity within the field.

Anthropological Approaches to the Study of Youth

The terms *childhood* and *youth* are context-dependent and highly contested categories in the contemporary world. The United Nations Educational, Scientific and Cultural Organization (UNESCO) defines youth as the period of time between fifteen and twenty-four years of age, and the term is more broadly understood as a "period of transition from the dependence of childhood to adulthood's independence" (UNESCO 2017). Childhood is defined in similarly flexible terms by the United Nations Convention on the Rights of the Child as a "separated and safe space" from adulthood, occurring up to eighteen years of age, and also refers to the conditions of one's life during this time (UNICEF 2004). Furthermore, the categories of childhood and youth are defined in gendered terms; while childhood is often depicted as feminized, with children seen as vulnerable and in need of protection, youth is often depicted as masculine and threatening (Pruitt et al. 2018).

As these definitions highlight, both childhood and youth represent fluid categories, rather than fixed, age-based groups, and must be considered with critical attention to social context and the overlapping categories of class, ethnicity, gender, and disparities of access to material goods and political advantage. While the young people represented here fit largely within the defined category of "youth," some also fit within the category of "children." I predominantly use the term "young people" to refer to my research participants who identify themselves and are identified by their peers as broadly falling within the category of youth.

The study of youth has drawn increasing recognition from social scientists in recent decades and has come to focus heavily on the processes of identity making undertaken by young people (e.g., Bucholtz 2002; Jenks 2005; Quijada 2008; Wulff 1995b). This attention suggests that the ways in which young people negotiate a sense of self and belonging have much to reveal, not only about the making of identities more generally, but also about the broader societies in which they live and about larger global processes. Examining practices of identification among young people can provide rich and significant insights into the processes of cultivating a sense of belonging and how that occurs in response to social contexts. In doing so it can also provide an important window into the specific manifestations of social issues on local and global scales.

Indeed, as Fass (2003, 2007) and others have pointed out, children and young people may be regarded as a driving force in the processes of globalization (see also Appadurai 1996; Katz 1998). Among the central means through which young people may influence globalization are the inventive ways they express themselves in terms of consumer habits, rejecting and embracing various forms of authority, and making strategic choices about style, music, and language. My research on identity and belonging among young people from refugee backgrounds in Brisbane speaks to pressing issues in Australia today, such as immigration policy and race relations, as well as to a broader world context, wherein the diasporic communities to which many of these young people ascribe are of relevance to their sense of themselves.

The study of youth provides a particularly powerful analytic lens within the anthropological landscape. As a category of analysis that represents a contested space that is lacking a clear, universal definition, youth acts, as Deborah Durham (2004) first termed it, as a "social shifter." As society determines who is to be considered youth and what that label entails, culturally specific determinations about social relationships, fields of power, and codes of morality emerge. In the contested and shifting space they inhabit, youth have been theorized as both victims of society and creative agents of social change (Abdullah 2005; De Bock and Honwana 2005). These opposing analytic positions get to the heart of one of the key issues anthropologists are trying to work out—do cultures make people or do people make cultures?

What the study of youth has the potential to highlight includes both the structural forces that impinge upon people's lives and their potential for innovation in confronting them. Issues of broad anthropological interest from media consumption to migration have been viewed through the prism of youth. Most recently, the field of youth studies has examined issues of identity and ethnicity among young people in increasingly globalized local contexts. Of particular relevance here, youth have been considered at the forefront, both literally and figuratively, of negotiating inclusion in modern multicultural contexts. The wide trends within the field of youth studies can serve as a kind of barometer measuring the importance of social issues over time.

Marking the earliest incarnation of youth studies in anthropology, Margaret Mead studied the phenomenon of coming of age among Samoan girls (Mead 1928). Following Mead, other anthropological works considered youth in terms of liminality, or a developmental life stage through which one would transition, rather than as a cultural category worthy of investigation (Evans-Pritchard 1969; Turner 1995). Sociological studies of youth have historically taken a problem-centered approach, focusing on sensationalized topics such as violence and sexuality and portraying young people as deviants, problems, or victims.

For example, Albert Cohen's *Delinquent Boys* (1955), a classic work that emerged from the Chicago School of Sociology, took an ethnographic approach to the study of deviant subcultures. This work influenced research emerging from the Birmingham School, established in the mid-1970s at the University of Birmingham in the United Kingdom, and is viewed as foundational to the fields of youth and cultural studies (Valentine, Skelton and Chambers 1998). The Birmingham School, working from a Marxist and post-structuralist take on working-class youth, focused heavily on class as the basis for youth culture (Bucholtz 2002). Some members replaced the term "youth culture" with the term "subculture," which they felt better captured the class dynamic of the cultural processes they were observing among young people (Hall and Jefferson 1976; Hebdige 1979). The concept of subculture helped to elucidate the emergent nature of culture as a process of becoming through highlighting the conscious and performative production of cultural forms. Early works of the Chicago and the Birmingham Schools demonstrated how subcultures served to facilitate a sense of community and commonality in response to challenges faced by young people, such as inequality, unemployment, and cultural conflict (Willis 1977).

Work out of the Chicago and Birmingham Schools on subcultural forms, which were extremely influential in early studies of youth cultures, provides peripheral insights into my work on young people from refugee and migrant backgrounds in Australia: it demonstrates youth resistance to adult narratives, as well as the multiplicity of self-conscious representations of identity that I regularly observed in my fieldwork. With its well-developed theorization of class, however, these early studies were widely criticized for depicting youth cultures as too deeply dependent on highly visible image markers such as music and fashion, at the expense of other defining elements of identification such as gender, sexuality, race, and ethnicity (Bucholtz 2002, 537).

With the shift of focus to these later categories of self-understanding and representation, scholarly studies of youth became more meaningfully aligned with questions of identification related to dominant national discourses of belonging. This disciplinary shift also marks the emergence of a reinvigorated anthropology of youth, which considers young people as social agents in the process of negotiating identity and belonging at the complex nexus of transnationalism and local cultures, where discourses of national belonging meet with individualized representations of race and ethnicity among young people. This is where youth studies scholarship is most relevant to my research.

Cultivating Ethnicity: Hybridity and Essentialism in Practice

As Stuart Hall's influential work, *New Ethnicities* (1992), helped to distil, ethnicity, as well as race, is socially constructed. It is negotiated in the context of community as people articulate similarities and differences between themselves and other groups of people. In the context of globalization, where different regional and national groups are drawn both together and apart in local settings, the boundaries of these articulations become increasingly unstable (Noble et al. 1999, 30). While ethnic affiliation may be presented on the surface as bounded and cohesive, as it often was by the young people involved in this study, it is indeed constituted out of fluid boundaries and strategic choices.

Such fluidity is the hallmark of the notion of hybrid identities. The concept of hybridity, also of key consideration in the identity-making practices of young refugees, has been conceptualized as the process by which new subjectivities are constructed through the overlapping and interweaving of different cultural forms (Bhabha 1994, 1996; Papastergiadis 1997). While these new ethnicities may emerge out of some degree of agency or strategic overlap, they are also shaped by the perceptions of others and the structural forces inherent in social, economic, and political processes. As Noble and colleagues (1999, 31) argue, "The celebration of fluidity is often made at the expense of registering the determining force of social relations and the role identity plays in responding to these."

The often criticized notion of essentialism is also crucial for the representation of ethnicity. While the concept of hybridity helps to demonstrate the ways in which people highlight the shifting and permeable aspect of their ethnicities (Werbner 1997b, 16), it is the use of self-essentialism in everyday circumstances that allows people to formulate and represent their ethnicities as fixed and immutable in different ways in different contexts and in response to the structural forces that frame their lives (Noble et al. 1999, 31; Spivak 1988, 1990). I use the terms hybridity and essentialism advisedly and engage in depth with the theoretical limitations of using this language in Chapter 3. However, as they have emerged out of the social theory relevant to identity, and more specifically in relation to the study of youth, hybridity and essentialism are useful concepts for examining the multiple ways in which ethnic identity may be represented in different contexts.

The mobilization of ethnicity is particularly evident in the imperative, sensitive, and often tense identity-making practices engaged in by young people. Through their avid consumption of style, commodities, and ideas and their creative interpretation of racial signifiers from resources and symbols that traverse national borders in their origin, many studies of youth and ethnicity locate young people and their hybridizing strategies at the forefront of the processes of globalization (Back 1996; Abner Cohen 1974; Nayak 2003, 2009; Wulff 1995a). While such studies of youth culture are certainly relevant to my study, the ways in which they depict young people constituting new ethnic identities by merging various cultural signifiers do not precisely fit, nor theoretically capture, my experience.

Rather than merging symbolic references in the formation of new ethnicities, I observed young people actively emphasizing and deemphasizing ethnic identity in a creative engagement with the broad messages of multiculturalism that sought to address their ethnic difference. Moreover, in my observations, while young people may speak back to structural constraints and reflect the experiences that frame their lives in their complex and often self-conscious representations of themselves, the ways in which they do so can be described at times as strategic, but at other times as a much more subtle and even subconscious positioning—reliant, in these moments, more on the kind of unconscious engagement and internalization of those structural constraints than a direct confrontation with them (Moore 2011, 209).

As I explore further in Chapter 3, to emphasize the dynamic relationship between these young people's sense of identity and the multicultural discourses that frame their lives, I utilize the notion of responsiveness. The literature on "everyday multiculturalism" and "multicultural drift" has established how daily interethnic encounters in multicultural spaces foster the capacity and habits for people of diverse backgrounds to live in relative harmony (Harris 2013; Werbner 2013; Wise and Velayutham 2009). The concept of "conviviality" in relation to "everyday multiculturalism" highlights the various national, cultural, and embodied structures that help to foster harmonious coexistence in multicultural settings (Wise and Velayutham 2013). Similarly, the concept of "everyday cosmopolitanism" highlights the "strategic practices of transaction in specific contexts," which create a sense of civic engagement and the possibilities for multiple forms of ethnic and national belonging to coexist together (Noble 2009).

In the context of everyday multiculturalism, youth are considered adept at developing "multiple identities," from which they have been theorized as "hybrid," "in-between," "fluid" (Bhabha 1994; Goffman 1959; Hall 1992, 1993, 1996), and "ambivalent" (Ngo 2010). I favor the notion of responsiveness, in a step back from the accepted notion of the hybrid and fractured nature of migrant youth identities. The notion of dynamic responsiveness in youth identity making provides scope to look beyond the prevalence of their multicultural encounters to underscore and unpack a level of engagement with the broader multicultural context through which such hybrid identities also emerge.

Having migrated to Australia, the young people with whom I worked have become part of a vast and contentious immigration context historically linked to articulations of whiteness and racial and ethnic division. Throughout the course of my fieldwork, a dynamic relationship between the fluctuating ways young people treated and defined their sense of racial and ethnic identity and the messages they regularly encountered, broadly framed in relation to multiculturalism, began to emerge. It is to this multicultural context, and the challenges of identity and inclusion it presents for young refugees, that I will now turn before concluding the chapter.

Multiculturalism, Youth, and the Refugee Experience

The management of diversity, which multiculturalism in its various manifestations has been implemented to address, is now the subject of widespread moral panic and political debate in Western settler nation-states. In Australia, the United States, the United Kingdom, Canada, and Europe, concerns regarding national identity, immigration, citizenship, and borders are ever present and growing. As I explore further in Chapter 2, concerns in these contexts are rooted in a fear of the cultural loss of European heritage and tradition and in political conflict over expanding populations due to both chosen and forced migration. Central to these debates is the proposed need for strategies designed to ease integration, to help people to live together with difference—difference that is often implicitly, but always undeniably, tied to race and ethnicity.

Youth scholars have argued that young people are at the forefront of negotiating inclusion in these modern multicultural contexts (Fass 2007; Gow 2005). Young people's lives, which unfold within the thick of difference and diversity in the schools and public spaces of multicultural cities, are regarded, in both popular understanding and scholarly discourse, as central to assessing the fate of multicultural living. From youth-driven race riots, of which the 2005 Cronulla riots in Australia are a primary example, to the sunnier and perhaps less frequent depictions of youth using diversity as a creative agent of cultural change, the lives of young people have been regarded as indicative of both promise and skepticism regarding the multicultural project (Harris 2013, 5).[2]

Despite their exposure to multicultural contexts, however, young people may be no more open or resistant to the ideals of inclusion than anyone else (Harris 2013). For young people, as Harris notes, within the diversity of their everyday landscape, "racism and prejudice sit alongside care and recognition" (2013, 3). The ways in which young people grapple with multiculturalism in their everyday encounters challenge profoundly the common portrayals of their inclination to embrace and consume diversity, on the one hand, and to incite racism, riots, and violence. on the other (Butcher and Harris 2010, 449; Herron 2018).

What has emerged as significant in my work with young people is, not only that they are formulating a sense of self and belonging in the context of racial, ethnic, and cultural diversity, but also that they are doing so in response to various approaches to manage that diversity. Their responsiveness to the implicit, but pervasive, messages that influence their lives in terms of how they negotiate their own sense of themselves highlights identity making as an attempt to create connection, affinity, and understanding. The ways in which young people align themselves with or position themselves against one another in accordance with, and against, broad social expectations allows them to forge connections with one another, with the broader Australian population, and with the transnational diasporas with which they also identify.

Young people from migrant and refugee backgrounds face the heightened complexity of defining a sense of self and of place at the intersections of national, ethnic, and cultural identity. As relative outsiders to the broad context in which their daily lives unfold, the dynamics of constituting a sense of self and belonging are, for these young people, especially challenging. Young people with refugee backgrounds must not only contend with the complexities of ethnic, national, and cultural identity, but must do so also in the context of rupture, trauma, loss, and the challenges of the resettlement experience.

Moreover, the fact of their migration effectively disrupts their perceived role as youth in need of protection, and the fact of this mold breaking creates the counterperception that they are risky. Their displacement, as well as their capacity to deal with diversity in a multicultural context, is also gendered; young men are more likely to be viewed as volatile and threatening in the society of their resettlement and young women more likely to be perceived instead as vulnerable. In what are often presented as crises of migration, media coverage centers around hordes of young refugees as a threat to the moral and social order and depicts young men in particular as welfare parasites at best, and terrorists at worst (Pruitt et al. 2018). In terms of both their lived experience and the ways in which they are more broadly represented and perceived, for these young people "belonging—to family, community and country—is always at risk" (Correa-Velez, Gifford and Barnett 2010, 1399; see also Jackson 2002, 33).

However, counter to the trauma-centered approach that is so prevalent in the literature, the impact of past experience is not the main factor in determining the psychological well-being of young people from refugee backgrounds (Gifford, Correa-Velez and Sampson 2009; McMichael, Nunn, Correa-Velez, and Gifford 2017). Among the most significant "indicators of belonging" put forward in Gifford's (2009) "Good Starts" study on the health and well-being of refugee youth in the initial stages of resettlement are perceptions of social status and a sense of belonging in their place of resettlement.

I take this perspective as a starting point for my research. For young people from refugee backgrounds, the pursuit of belonging is undertaken in relation to the national context in which they currently live and is influenced by a range of other factors related to the whole of their life experiences. The lives of the young people represented in this book were quite overtly politicized through their resettlement in Australia. In the Australian context, young people are confronted with various expectations and pressures which, like the anthropologist Ghassan Hage (1998, 2003; see also Povinelli 2002), I locate in the current policy framework of multiculturalism. As I explore in depth in Chapter 2, the social values of integration and tolerance have emerged to confront ongoing tensions over immigration at various points in Australia's history and provide the basis for those expectations that young people, in turn, perceive, engage with, and manipulate in their everyday practices. It is at this juncture between broad social influences and the everyday practices of cultivating a sense of belonging that I locate the study and where both are rendered meaningful.

2

Multicultural Australia and the Refugee Experience

Ethnographic Settings

Let me begin the task of contextualizing my research on refugee youth identity in Australia by briefly explaining how I came to do this research, in this place. Immediately before having moved to Australia, I completed a master's degree at Oxford University on what I broadly described as the anthropology of childhood. I examined the notion of agency in children's lives; how the processes of socialization that draw them into the dominant culture are counterbalanced by the decisions and awareness they draw upon to affect that culture.

Early in 2005, with a freshly awarded degree in hand, I found myself living in Brisbane with my now husband, an Australian, born and raised in Brisbane. Brisbane at that time had seen a recent influx of Sudanese refugees, particularly in the suburb in which we lived. It was noticeable enough so that a relative, also living in Brisbane, and aware of my recently completed research on young people, suggested to me that I might next do some kind of work with the very tall, very black young people who suddenly appeared on her suburban streets amid the very white population already living there. I liked the idea, and so I began to volunteer extensively in the refugee community, tutoring school-aged children and working in an agency that provided settlement services to newly arrived refugees. I thought about the young people I was working with in those capacities as my mind started to drift back toward embarking upon more study and pursuing a doctoral degree in anthropology.

Eventually, I married my newfound interest in the young refugee communities of Brisbane with my master's research and submitted a proposal to my soon to be doctoral committee. My research question centered on how these young people from different backgrounds form a culture among themselves that stands apart from the many social organizing categories—their race and ethnicity, their nation of origin, their status as refugees—that frame their lives. As I came to realize, and as I briefly touched upon in the previous chapter, they don't. As the core premise of this book suggests, in fact quite the opposite is true.

Young people develop a sense of who they are and how they fit in social place, at least in large part, by responding to the various ways in which their lives are framed in social context; which was made apparent to me through my observations of their interactions with each other that were heavily focused on issues of race and belonging. Their sense of identity and various paths to belonging were certainly influenced by a range of factors encompassing the whole of their life experiences, including their countries of origin, their family lives, and their experiences as refugees, all of which I explore in this chapter. What I came to understand as most relevant to their identity-making processes in my research, however, and what is consequently at the core of the book's findings, was the sociopolitical context of these young people's place of resettlement and how their lives were treated, managed and framed in that context.

Australia proved to be an ideal place in which to study the dynamics of identity formation among young people from refugee backgrounds. Its unique combination of demographics (over half the population are born overseas or have a parent who was), and recent social history (multiculturalism emerged in the 1970s as a formal political policy related to immigration) established a set of sociopolitical ideals that markedly surfaced in the lives of these young people. The social and political context of Australian multiculturalism forms the backdrop against which these young people engage with one another in the pushes and pulls of belonging.

Before delving into the ethnography, let me first detail the emergence of the Australian sociopolitical context which figured so prominently in the identity practices of these young people. I begin by examining Australia's fraught immigration history and politics from which the current system of multiculturalism has emerged. In doing so, I seek to demonstrate how current multicultural policy in Australia rests upon a set of discursive and institutional norms which are implicitly tied, not only to national and ethnic heritage, but to race. The power dynamics of this political framework reveal multiculturalism as a kind of nation-building exercise that is deeply rooted in whiteness (Hage 1998, 2003). I argue that messages, reflective of the ideals of integration and tolerance, emerge from the broad moral backdrop of Australian multiculturalism and that young refugees intuitively perceive and express this in their identity formation.

Following this, I explore some relevant background information about the national context from which the young people in this study have migrated to Australia. I seek here to demonstrate the ways and degree to which social, political, and familial tensions related to and emerging within these young people's everyday lives manifest and are reflected in the shaping of their identities and in their pursuit of social belonging.

Australian Immigration History and Politics

Australia's population is reported to be approximately 24.5 million, according to the 2016 census, and includes a broad diversity of cultural, national and ethnic groups (Australian Bureau of Statistics [ABS] 2017). There are over three hundred languages and over three hundred ancestries represented in Australia today (ABS 2017; Australian Department of Home Affairs 2017). It is among the world's most diverse societies, considered "a nation of immigrants" to a greater degree than any country other than Israel (Hollinsworth 2006, 196). One in four Australians is an immigrant and an additional one fifth of the population has at least one immigrant parent (Castles, Hugo and Vasta 2013).

Since the Second World War, Australia has had one of the largest and most diverse immigration programs in the Western world (Collins, Noble, Poynting, and Tabar 2000). Approximately 7 million people have migrated to Australia since 1945 (Australian Department of Immigration and Citizenship [DIAC] 2011a). Of those 7 million permanent residents who have migrated to Australia since 1945, 700,000 are considered refugees or displaced persons (Castles et al. 2013). As in many Western settler nations, immigration, while crucial to transformations in Australia's economic and social welfare systems, has been the source of much political and social controversy.

White Australia Policy

In detailing the evolution of Australia's immigration programs and policy, it must first be noted that Australia's current wealth and position as a Western nation was built upon the systematic breakdown of its Indigenous population through colonization and subsequent immigration (Hage 1998). This is relevant because it has arguably contributed to what Ghassan Hage (2003) describes as "White colonial paranoia"—a national vulnerability and fear of loss, rooted in the nation's emergence through conquest. According to Hage's conceptualization, being Australian has to a large degree, relied upon expressions of "Europeanness" or "Whiteness" (Hage 2003, 48). As such, throughout the nation's history issues of race and ethnicity have played a central role in Australia's immigration policy (Collins et al. 2000; Hage 1998, 2003; Hollinsworth 2006, 196).

The pervasiveness of racial and ethnic based rhetoric regarding nonwhite immigration may be traced back to the White Australia Policy, a Commonwealth of Australia Constitution Act passed by the Parliament of the United Kingdom in July 1900 and implemented at the time of Australia's federation in January 1901 (McMaster 2001, 41). It was designed to prevent the immigration of nonwhite people and meant that the "Commonwealth Parliament could pass laws to ensure that, with few exceptions, nonwhites would not be permitted to settle, work, or live (temporarily or permanently) in Australia" (McMaster 2001, 41).

After the Second World War, while still under the White Australia Policy, Australia implemented a broad immigration program through which immigrants were actively sought under the social mandate to "populate or perish" (Tsolidis and Pollard 2009, 429). Waves of European immigrants predominantly from Western European countries such as Britain and Ireland arrived under this program in the twenty years following the war. When the desired numbers did not arrive from these preferred countries, immigrants then arrived from southern European countries such as Greece, Italy, and the former Yugoslavia. During the postwar period, immigrants were mainly of European descent, and issues of race and ethnicity continued to play a role in attitudes toward them. Discrimination was aimed at Greek and Italian migrants, who were considered "not completely white" but sufficiently white to be accepted as second-choice migrants after the Western Europeans (Tsolidis and Pollard 2009, 429).

The White Australia Policy served particularly to assuage anxiety over Australia's proximity to Asia, and to attempt to prevent it from becoming a preferred destination for Chinese immigrants who might "dilute" the Australian culture and lifestyle in relationship to its British heritage (Tsolidis and Pollard 2009, 429; see also Jupp 2000, 97). Australia's immigration history has long been plagued by a fear of being overtaken by Asian countries in what has been popularly referred to as an "Asian invasion." The pervasiveness of this racial and ethnic based rhetoric regarding nonwhite immigration rooted in the White Australia Policy, and a sense of national vulnerability or fear from which it emerged, is widely evident as it has regularly resurfaced in political policy and debate in more recent times.

For example, in this continued political climate even after the White Australia Policy was dismantled, conservative Australian historian Geoffrey Blainey asked the question, "Should Australia continue to be dominated by Anglo-Celtic peoples and the English language and institutions? Or should it become a new Eurasia?" (Blainey 1984, cited in Hollinsworth 2006, 227). Later, the One Australia Policy (beginning in the late 1980s), mandated migrants to fully "assimilate" into what was perceived of as mainstream Australian culture. Taking an even stronger stance, Pauline Hanson's One Nation Party (beginning in the late 1990s), was premised upon Hanson's segregation of Aboriginal people, Torres Strait Islanders, and people of Asian backgrounds from her constituency because of their perceived lack of ability or willingness to assimilate into a Western European cultural norm (Hollinsworth 2006, 230).

The White Australia Policy was officially dismantled under the Whitlam Labor government in the early 1970s. This was precipitated by Vietnamese "boatpeople" traveling south following the fall of Saigon (Hollinsworth 2006, 210). Vietnamese migration to Australia was the nation's first significant experience with asylum seekers and refugee claimants deemed to be entering Australian territory illegally (Crock 2006:74). During this time, the task of limiting nonwhite migrants shifted to restricting the number of refugee arrivals in Australia. Australia began to develop what Crock (2006) refers to as a "culture of control." This control is manifested in the strict guidelines and policy developed to determine who is permitted to enter Australia and settle as a refugee claimant or asylum seeker through policies such as temporary protection visas, mandatory detention, and the offshore processing of refugee claims (Crock 2006; Thompson 2011). Such measures around refugee intake continue to be highly controversial in Australian politics. By way of background, I will provide some detail here on what it means to be a refugee in in the international context, and on Australia's evolving and contentious policy toward refugee intake.

Refugees in Australia

The international definition of a refugee, as outlined in the United Nations High Commissioner for Refugees (UNHCR) 1951 Convention Relating to the Status of Refugees, to which Australia is a signatory, Art 1A(2), states that the term refers to all people for whom: "owing to a well-founded fear of being persecuted for reasons of race, religion, nationality, membership of a particular social group or political opinion, is outside the country of his nationality and is unable or, owing to such fear, is unwilling to avail himself of the protection of that country; or who, not having a nationality and being outside the country of his former habitual residence, is unable or, owing to such fear, is unwilling to return to it." (UNHCR, cited in Crock 2006, 169, see also Fiddian-Qasmiyeh, Loescher, Long and Sigona 2014)

The term *refugee*, as it is broadly defined and used in public policy contexts, is neither neutral nor comprehensive in spite of this seemingly straightforward definition. It carries with it a range of meanings, expectations, and connotations, and it is continually amended in both a national and international framework in terms of the rights it entails for, or excludes from, those who are deemed to fall within its parameters. While in previous centuries migration may have occurred on a larger scale, today there are fewer places to which "extra" people may move (Harrell-Bond and Voutira 1992; see also Bauman 2016; Gatrell 2015; Gemie 2010; Maley 2016; Ong 2003; Taylor 1994). The UNHCR was established in response to mass movements of Eastern Europeans during the Cold War and caries the underlying assumptions of humanitarian regimes, that refugees represent a situation of disorder which is transitory and temporary (Harrell-Bond and Voutira 1992, 7).

The validity of the category of refugee and the question of who may be considered to be one is of great relevance in a global context through which concerns over national borders are emerging with increasing intensity. Moreover, an understanding of the refugee experience as distinct from general migration is of great anthropological concern in the context of modernity. As Harrell-Bond and Voutira argue, "in anthropological terms refugees are people who have undergone a violent 'rite' of separation and unless or until they are 'incorporated' as citizens into their host state (or returned to a state of origin) find themselves in 'transition' or 'liminality'" (1992, 9). The work of incorporation involves adapting to radically new conditions both socially and materially and has a strong impact on international power dynamics (Harrell-Bond and Voutira 1992, 9).

A person officially defined as a refugee claimant or asylum seeker in the current formulation is someone in the process of applying for protection as a refugee under the UNHCR 1951 Refugee Convention. If their application for such status in Australia is successful, they will be deemed a refugee and gain permanent residence after the completion of health and character checks. If refugee status is not confirmed, these people have limited options but may seek protection under other international agreements (Fiddian-Qasmiyeh et al. 2014). All but two of the young people who participated in my study (one born in Australia and one a migrant from Papua New Guinea) had confirmed refugee status.

Australia's refugee intake currently averages around 17,000 humanitarian entrants per year (Refugee Council of Australia 2016a), approximately one quarter of whom are young people aged between ten and nineteen years (Correa-Velez et al. 2010, 1399). Australia recognized 2,377 asylum seekers as refugees in 2015; 0.1 percent of the global total (Refugee Council of Australia 2016b). Despite relatively modest numbers Australia's refugee intake has been the source of much public debate and political controversy. In recent years refugees to Australia have primarily been settled from Africa, Asia, and the Middle East (Refugee Council of Australia 2016b).

Sudanese refugees represent one of Australia's fastest growing refugee populations (Marlowe 2010), and at 2006 constituted 73 percent of Australia's humanitarian entrants (Australian Bureau of Statistics 2017). Since 1996 over 20,000 Sudanese refugees have immigrated to Australia under the Humanitarian Program visa system (DIAC 2007; Marlowe 2010). Additionally, Australia hosts a steadily growing number of Karen and Chin—persecuted ethnic groups previously residing primarily in Burma, Thailand, and Malaysia—as well as an established number of refugees who identify as Burmese (STARTTS 2007).[1]

The majority of refugees from Northeast Africa and Burma, including my research participants, currently come to Australia under the Humanitarian Program. The Humanitarian Program issues visas under two classes: (1) onshore applicants—those applying for visas after they have arrived in Australia; and (2) offshore applicants—those applying for visas from the source country (DIAC 2011b). All of the young people with confirmed refugee status who participated in my study were classified as offshore applicants.

The most fraught political debate and controversy over Australia's Humanitarian Program emerges in relation to onshore visa applicants, and particularly those who make the journey to Australia "illegally" on asylum seeker boats controlled through those commonly referred to as "people smugglers" (Bauman 2016). During the course of my fieldwork, in June of 2012 alone, two boats of asylum seekers attempting to arrive on Australian shores capsized in a dangerous stretch of sea between Indonesia and Christmas Island, a common route for asylum seekers transiting to Australia through Indonesia. A number of asylum seekers were rescued and close to one hundred were estimated to have died on these two boat journeys (Gartrell 2012; Matt Johnston and Maley 2012).

Such tragedies continue to occur and fuel ongoing debate about how to process asylum seekers arriving on Australian shores without visas in order to most effectively deter these dangerous boat journeys. A number of controversial measures have been implemented in recent decades in order to curtail illegal entrants onto Austrian shores. Such measures include temporary protection visas, which severely restricted the rights, entitlements, and services available to asylum seekers to aid in the process of resettlement, as well as a number of strategies for processing asylum seekers in offshore detention centers, rather than allowing them to enter mainland Australia upon arrival.

Two of the most notable measures to implement offshore processing of refugee claims are the Pacific Solution, implemented from 2001 to 2007, which used detention centers in Papua New Guinea and on the island nation of Nauru to process refugees; and the Malaysia Solution, which proposed, in 2011, to send 800 unprocessed refugees arriving in Australia to Malaysia for processing, in exchange for receiving 4,000 "genuine" refugees awaiting resettlement in Malaysia (Crock 2006; Dao 2012; Thompson 2011).

Although neither of these solutions are currently implemented, this remains a live debate under the conservative government at the time of writing. Elements of both the Pacific Solution and the Malaysian Solution are still in place, and variations of those solutions as well as temporary protection visas are regularly proposed. For example, deals with other countries, including, at the time of writing, the United States (which has agreed to the terms of resettlement), are being considered for the exchange of refugees and refugee claimants (Innis 2016). Additionally, fining and banning undocumented asylum seekers arriving by boat from future reentry to Australia was recently proposed (Doherty 2016), and detention centers for the offshore processing of refugee claims are still opened on Nauru and in Papua New Guinea, in addition to a number of refugee detention centers on mainland Australia.

The offshore processing of refugees and the use of detention centers and temporary protection visas are highly controversial practices, which are argued to be detrimental to the psychological well-being of asylum seekers as well as ineffective in their goal of deterring illegal entrants (Onselen 2012; Vasek 2011). At the time I conducted this research and following the asylum seeker boat tragedies and various incarnations of potential mitigating solutions described previously, the UN Human Rights commissioner, Navi Pillay, expressed deep concern and condemnation in regard to Australia's temporary protection visa scheme and offshore detention centers. She argued that such strategies express "a strong undercurrent of racism in the country" ("UN Rights Chief Slams Racist Australia" May 26, 2011).

Intense political debate regarding refugee intake in Australia, despite its relatively small numbers of humanitarian entrants, is indicative of Australia's contentious relationship with refugees in particular, and immigration more broadly. Dandy (2009) argues that despite the public- versus policy-related differentiation between the terms *immigrant, refugee*, and *asylum seeker*, the broad attitudes of Australian society demonstrate little of this differentiation in terms of perceived threat. Congruent to this lack of differentiation (and while it may be significant that research participants with refugee status were, in all cases, offshore applicants), the young people in my study did not appear to make a distinction between a perceived stigma related to being a refugee and that related to the broader categories of being a migrant or ethnic minority.

While the vast majority of my participants came to Australia under official refugee status, it is the political and moral implications designed to address immigration more broadly from which the messages I analyze in relation to these young people's identity practices emerged. In the course of my research with them, I did not find these young people to be reflecting the negative stigma associated with the politics of refugee status, as much as the stigma of being an outsider or immigrant in more general terms and the implications associated with that status. Therefore, it is the dynamics and attitudes emerging from Australia's general immigration history and political underpinnings where I focus much of my analysis.

The Emergence of Australian Multiculturalism

Australian immigration policy has changed from a postwar emphasis on "assimilation," which encouraged migrants to adopt the cultural practices of the Anglo-Celtic majority, to a shift toward "integration," which supported migrants to maintain more of their own cultural practices for a time before ultimately assimilating, and currently to a policy of multiculturalism and cultural diversity. Multiculturalism was officially implemented in the early 1970s and encourages migrants to preserve the cultural practices of their home countries (Hage 1998, 2003). Assimilation, integration, and multiculturalism all engage to varying degrees with the notion of tolerance, and throughout Australia's immigration history have been both controversial and racialized (Collins et al. 2000; Hage 1998). Indeed, multiculturalism, in terms of both current immigration policy and as a broader social and moral framework, is deeply imbued with issues of racial and ethnic difference.

The varied attempts to restrict immigration based on skin color that have occurred alongside Australia's large and robust immigration program—discussed previously in relation to the White Australia Policy, the continuing political and public debate over refugee arrivals, and the general fear of cultural loss, which has arguably helped to prompt waves of discrimination against various nonwhite immigrants throughout its history—may be characterized as nation-building exercises. Such policy and attitudes represent, as Hage and others have argued, a construction of national belonging which is rooted in the establishment of whiteness as central to being Australian (Hage 1998, 2003; Kapferer 1998).

In opposition to the popularly held view that Australia's current immigration policy framework of multiculturalism marks a departure from nationalism, multiculturalism instead relies upon a distinct kind of nationalism (Hage 2003; Povinelli 2002). This is a nationalism that places whiteness as an implicit stipulation of belonging from which the moral obligations of inclusion and tolerance are exercised. Most simply, whiteness represents the power and privilege afforded to those who identify as white (McIntosh 1990). The sense of entitlement that allows people the capacity to exercise nationalist practices rests upon the capacity to accumulate more or less whiteness—of which white skin color may function as only one example (Hage 1998, 53). In terms of how it is both supported and upheld, and how it is denigrated and torn down, multiculturalism at present marks a crisis in white identity politics.

As I explore subsequently, it is the construction of whiteness that preserves the dominance by which race dictates the political and social boundaries of multiculturalism (Moreton-Robinson 2004). In the section that follows, I examine the particular manifestation of multiculturalism in the Australian context and explore its relationship to whiteness as well as what makes it similar to, and distinct from, that of other Western, settler nations. Issues of race, ethnicity, and whiteness inherent to the Australian multicultural context are at the core of the identity-making practices of young people from refugee backgrounds.

Multiculturalism and Whiteness in the Settler Nation

Multiculturalism emerged in the political and popular discourse of the Australian context, particularly in relation to immigration, after it was introduced as a policy framework by Al Grassby, immigration minister during the Whitlam Labor government in the early 1970s. Following the dismantlement of the White Australia Policy, Grassby (1973) advocated from a political standpoint for the maintenance of cultural heritage and social identity among migrants for broad social benefit. Since Grassby's initial introduction, multiculturalism in the Australian context has been a source of wide public controversy and intellectual debate (Jakubowicz 1985, 1).

When Australia abandoned the White Australia Policy, it became one of only a handful of Western nations to implement an official state immigration policy framework of multiculturalism (Joppke 2001). Along with Canada, Australia provides one of the most prominent examples of nations with an explicit, policy backed approach to multiculturalism (Joppke 2001). Multicultural policy may be described as providing a framework for addressing various forms of diversity in the context of universal rights and inclusion in a nation-state. As a political and social policy, multiculturalism has been widely theorized in democratic nations in terms of the extent to which it helps to define a "relationship between constitutional democracy and a politics that recognizes diverse cultural identities" (Gutmann 1994, ix).

The United States, on the other hand, provides an example of implicit multiculturalism. Multiculturalism in the U.S. context differs from that of Australia and Canada in both the political backdrop from which it was conceived and in the ways in which it is enacted. It does not emerge from a colonial mindset, and rather than being formalized through policy, multiculturalism in the United States relies instead solely on its moral impetus of inclusion and equality (Gunew 1993). While implicit multiculturalism is deeply entrenched as an ideological framework in the United States, U.S. citizenship does not claim an explicit multicultural component such as is the case for Canadian and Australian citizenship. While U.S. founding myths are based on the ideals of liberty, democracy and equality for example, British Commonwealth nations instead emphasize the pragmatic benefits of cultural diversity for what sociologist, Christian Joppke, describes as a "post-British nation-building commitment to multiculturalism" (Joppke 2001, 440–441).

Explicit multicultural policy in the Canadian context serves the primary "de-ethicizing" purpose of separating the dominant national language from the privileges of historically dominant groups (Joppke 2001, 31). Rather than being geared toward minorities, the bilingual framework of Canadian multiculturalism is designed as having an integrative capacity for society. Australian multicultural policy stresses further the limits of diversity and has an arguably more prominent nation-building agenda, with a particular focus on issues of minority integration, then present in the Canadian example (Joppke 2001).

Australia's National Agenda for Multicultural Australia, passed by the Labor government in 1989, states that "multicultural policies are based on the premise that all Australians should have an overriding and unifying commitment to Australia, to its interests and future first and foremost" (Joppke 2001, 438). Australia has, over time, loosened constraints in the naturalization process that previously aligned more explicitly with racial selectivity, such as lowering the language requirements and expectations of full cultural assimilation. To that end, the Australian multicultural policy framework, despite its capacity to ignite debate, has been documented as contributing to the successful integration of immigrants to Australia (Collins 2013; Kymlicka 2012).

In its formulations as both purely implicit and ideologically imposed, as well as explicit and policy based, modern, Western multiculturalism is currently under intense scrutiny. The rise of multiculturalism over recent decades through events like the demise of the White Australia Policy, the civil rights movement in the United States, and the opening up of borders in the European Union is now being reexamined (Taub 2016). The success, or lack thereof, of multiculturalism, in its many manifestations is marked by its ability to mitigate and manage diversity on the one hand, and to encourage and celebrate it on the other. From both perspectives, it is an emotionally charged battle, evoking waves of populism and a kind of turning point in white identity in the political epicenters of the Western world.

Donald Trump was elected president of the United States; the United Kingdom voted to exit the European Union; right-wing white nationalism is on the rise in a number of other European nations, including Norway, Hungary, Austria, Germany, and Greece; and Australia continues to struggle with a perceived crisis of refugee intake and integration (Bauman 2011, 2016; Roger Cohen 2016; Taub 2016). Each of these movements is the result of their own distinct conglomeration of issues broadly encompassed by race, class and gender. What they seemingly share, however, is the centering of what is depicted as a problem with multiculturalism—and at the heart of that problem, the consequent grappling with a perceived slippage of the status that a white identity once invariably secured.

A major part of Trump's platform relies on issues of immigration; the promise to deport large numbers of illegal immigrants and the practice of "extreme vetting" of refugees, especially from certain Muslim majority countries. The extent to which the popularity of this stance reflects economic disenfranchisement versus racism per se, is the subject of much of the current debate in the United States. The most likely explanation is that the two are deeply entangled with one another. A focus on problems broadly framed as a part of multiculturalism, such as illegal immigration, loss of jobs, and increased crime, represents an acceptable way for people to articulate their fear over what they perceive as a crisis for the white majority, without being accused of racism (Taub 2016). This rings true also for the current political debates on Australia's refugee problem, in which arguments for stopping the arrival of refugees continue to resurface in terms of protection from people smugglers and fairness to those waiting in an imaginary queue (Roger Cohen 2016; see also Hage 2018).

In the United States, as in Australia, white people are struggling with a sense of the loss of their foothold as the majority and all of the privilege that that entails. Although race is certainly part of it, the fear is better examined then easily dismissed with the label of racism or bigotry. As Taub (2016) argues, "being part of a culture designed around people's own community and customs is a constant background hum of reassurance, of belonging." With the perception of that hum of reassurance losing its potency, white people are being forced to contend with how they fit within the rapidly changing demographic makeup of their multicultural cities.

It would be inaccurate, however, to argue that all majority white populations struggle with cultural diversity in this way. Many embrace the moral objective of the multicultural project to promote diversity and an ethic of tolerance. So, let's leave behind, for a moment, the fraught political atmosphere in so many parts of the Western world where the legitimacy of multiculturalism itself is so hotly contested. Let's assume that the broad goal of equality in the face of diversity is established and accepted. And let's turn instead to the deep story of the power dynamics at play in how multiculturalism is implemented, and indeed, how it is experienced by those for whom it is most explicitly aimed at impacting. To do this, we need to start by looking at how race and ethnicity are intertwined with national belonging in multicultural contexts. This demonstrates how the messages that emerge from multiculturalism can be analyzed as a nation-building exercise enacted through the position of whiteness and the privilege it affords.

Managing Diversity and the Multicultural Ideal

Multiculturalism is widely and implicitly understood as a black or brown issue, with whiteness placed squarely at the other end of the spectrum. In popular understandings, multiculturalism is about how to manage, incorporate and deal with "multicultural" people—those of racial and ethnic backgrounds in need of management and inclusion—while whiteness is framed as the default norm. The inherent contradiction in this formulation in the Australian example, however, is in its implicit aim at nonwhite people. It is an aim that serves to racialize at the same time as it seeks to underscore the inconsequence of race as a broad moral aspiration of the Australian multicultural project.

Australian multicultural policy demonstrates this contradiction by providing a set of ideals that seek to both counter the relevance of race in achieving "Australianness" on one hand, and on the other, and to celebrate diversity in an emphasis of Australia's tolerance. The disconnect between the implementation and the expressed purpose of multiculturalism can be analyzed through the alternating messages, inherent to Australia's broad multicultural discourse, of the impetus for integration of those of nonwhite backgrounds and the need for tolerance among the white population. It is the more abstract sense of entitlement represented by whiteness that allows for the hierarchy of power through which some may lobby for better integration or, alternatively, exercise tolerance in their engagement with others.

The concept of whiteness is central to understanding both the messages projected through multicultural discourse and young people's engagement with those messages in the Australian multicultural context. Messages urging for smooth integration into what is broadly couched as mainstream, white Australian society, or alternatively, messages celebrating the perceived tolerance of that population are central to Australian multiculturalism. Such implicit messages are encountered at a discursive level in the terrain of young refugees' daily experiences as well as in the more formal, policy-level articulations of national belonging they confront in the process of obtaining Australian citizenship.

In my conceptualization, it is a power dynamic afforded by whiteness in the Australian multicultural context that generates the messages of integration and tolerance young people of minority backgrounds perceive, engage, and reflect in their own articulations of identity and belonging. I refer to such messages of integration and tolerance emerging from Australian multiculturalism more broadly as the moral framework of multiculturalism. The varied and complex ways in which these messages emerge and are perceived by young people provides the ethnographic crux of the book and the subject matter of the chapters that follow. Here, however, I will briefly unpack the discourses of integration and tolerance and how they surface in these young people's lives through what I refer to as the broad moral framework of multiculturalism.

Integration, Tolerance, and Belonging

I locate the particular ways in which tensions emerge for young people around the articulation of belonging as within the discourses, closely bound to multiculturalism, of integration and tolerance. Throughout the course of my fieldwork I became increasingly aware of messages, promoted in social discourse and broadly linked to multicultural policy, that sometimes ran counter to the popular multicultural agenda of equality and social cohesion. The delivery and interpretation of the messages of integration and tolerance can contribute to a sense of discord between the officially stated intention of multiculturalism and the varied ways in which it is experienced.

I take these messages as a focal point from which I analyze the identity-making practices engaged by young people. Messages of integration and tolerance operate at the national level of multicultural policy and the social and moral ideals it helps shape. They filter down to young people in their daily school environments, as well as through the more unique experiences related to being a refugee or migrant, such as that of the citizenship ceremony.

The discourses of both integration and tolerance serve to designate the need for social inclusion in national space. In doing so, a distinction emerges between those who ought to belong—and how their belonging might be approached through explicit political and social aims—and those who simply do belong. Messages of integration and tolerance are experienced by young people of nonwhite minority backgrounds as a means by which to differentiate between those whose difference is in need of governance and those who are to do the governing.

Integration and tolerance have come to encapsulate the abstract ideals of multiculturalism to foster universal rights and equality in the face of cultural diversity. They also represent the inherent contradiction in how multiculturalism is experienced by those it is implicitly designed to impact. In the Australian multicultural context, the expectations and pressures placed on young people from refugee backgrounds to integrate with the majority-white population and obscure their racial difference on the one hand, and to emphasize and celebrate it on the other, are paradoxical. The ideals of integration and tolerance are conflated with one another in the popular support of multiculturalism, reinforcing a power dynamic through which the boundaries of national belonging are established.

An article published in the *Sydney Morning Herald* (Megan Johnston 2011), citing Dunn's Challenging Racism project (2001–2008) began by posing (and then responding to) the question, "Is Australia a racist country? The answer to this troubling question turns out to be: overall, no." But the details of this initial claim were not so straightforward. The article went on to unpack the research findings, based on extensive quantitative data collected over a decade, which indicated that the majority of people surveyed were found to be tolerant of cultural difference, despite an undercurrent of "a problem with racism" in the country (Dunn, quoted in Megan Johnston 2011).

According to Dunn's research, approximately one third of Australians support "multiculturalism" at the same time as "assimilation" (Megan Johnston 2011). While people broadly support multiculturalism in terms of a tolerance for the desirable elements of diversity, many still see assimilation and integration as necessary for social cohesion. As mirrored in the results of this vast study on attitudes toward race, although current policies of multiculturalism and cultural diversity are characterized as breaking from the previous, less tolerant approaches of assimilation and integration, they contain a great degree of ideological overlap (Ang 2003; Ang, Hawkins and Dabboussy 2008; Butcher and Thomas 2006; Hage 1998; Kapferer 1998).

The structural similarities of the seemingly contradictory ideals of integration and tolerance are at the heart of the broad nation-building ethic of the multicultural project. As Hage argues, the "practice" of tolerance is itself a nationalist practice not dissimilar to the more obviously nationalist perspective inherent in an assimilationist or integrationist mentality. In alignment with Bourdieu's conceptualization of "strategies of condescension" (Bourdieu 1990, cited in Hage 1998, 87), Hage frames tolerance as "a strategy aimed at reproducing and disguising relationships of power in society" (1998, 87). For Hage (1998, 87), "Multicultural tolerance, like all tolerance . . . is a form of symbolic violence in which a mode of domination is presented as a form of egalitarianism." That is, the very capacity to exercise tolerance relies upon a perceived position of dominance and power in an imagining of the nation (Modood 2016). The mechanism that enables people to practice tolerance is the same that enables people to call for others to integrate, or indeed, to practice intolerance.

Discourses of both integration and tolerance manifest in the everyday experiences of young people from refugee backgrounds in Brisbane. And in their self-conscious representations of self, through which the boundaries of belonging are sought and policed, they hear, engage, and manipulate these messages. Through an analysis of their engagement with such discourses at school and in the broader national context, which is the subject of the chapters that follow, young people's identities emerge in dialogue with the multicultural agenda they encounter in their daily lives.

Integration and Tolerance in Context

Twenty of my informants became Australian citizens and attended a citizenship ceremony, seven during my fieldwork. The ceremony emphasizes that those obtaining citizenship are lucky to do so and to be in a superior nation, by virtue of its democratic nature, than that from which they came. At a ceremony I attended in March 2009, the lord mayor commented that here there are men in uniform to protect people, while in many parts of the world from which many people in the audience may be fleeing, this is not the case. He went on to state that "we are excited that you have a different religion, dress differently, eat different foods," that in Australia everyone will be given a "fair go" and that ideal citizens should join a political party, and participate and volunteer in their communities in order to "promote understanding, tolerance, and a cohesive community." At the ceremony, the benefits of multicultural tolerance and the celebration of difference were promoted in juxtaposition to the overriding message of the impetus to integrate into Australia as a superior nation-state.

Sentiments of national pride, expressions of tolerance, and assertions of the need for new arrivals to integrate into their new society invoked in relation to citizenship are replicated in popular and media debate. They emerged most prominently for young people in their local school environment, through anti-racist rhetoric, and the alternating promotion of Australian cultural values and tolerance for difference.

The notions of integration and tolerance, formally invoked at the citizenship ceremony and rooted in national immigration policy, were indeed echoed at Paddington High, where I conducted a significant part of my fieldwork. It was here that calls to integrate and the alternate promotion of tolerance were most immediate and relevant to the lives and identities of these young people. As many scholars have argued, for young people schools are sites where existing power dynamics and inequalities are learned and reinforced (Bourdieu and Passeron 1990; Simmons, Lewis and Larson 2011; Willis 1977). In my research experience, schools served as a primary site where the discourses emerging in national context were perceived and engaged by participants with both positive and negative consequence.

Paddington High had a strong antiracism rhetoric and a policy of "mainstreaming" English Language Learner (ELL) students. On my first day of fieldwork in February 2009, an ELL teacher told me that "race is not an issue at this school" and "we've hardly ever had any racist incidents here." There were so many young people with "different issues" at the school, it was explained to me, that race was simply "part of the mix." As the teacher went on to say, "This one has a disability, this one's in a wheel chair, this one can't read . . . it's like, 'come on, what do y'got?'" In this teacher's classification, race was akin to any other difference a student may experience—with difference positioned as an obstacle one must overcome in the quest for integration.

Race, for this teacher, was not used against fellow students, nor should it have been used by students to account for any aspect of their experience. Downplaying the relevance of race, emphasizing the rhetoric of antiracism, and the mainstreaming of ELL students all represent the broader attempts of the school to promote integration within the student community. In contrast to promoting integration, mobilizing the language of tolerance served to distinguish and celebrate young people's difference in reference to their ethnic identities, and indeed, their experiences as refugees.

An ethic of tolerance was promoted in the school environment through events that celebrated young people's ethnic backgrounds, such as "Multicultural Night," as well as providing a multitude of opportunities for them to tell their life stories or recount various aspects of their journeys to Australia. Similarly, tolerance was inherently promoted at another school where many of the young people who attended Kedron Club were enrolled. Instead of mainstreaming, at this school young people were segregated in an ELL learning stream. Within the discourses of integration and tolerance where the significance of skin color was explicitly denied, young people were also simultaneously singled out and bound to their refugee status in ways that were not always in line with their own sense and representations of self.

The discourses of integration and tolerance act upon the lives of refugees and migrants at the local, community and national level, while they are framed as both problems and victims based on racial signifiers (Rios-Rojas 2011). The young people represented in this book were defined through the ways in which they were cast as other through the discourses of integration and tolerance invoked in the school and community environment. Conversely, race, as a defining feature of their ethnic identities was at the same time denied through the mobilization of the discourses of integration and tolerance. Consequently, young people have to make sense of competing and contradictory messages, and as I will explain in the ethnographic chapters that follow, in doing so constitute their own sometimes explicitly racialized identities.

My ethnographic focus is on how the tensions of creating a sense of identity and belonging surface in the lives of young people in the context of their complex and often seemingly contradictory relationship with expectations and pressures emerging from Australian society more broadly. However, despite the degree to which it was or was not acknowledged by the young people themselves, their migration is an undeniably formative experience. So, in addition to the influence of national policy frameworks, social discourses and local experiences in their host country, young people also cultivate a sense of identity out of influences emerging from the pre-migration contexts of their lives. That is, their experiences as members of other national spaces and their journey to Australia. It is to this contextual background that I will now turn before moving on to my theoretical conceptualization in chapter 3, and the ethnographic material of the proceeding chapters.

Country of Origin and the Journey to Australia

The young people represented here contend with a number of unique influences on their lives related to where they came from, how and why, and the associated influences of home and family, class and gender. This range of influences impact upon what it means for them to be refugees despite their apparent disregard or general reluctance to self-identify as such. Elements of their lived histories and backgrounds, in addition to the influences of Australian sociopolitical frameworks and attitudes, form the backdrop against which they seek a sense of identity and social belonging. In the sections that follow, I provide brief introductory material to the ethnic backgrounds and countries from which these young people have migrated for readers unfamiliar with these places, as well as detail certain aspects of their experiences as refugees. This material is intended to locate young people's experiences in the Australian context by providing relevant details of their pre-migration lives and their journey to Australia.

I provide this information with some hesitation however, because such brief introductory material is inevitably simplistic, and because, as explained in chapter I, it was outside of the scope of my research design to conduct in-depth explorations of my participants' lives before resettlement. However, elements of the pre-migration aspects of their lives that emerged as significant to their sense of self and identity are revisited in greater detail in the ethnographic chapters that follow. For more in-depth analyses of the information I only briefly touch upon here, I refer the reader to the references cited throughout the sections that follow. I have organized this material both geographically and topically to distil what I observed as the most salient aspects of the young people's experiences.

African Participants

Before being resettled in Australia, a number of my Sudanese research participants lived in the Kakuma Refugee Camp in Northern Kenya, some lived in the Kiryandongo Refugee Settlement in Uganda, and others were temporarily settled in the urban center of Cairo, Egypt, where they faced racial discrimination and police violence. In addition to the twenty-three Sudanese participants, one participant migrated to Australia from Sierra Leone, via Guinea, and two from Uganda, via Kenya. The majority of Sudanese refugees come from Southern Sudan and immigrated as a result of the twenty-two-year civil war between rebel groups in the South and government forces in the North (Duffield 2003; Marlowe 2010; Obongo 2014). Many spent years in refugee camps before being settled in the United States, Canada, Australia, and the United Kingdom under humanitarian visa programs (Marlowe 2010).

Anecdotal information from teachers and the young people themselves indicates that many of my African participants spent some portion of their lives in refugee camps. However, life in refugee camps, and refugee status more broadly, was not directly or usually prominent in the represented identities of my African participants. On the other hand, as I detail subsequently, the interim countries in which these participants lived before coming to Australia were a constant source of discussion, comparison, and sometimes rivalry between participants.

All twenty-six of my African participants were Christian and the majority attended church (Anglican, Catholic, or Presbyterian) regularly with their families. They came from several different tribes including the Dinka, Nuer, Nuba, and Anuak of southern Sudan and the Acholi of northern Uganda. For some, discussing tribes was a regular source of amusement, camaraderie, rivalry, and general interest, while others preferred not to identify in this way (at least not in my presence). All of my African participants had some formal education, although there was, apparently, a significant amount of variance in how much and what kind.

Karen, Chin, and Burmese Participants

All eight Karen, one Chin, and two Burmese research participants were either born or spent most of their lives in refugee camps on the Thai-Burma border. As a result, these participants have had very little formal education. They share similar stories of fleeing Burma for Thailand and the majority grew up in the Tham Hin refugee camp, on the Thai-Burma border, before coming to Australia. Many knew of each other from the camp before their arrival in Brisbane. Having spent so much of their youth in the camp and having similar stories of their lives in and journey to the camp, these participants readily discussed and identified with their experiences of refugee camps, and they regularly shared news of friends and acquaintances still living there.

There are over 140,000 refugees living in camps along the Thai-Burma border. A majority are from the ethnic minority Karen (Karen Buddhist Dhamma Dhutta Foundation). Karen people are predominantly from southern and southeastern Burma and have endured six decades of civil war (Australian Karen Foundation). The imposition of the Burmese government military regime in 1962 resulted in the persecution of ethnic minorities and gross human rights violations that forced thousands to flee the country for neighboring refugee camps. The Chin people of northwestern Burma, a population of approximately 1.5 million, have endured a similar fate at the hands of the Burmese military regime (Bagnall 2010).

Most Karen and Chin refugees that resettled in Australia are Christian. All of my Karen and Chin participants were practicing Catholics. My two Burmese participants were Muslim. I discuss the various and complex ways these young people address and downplay religion within their friendship groups in chapter 4.

The common experiences of research participants in terms of the pre-migration contexts of their lives arguably evoked varying degrees and different forms of impact on their sense of self, identity, and belonging to their present social context. While they are not an explicit focus of the research, I provide these experiences and characteristics here for a more comprehensive understanding of the background of research participants and to substantiate the claim that they contend with such a range of influences originating from beyond the boundaries of the Australian national framework.

Moreover, as I detail later, the similar variability with which young people identified with their refugee status itself is broadly mirrored in its fluctuating and arbitrary assignment through national and international frameworks. I consider such broad defining experiences through which my participants' lives are framed in the context of their host country (e.g., being from war-torn countries, having lived in refugee camps or alternative transitory settings, being of a particular religious faith and having little to no access to formal education) in terms of the ways in which they gain shape and meaning in the lived contexts of their daily lives through, for example, the dynamics of family life.

Being a Refugee, and Family Life

All of the young people discussed in the book were living in some form of family arrangement. Of the eleven participants of Karen, Chin, and Burmese backgrounds, eight came to Australia with both parents and siblings, two came with only their mother, and one arrived and lived with only an older sister. Of the twenty-six African participants, fifteen lived with only their mother or a "stepmother" and siblings, eight lived with both parents and siblings, two lived with their grandmothers, and one lived with only older siblings. In the process of their journey to Australia, the familial relationships of many of these young people underwent a process of restructuring (e.g., cousins were represented and/or perceived as siblings, aunts were represented and/or perceived as mothers, and mothers were represented and/or perceived as "stepmothers"). Family dynamics were of central importance to young people's sense of themselves and where they fit in their social environment, as familial expectations and discourses both conflated and clashed with local and national discourses, frameworks, and pressures, as well as those stemming from peer groups.

As my central focus is on the tensions of belonging that emerge between young people, especially in the school environment, I explore the influence of family dynamics and pressures as they arose and were engaged by young people in this context. Dating, for example, was a significant issue for young people in which family dynamics were prevalent. As I will expand upon in chapter 4, one of the more regularly occurring ways in which young people expressed their desire to assert themselves as the same or different from other young people, usually based on some element of race or ethnicity, was through dating. When this clashed with parental expectations, conflict arose. Family dynamics form an important backdrop through which young people engage in a process of constituting belonging with one another and engage other defining aspects of their lives such as gender and class. Schools act as places where both young people and their parents are forced to negotiate relationships with people of different cultural backgrounds and socioeconomic positions (Neal and Vincent 2013). Moreover, for these young people it was the family that provided the most direct and relevant ties to their country of origin.

Unlike young people from second- and third-generation migrant backgrounds who also encounter intergenerational tensions but often have intangible associations with a "home" country, young people from refugee backgrounds frequently have strong ties to their country of origin and members of their family who still reside there. Therefore, they may be faced with a range of challenges, such as retaining the language and culture of the country from which they fled, while becoming accustomed to the country to which they have fled (Guerra and White 1995). Contributing to these complexities, young people from refugee backgrounds are more susceptible to high unemployment rates, low educational achievement, and the effects of trauma, post-traumatic stress disorder, loneliness, isolation, and depression (Broadbent, Cacciattolo and Carpenter 2007; Mosselson 2009).

Due to these complexities, much of the literature on young people from refugee backgrounds takes a problem centered approach in which young refugees are portrayed as victims or in constant tension as they are "torn between two worlds" (Ngo 2008, 4; see also Guerrero and Tinkler 2010; Ngo 2010; Rajaram 2002). I do not disagree that young people from refugee backgrounds are indeed marginalized in ways that are unique to their refugee status, and that such marginalization often becomes deeply entrenched. I accept, as Mosselson contends, that "refuge youth are rendered peripheral in their societies and have learned this marginalization in their new host countries" (2009, 451; see also Badea, Jetten, Iyer and Er-rafiy 2011).

Despite these challenges however, the young people at the center of this book did not always perceive themselves as marginalized, and when they did this marginalization was not always or directly attributed to their refugee status. Instead, when discussing refugee status specifically, or marginalization generally, young people would frequently slip into discussions of their race, ethnicity or socioeconomic positioning highlighting the importance of social class in the analysis of multicultural perspectives (Neal and Vincent 2013). The term *refugee* was often used, even by young people of official refugee status, to describe others—they sometimes described living, for certain periods of their lives, "like a refugee." This distancing from the category of refugee is likely at least in part the result of what Jackson (2002, 91) notes as the phenomenon through which life, in experiences of rupture, crisis and trauma, "all but ceases to be warrantable." The refugee experience of flight often erupts so profoundly out of context to the lives of people before and after such events, that it lacks the coherent framework necessary for its retelling.

Nonetheless, and while I did not actively pursue them, young people did on occasion offer narratives of flight and trauma in association with the refugee experience. I interpret their narrative accounts as helping them to transcend the objective label of refugee. Through the process of retelling stories of their experiences as refugees, those experiences are actively reformed in ways that might integrate their personal narrative with the ways in which they are externally framed (Jackson 2002, 15). I consider young people's overlapping narratives of their refugee experiences with the ways in which their lives are framed in the Australian context in the ethnographic chapters that follow.

In this chapter, my aim was to discuss the broader social and political contexts through which the young people in my study engaged in the processes of constituting a sense of themselves and belonging. I began by providing an overview of immigration history and attitudes toward migrants and refugees in Australia and how multiculturalism arose out of this fraught context. Contested as multiculturalism often is in the modern, Western world, I identified the discourses of integration and tolerance as emerging from the current policy framework and moral landscape of Australian multiculturalism. In line with Hage (1998) and Povinelli (2002), among others, I identified both integration and tolerance as nationalist practices emerging out of a position of whiteness. I argued that discourses of integration and tolerance are demonstrative of the power dynamics which act as barriers in belonging to the Australian national space for these young people.

The various contexts which constitute the ethnographic setting through which the book takes place—host country, country of origin, the experience and status of being a refugee, and family life—all offer (and exclude) some form of what can be described as symbolic capital (Bourdieu 1986). It is symbolic capital that permits the kind of cultural competence that ultimately allows for an enhanced sense of being or belonging in social context. While a primary focus of this chapter was on the various ways in which a sense of belonging is both limited and made available to people in the Australian national space, the accumulation of being and belonging is not simply a passive process. Rather, it emerges as people respond to and actively engage with the constraints and opportunities particular to the social contexts in which they arise.

In chapter 3 I will establish the conceptual lens of youth responsiveness to sociopolitical context and examine relevant theoretical perspectives. In the proceeding ethnographic chapters, I examine young people's identity work with a focus on how the narrative framework of Australian multiculturalism affects that process. It is their constitution and representations of themselves that emerges in response to the Australian multicultural context that is the key focus of the book and the subject of the central research findings in the chapters that follow.

3

Identity in Theory

Responsiveness and Belonging among Refugee Youth

From early on in my fieldwork, it became apparent that race was a central frame of reference for the young people in my study. Whether they were explaining to me how and why skin color was an essential component of their experience, critical to everything from how they chose their friends to the development of their world view; or whether they were doing the opposite and explaining how skin color had exactly zero relevance to their lives, they talked about it constantly. At the same time, it became increasingly apparent that race was a particularly loaded topic in the public moral discourses that framed their everyday lives.

As described in chapter 2, young people's experiences at school and in other aspects of their lives after resettlement in Australia were peppered with attempts toward, and talk about, integration and tolerance. I frame the concepts of integration and tolerance as discourses emerging from a multiculturalism that manifested in young people's daily lives. Through messages of integration and tolerance, these young people were called upon to both downplay the relevance of race for successful assimilation, as well as to emphasize and celebrate their racial and ethnic difference when called upon to do so.

Over time, I began to see these two phenomena—young people's talk about race, and the ways in which race was treated or managed in their daily environments—as linked. Young people's sense of identity, of course, develops from a vast entanglement of influences, experiences and beliefs. Yet certain ways in which they represented themselves seemed to emerge in a dynamic relationship with the ways in which their status as minority and refugee youth were addressed in the public and political sphere. In this chapter I seek to establish the mechanisms through which the relationship between refugee youth identities and the Australian multicultural context arises.

In doing so, I examine relevant theories of identity and develop my conceptual lens of dynamic responsiveness as a key element of the identity work of young people from refugee backgrounds. I utilize the notion of dynamic responsiveness to explore the role of social context in the identity-making practices of these young people. Central to this conceptual lens, I explore the concepts of hybridized and essentialized representations of identity and how they are mobilized by young people in dynamic response to the sociopolitical backdrop of their lives. Also, of key significance to the ways in which young people represent themselves, I explore Bourdieu's (1986) concept of "capital" and the role it plays in helping these young people establish a sense of belonging.

I conceptualize hybridity and essentialism as modes of self-representation which allow a kind of agency or participation in the ways in which these young people are represented in the Australian national context. I utilize the concept of capital to highlight how young people's hybridized and essentialized self-representations demonstrate a degree of cultural awareness as they establish a sense of themselves and cultivate a sense of belonging in Australia. A note of warning, in unpacking these overlapping and sometimes theoretically dense concepts, I shift between abstract analyses of their broad relevance to the anthropological literature, and explanation of their relevance to the identity work of these young people. I do so to locate young people's identity work in this ethnographic context, within the scope of scholarship on broader social processes.

The often highly self-conscious representations of self that ensue between young people can be understood at once as the inevitable consequence of social and historical contexts, and also as the work of partially knowing actors who playfully engage and respond to these contexts with one another. As such, elements of structure, culture and agency converge in potent ways in the spaces where young people approximate identity and belonging through responsiveness.

Young people's hybridized and essentialized representations of themselves emerged with reference to their sense of racial and ethnic identity. Before delving into my theoretical framework on identity and responsiveness, it is important to briefly highlight the conceptual slippage between the terms race and ethnicity in sociopolitical usage, as well as in how they were employed by my research participants and how I in turn use them in the analysis presented here.

Race and Ethnicity: Untangling the Terms of Conceptual Overlap

I use the term *race* to signify skin color explicitly where it was similarly mobilized by participants. I use terms such as *ethnicity* or *ethnic identity* to indicate elements of language or culture, and the term *racialized* to signal the overlap between young people's references to skin color and ethnic heritage.

While there is no standard definition of what constitutes an ethnic grouping, ethnicity is usually associated with (but does not require) a distinguishing name and other shared traits such as: past history, common heritage, language, religion, nationality or territory, world view, and aspects of physical appearance.

While ethnicity is decidedly rooted in culture, the concept of race has drawn much critical engagement from scholars in recent decades due to its association with biology. It is now largely dismissed as a social construct with no biological basis.

To say the least, "race" is a highly controversial concept. In its ugliest form, it has been used to inaccurately categorize genetic variation from which racist stereotypes and power structures have been justified. Most recent developments in genetic research suggest possible links between race and DNA but purportedly maintain that such links should not be used to support current racial stereotypes, and advocate for a new way to talk about race and genetic difference that does not lend itself to racism (Reich 2018). As critics have pointed out, these most recent attempts to resurrect the category of race as more than a social construct, capitalize on geographically based genetic variation but fail to demonstrate a precise correlation with biological or social definitions of racial categories (Goodman and Darnovsky 2018). Social scientists largely maintain that a belief in innate difference between humans based on decisive "racial" characteristics is not only theoretically untenable, but also a misconception with profound implications (Billinger 2007, 6). Careful attention to historical contexts and a range of sociocultural factors demonstrate that race as a defining category must be analyzed primarily as a social construct. However, despite ongoing debate over the biological implications of race, as a paradigm upon which human difference is often categorized, it cannot be ignored that race remains a dominant conceptual framework.

In theory, political institutions in Australia and elsewhere utilize the concept of race to describe observable physical characteristics such as skin color, and ethnicity for characteristics such as language and country of origin. However, in practice there is a great deal of policy overlap as racial and ethnic markers are often used interchangeably; for example, people may be classified as of European heritage or white, or of African American heritage or black (Bucholtz 2011, 6; see also Omi and Winant 2011). Likewise, there was a great deal of conceptual slippage among the young people represented here in their identification with racial or ethnic markers—they defined themselves as African or black, as Karen or "not a white," and as Burmese or "a brown skin."

I utilize each of these terms in the instances and ways in which the young people themselves did so, and commonly indicate this through quotation marks. Of critical note here, is my participants heavy use of the term "African" as a descriptor, and how this sits in contrast to the Karen young people's lack of use of the term "Asian," despite its currency as a category of identification in Western nations. When using the term African to refer to themselves, my participants appeared to be establishing solidarity with one another through a transnational, diasporic identification in similar fashion to how they utilized the descriptor "being black." Such positive and binding association with the

Western categorization of "Asian" appeared not to exist in similar fashion for Karen participants. Indeed, the only time I recall and recorded a Karen, Chin, or Burmese young person use the category of Asian as a descriptor was when Wah Wah described how she hoped to date an "English, not Asian boy." Asian, as a category, appeared not to carry the cool or desirability of an African identity as young people of Karen, Chin, and Burmese backgrounds opted instead for ethnic or nation specific terms to describe themselves. Their choices of identifying terms here serve to further highlight the dynamic processes of identification.

These young people perceived and experienced a kind of external labeling of their ethnicities which indirectly emphasized and alternately denied the significance of race and ethnicity. It was in part in response to this external marking of their ethnicities that young people emphasized hybridized and essentialized representations of themselves, often with significant reference to race. Moreover, their practice of alternately evading and inhabiting racialized identities serves to further highlight the inherent link between whiteness and multiculturalism and the subtle ways in which young people may both resist and echo this nexus. That is, slippage between race and ethnicity in policy related and broader social narratives was also reflected in the complex identity-making practices engaged by these young people.

Let me now approach this complexity. In doing so, I seek to establish my conceptual lens of responsiveness by exploring some broad theoretical perspectives of identity in the anthropological literature, through which I demonstrate how identity emerges in response to social environment. I will then explore the concepts of hybridity and essentialism in the anthropological literature and as I utilize them in analyzing the identity work of young people from refugee backgrounds. I argue that hybridized and essentialized representations of identity are mobilized in response to the social and moral framework of the multicultural landscape, thereby acting as a form of capital which aids in the cultivation of belonging for these young people.

Identity through Dynamic Responsiveness

Cultivating a sense of identity is at its core a subjective, comparative process. It involves emphasizing similarities to certain people in certain contexts, and differences to others. Similarity and difference are not objective attributes of course, but rather perceptions and products of people's interactions with one another (Gilroy 1997, 315; see also Brubaker and Cooper 2000; Gilroy 1993, 2005).

In a broad anthropological perspective, the cultivation of identity through an emphasis on difference manifests in socially established categories such as race, ethnic groups, or gender. Difference allows groups to define themselves in opposition to other, often dominant groups. A prominent example of this in the anthropological literature is Fredrick Barth's (1969) classic work on ethnic identity. In it, he detailed the strategies and production of cultural forms invoked by ethnic groups in northwest Pakistan, for maintaining their distinctiveness and boundaries in relation to other groups. Barth emphasized that establishing difference is central for the maintenance of a collective group affiliation (Barth 1969; Jenkins 2008). Likewise, Stuart Hall argued that a sense of groupness is constructed through defining who the group is not, rather than through defining who it is (1996, 17). This process of exclusion, as Hall also noted, emerges from the power dynamics of particular social contexts (Hall 1996:4)

Conversely, the cultivation of identity through an emphasis on similarity in the creation of community and solidarity, as notably demonstrated in the work of social theorists Benedict Anderson (1991) and Michael Billig (1995), is also deeply political and results in such powerful ideologies as nationalism. In his conceptualization of "imagined communities," Anderson (1991) argued that nations are not inherent groupings but represent socially constituted distinctions in that the communion they imply exists in the minds of those who imagine themselves a part of it. While they may emerge as "imagined" however, such ideologies do not merely function in the imaginary (Jenkins 2008). Instead, the cultivation of commonality can act as a powerful motivating force in people's lives with such far reaching implications as to define what constitutes a nation and why (Billig 1995). The creation of community through assertions of similarity is an all but straightforward process—a process, however, that for reasons difficult to define, is ever important to individuals (Skey 2011, 9).

This process of emphasizing similarity and difference that the work of establishing identity entails, represents, in effect, a response to social context. As I apply the concept of responsiveness to identity making, I seek to highlight the reactive and evolving nature through which a sense of self or group emerges. Identity is not objective, and it does not emerge in a bubble. It is established against and in accordance with the predominant social stimuli of a given social context. Dynamic responsiveness is especially relevant when theoretically leveraged in the analysis of youth identities. It usefully captures the sensitivity and perception required to cultivate a sense of self-definition and inclusion in social context—an impetus at the heart of the process of identity making. This drive for inclusion and a sense of self-definition is particularly salient for young people at the transition into adulthood; a time when how we are perceived by others is of great consequence.

For my research participants, who were effectively between national contexts and who constituted different racial, ethnic, and language groupings, asserting sameness and difference in regard both to each other and to others in the broad landscape of their social environments was particularly fraught, complicated, and indeed, significant to their sense of self and social belonging. Young people from refugee backgrounds are in between a number of identifying categories and therefore have a range of choices in whom they may align themselves with and differentiate themselves from, and for what purposes they may choose to do so (see also Badea et al. 2011, 586). For example, they are often viewed as different in their host country due to various racial- and ethnic-based signifiers, yet they are also often viewed as different within their own families (both in the host country and still residing in their country of origin), who see them entering and adapting to a new cultural space. They are not quite one, not quite the other.

How then did these young people create belonging by emphasizing sameness and difference, to different people and in different ways, in their multifarious self-representations? And how did these identity-making practices act in dynamic response to their social context? In many ways, these questions are at the heart of the content of the chapters that follow. In order to develop the conceptual platform from which I interpret their identity work, however, I must provide some details of the ethnographic punch line here.

In some instances, young people articulated difference from the broader population and similarity to one another in the creation of a collective group identity and a sense of belonging with one another. They did so by emphasizing ethnic signifiers, such as skin color, through which they mobilized racialized, essentialized self-representations. On the other hand, they sometimes articulated a sense of similarity to the broader population and difference to one another as they emphasized a sense of integration and connection with wider Australian society. They did so often by explicitly downplaying those same ethnic signifiers and putting forth what they described in terms of a "mixed," or, as I conceptualize it here, a more "hybridized" representation of themselves.

Hybridity and essentialism are central themes related to scholarship on identity in social science research. Here, I detail the broad emergence and application of these concepts as well as the critique they have drawn. In doing so, I explain and justify my use of hybridity and essentialism for analyzing the complex relationship between identity and social context among these young people from refugee backgrounds.

The Hybridized Response: Merging and Acknowledging Difference

Firstly, it is worth noting that the term hybridity has a loaded historical association as it was used to signify "racial mixing" in colonial ideology (Papastergiadis 1997). In current trends however, the concept of hybridity has been largely shifted from this earlier association. In the last two decades, particularly in the fields of cultural theory and postcolonial studies, most prominently through the works of Edward Said (1979), Stuart Hall (1993), and Homi Bhabha (1994, 1996), the term *hybridity* has been used to demonstrate a kind of duality which can emerge in an individuals' sense of identity. It was initially applied to analyze the dynamics of interchange between colonizers and colonized, and then extended more broadly to the current world context (see also Werbner 1997b).

Hybridity has come to represent the fluid and emergent nature of social selves as depicted in current theoretical frameworks and in the context of the global overlapping of ethnicity, race, and culture in local settings (Bhabha 1994; Papastergiadis 1997; Young 2006). The concept is now widely used in scholarship to connote a positive process of merging, mixing, combining and overlapping different representations of ethnicity and cultural identity in the creation of new representations. In its recent appropriation for representing ethnicities, scholars use hybridity as a way of countering the simple dualities of hyphenated identities and emphasizing the dynamic and complex nature of ethnic identity (Noble and Tabar 2002). Considering this evolution of the concept, Papastergiadis urges that "we now have the confidence that Hybridity has been moved out from the loaded discourse of 'race,' and situated within a more neutral zone of identity" (1997, 257). It is in its relationship to self-understanding and identity making that the concept of hybridity is useful in approaching the complexity and multiplicity of the subjective positioning of young people from refugee backgrounds. Even in this more productive application to understanding identity however, hybridity has still been subject to wide debate and critique—and rightly so.

While it is a useful tool for highlighting the degree to which identities are the result of overlapping cultural influences in the modern, globalized world, hybridity is an insufficient concept for gaining understanding about how specific identities emerge or how belonging is approached. As anthropologist, Henrietta Moore (2011) states, "Its advantage is that it appears to capture differences in reception and response to external influences of all kinds, but its weakness is that it gives little insight or understanding into how or why these specific differences should be generated" (Moore 2011, 63). In other words, simply claiming that identities are "mixed" or "in-between" does not give us much analytic leverage. It does not help us to understand how or why or the processes by which such mixed identities emerge.

Considering this shortcoming, I use the term *hybridity* not simply to represent a merging or mixing of cultural symbols in the presentation of a new sense of identity, as it has been applied most recently to scholarship on identity. Instead, I reserve the term to capture people's own emphasis on the flexibility with which they constitute a sense of themselves and belonging to others, albeit through a range of symbolic cultural resources. That is, I use hybridity to capture a kind of self-representation in alignment with mixing and merging, rather than to describe new formulations of identities through actions of mixing and merging as such.

In a footnote to her argument, Moore states that her aversion to the concept of hybridity, in its application as an analytic framework, is related to hierarchies of power in postcolonial contexts, not as it emerges in "those social and national contexts where the concept of hybridity has been part of lived experience and woven into nationalist discourse of identity and citizenship" (2011, 209). As she goes on to argue, "hybridity as a sign and as a marker of cultural identity has . . . become part of a series of identifications and possibilities for self-fashioning . . . which also includes the use of cultural difference as a form of governmentality, as in policies of multiculturalism" (2011, 210). I maintain that unless demonstrated as relevant to and emerging out of people's self-identification, the concept of hybridity is without analytic merit. I offer justification for my use of the term *hybridity* in line with Moore's exception. That is, hybridity has a specific, localized context of meaning for young people from refugee backgrounds in Australia.

I use the concept of hybridity in terms of its "regional" value—it emerges in Australian multicultural discourse through the value placed on mixing and merging inherent to the notion of integration—and in terms of the doubling back wherein my informants employ flexibility as a foundational, explanatory element of their self-identification. That is, I use hybridity as a way of demonstrating young people's own emphasis on their capacity for flexibility, rather than to depict elements of their fixed identities which I, as a researcher, have deemed to derive from a process of mixing or merging. My conceptualization of hybridity refers to the ways in which young people presented themselves as flexible, and the ways in which they emphasized an ability to bridge or incorporate difference in representations of themselves and thus fit their conceptualization of the mainstream population.

The concept of hybridity is often depicted as positive and progressive in the scholarship on identity, as opposed to negative and regressive depictions of essentialism (Noble and Tabar 2002, 133). As Pieterse puts it, hybridity is conceived as, "the antidote to essentialist notions of identity and ethnicity" (1995, 55). I do not celebrate hybridity as entirely emancipatory. And to be sure, in other contexts participants also emphasized their lack of tolerance for difference as they enforced (ever shifting) boundaries on themselves and one another through their essentialized self-representations. Let's now turn to the scholarly roots of essentialism and my application of this concept for analyzing refugee youth identity.

The Essentialized Response: Merging Difference, Emphasizing Sameness

Scholarly opposition to essentialism, as it relates to cultural identity, is due to the fact that the concept is based upon the now widely discredited notion that cultural identities are fixed and immutable (Bhabha 2006; Noble and Tabar 2002; Werbner 1997a). In its most common usage, essentialism is the act of applying given properties to an individual or group and carries the implication that such individuals or groups may be singularly characterized. Werbner (1997a, 228) defines the act of essentializing as: "to impute a fundamental, basic, absolutely necessary constitutive quality to a person, social category, ethnic group, religious community, or nation. It is to posit falsely a timeless continuity, discreteness or boundedness in space, and an organic unity. It is to imply an internal sameness and external difference or otherness."

In this most basic form, when it is used as a mode of representation of one group, and applied by another, essentialism is an oppressive act. Moreover, as Werbner points out the objectification inherent in essentializing is as necessary in progressive political agendas such as citizenship rights and multiculturalism as it is for divisive acts of racism (1997a, 229).

In response to oppressive acts of essentializing, particularly with regard to race and ethnicity, antiessentialism emerged as an intellectual trend in academic discourse (Werbner 1997a). Antiessentialism provides an alternative to racist discourse, which seeks to apply precise defining attributes to race and ethnicity, and thereby seeks also to deny the fluid, open, hybrid nature and context driven modes through which these categories are now commonly believed to be constituted (Werbner 1997a, 226). However, as Werbner points out, essentialism should not itself be essentialized—that is, who is doing the essentializing, to whom, and for what purpose must be considered in the essentialism/antiessentialism debate (1997a, 226). It is at the crux of this argument where essentialism is made relevant to the identity-making practices of these young people.

There is a distinction between self-essentializing practices through which people depict themselves as static and unchanging despite the flexibility through which such depictions are often created, versus external, racist essentializing practices in which the explicit purpose is to represent other people in ways that do not allow for change or flexibility. As Werbner (1997a, 248) states, "Self-essentializing as a mode of reflexive imagining is constitutive of self and subjectivity. It is culturally empowering. But it is not, unlike racist reifications, fixed and immutable." The term *self-essentializing* represents a positive act through which people may create an "imagined community" for some beneficial purpose (Werbner 1997a, 230). Such an imagined community is often presented as unchanging and immobile, for the purpose of creating solidarity, and through emphasizing the commonality and similarity of its members.

"Strategic essentialism" is a term for self-essentializing that prominent social theorist Gayatri Spivak (1990) first used to describe the ways in which marginalized groups create and invoke solidarity in order to respond politically to their marginalization. Spivak's work illustrates that although it may be theoretically incorrect to represent marginalized groups in essentialized ways based upon race, gender, so forth, it is often the case that those groups do just that themselves, and they do so often for specific political purposes (Hollinsworth 2006; Spivak 1990). The concept of "strategic essentialism" can also be applied in a critical understanding of how marginalized groups may adapt an essentialized otherness in their everyday practices to create a sense of self and belonging (Noble et al. 1999, 31).

While presented as static and unchanging, the defining terms of an essentialized group may shift and evolve over time and across contexts. As Hollinsworth illustrates in reference to marginalized groups, "In the process of demanding recognition, these groups often come to depend ideologically and organizationally on Essentializing that difference, denying any common ground with their category's opponents" (2006, 59). The category of "opponents" in acts of self-essentializing is also shifting and lacking in clear boundaries. As a result, relationships that infer sameness and those that infer difference are dynamic and context dependent.

The concept of "strategic essentialism" as well as that of hybridity helps to explain the identification processes of "switching between 'same' and 'different' in multiple and unpredictable ways" (Hollinsworth 2006, 61). Both hybridized and essentialized self-representations evolve through a process of merging differences, however in hybridized representations that process of merging differences may be acknowledged and in essentialized representations it is often denied.

It should be clear, then, that the concepts of hybridity and essentialism contain a great deal of overlap and are not entirely dichotomous or oppositional. Instead, as I employ them here, these concepts are useful in highlighting different *emphases* in young people's representations of themselves and the ways in which they characterize their own processes of identification with others. Hybridity as a *process* is evident in both essentialized and hybridized self-representations—the merging of some inherent differences is necessary in constituting a sense of self or commonality with others. What I am interested in is the ways in which young people acknowledged and maintained this initial merging of difference in their hybridized representations of identity or denied it in their essentialized representations. Taken together, the variability with which difference may be merged in the representation of cohesion and unity might, depending on emphasis, be described in terms of hybridity or essentialism. For these young people, hybridized and essentialized representations of identity were almost always projected as they either emphasized or denied the relevance of race and ethnicity to their sense of themselves.

Race, Ethnicity, Choice, and a Note on Intersectionality

To be sure, the conceptual terms I've discussed thus far are both fraught—hybridity, in its historical association with race and its imprecise characterization of cultural mixing, and essentialism, in its simplification of complex and evolving racial and ethnic identities. Despite and even because of their explanatory shortcomings, these terms are both of particular relevance here. As noted earlier, I conceptualize hybridity and essentialism not only or exactly in terms of observations of young people's actions, but more precisely as a means of interpreting and analyzing their own reflections of how their sense of identity comes to be. Such self reflections allowed for a kind of participation in the dominant scripts of the broader national context in which their lives unfolded.

Central to this dominant script are questions about race, ethnicity, and how to manage and live with diversity. These young people reflected alternating fixed and flexible representations of their sense of an ethnic and racial self in relationship to their perception and experience of a sometimes overt, sometimes more indirect, racialization of their ethnicity in the Australian context. Their ability to emphasize and deemphasize their racial and ethnic identities through hybridity and essentialism points to the concept of "ethnic choice" (Song 2003). Ethnic choice speaks to the complex ways in which people from what are commonly conceived as ethnic minority backgrounds, can negotiate their own self-image and sense of themselves in the context of structural constraints or racial and ethnic labeling perceived as emerging from the broader community.

The notion of ethnic choice illustrates how, despite constraints, people exercise a considerable amount of agency in how they portray and represent their ethnicity for creating belonging in social life. As Song argues, people engage an array of "strategies" to respond to the limitations and manipulate the meanings of externally assigned ethnic categorizations. Among these strategies, people may choose, in Song's terms, "adherence to the dominant scripts" or "opting out" (2003, 55–57). These labels capture the degree of flexibility in how much one chooses to match the dominant representations of a particular ethnic group or demonstrate an alternative representation. Of course, the fullness of such "choices" concerning race and ethnicity must be tempered with the reality that the expectations of other members of an ethnic group, or indeed those outside of it, will limit and police an individual's ability to make choices that go against the dominant scripts.

Moreover, people must contend themselves with a number of scripts that both inform and inhibit the extent of their ethnic choices. For the young people represented here, their status as youths as well as their gender, socioeconomic class, and migration status intersect in the formation and representation of their racial and ethnic identities. The concept of intersectionality captures such multiple positionings and the inherent power dynamics they entail (Carroll 2017). Migrant youths in particular are faced with the dominant scripts of the mainstream culture of their place of resettlement, as well as the often competing expectations of their families and culture of origin. This complexity is especially true as it relates to race and gender among young migrants and refugees.

At the intersections of race and gender—both of which are relational, fluid, social constructs—the neatness with which young people understand themselves as same or different in comparison to broad, cultural expectations is disrupted (Cho, Crenshaw and McCall 2013). In other words, analyzing young people's racial and ethnic identity, as it intersects with other aspects of their identity such as gender, complicates both their essentialized depictions of sameness and their hybridized depictions of difference to the broader population. Beyond this, the complex ways in which young people may emphasize or vacate their racial identities may indeed be gendered. Are girls more likely to be urged toward tolerance or integration than are boys? How does this affect their representation of hybridized and essentialized identities? While these considerations are valid and indeed worthy of interrogation, the range of research informants represented here did not reveal a definitive gendered component to their hybridized and essentialized representations of racial identity.

What was exceedingly clear throughout the course of my fieldwork, however, was that these young people represented themselves in different and often seemingly contradictory ways, in different contexts through their near constant references to race and ethnicity. These ethnic and racial choices were determined through young people's mobilization of what I have described in terms of hybridized and essentialized depictions of their interactive selves.

In other words, these young people cultivated essentialized representations of themselves in their daily interactions as they sought to fix themselves in relationship to one another often with reference to race and ethnicity. Paradoxically, the processes through which they created a sense of fixed and immutable identities were often heavily reliant upon hybridizing strategies. The ways in which they emphasized a sense of sameness to one another in their essentialized self-representations, or a capacity to incorporate difference in their hybridized self-representations, is indicative of a responsiveness to the political context of their lives. The oscillating hybridized and essentialized self-representations through which these young people cultivate a sense of identity ultimately act as a form of capital through which they respond to their social context and approach a sense of belonging.

Dynamic Responsiveness as Symbolic Capital

As Moore argues, "the interconnections between personal fantasies and social imaginaries have to be analyzed within specific social, economic and political circumstances" (2011, 61). I interpret these young people's choices in how they represent their sense of racial and ethnic identity as related to the ways in which notions of racial essentialism and hybridity are engaged in their broad social landscapes. Consequently, their own hybridized and essentialized self-representations reflect the perception and accumulation of a kind of symbolic capital which emerges in dynamic response to certain ideals of multiculturalism. To understand the notion of "capital" and how it relates to the identity work of these young people, it is necessary to briefly outline the emergence of the concept in the work of prominent social scientist Pierre Bourdieu.

Capital and the Field

First, I understand the Australian national space in ways that align with Bourdieu's conceptual framework of "field" (see also Hage 1998, 53). The field represents a lens for analyzing individuals and groups as positioned within a relationally constituted structure, in which they engage in competition for various forms of material and symbolic goods deemed valuable within the field (Bourdieu 1984, 228; Bourdieu and Wacquant 1992, 96). The Australian multicultural context itself may be described as a "field" because it represents a space where people of diverse cultural and ethnic backgrounds struggle to define what constitutes belonging and how resources and rights are best allocated. As Harris describes, Australian multiculturalism represents "a dynamic, lived field of action within which social actors both construct and deconstruct ideas of cultural difference, national belonging and place-making" (Harris 2009, 187). The Australian multicultural space may also be understood as an especially important field for the domain of youth where power dynamics and individual agency converge in localized settings (see also Bottrell and France 2015). The field, in Bourdieu's conceptualization, represents a space where "capital" is distributed. Resources, both symbolic and material, deemed valuable within the field, are considered "capital."

Bourdieu's formulation of cultural and social capital refers broadly to valued preferences within a given field, in terms of embodied and dispositional characteristics (such as, in the national field, appearance, accent, preferences for behavior, etc.) and material cultural goods (e.g., art, books, etc.), as well as how these resources equate to a sense of belonging and membership within a group (Bourdieu 1986, 243–248). The accumulation of social and cultural capital when recognized and valorized by others is transformed into symbolic capital, defined by Hage as "the recognition and legitimacy given to a person or group for the cultural capital they have accumulated" (Hage 1998, 53). I utilize the concept of "symbolic ethnic capital" to describe the ways in which young people represented highly racialized depictions of their ethnic identity through performance in chapter 5.

The embodied and dispositional characteristics provoked in response to particular fields and in relation to symbolic capital is known in Bourdieu's analysis as "habitus." Otherwise defined as "a socially constituted system of cognitive and motivating structures" (Bourdieu 1977, 76), habitus reflects both a fundamentally embodied practical sense or reading of social context (e.g., how one moves and carries themselves in particular fields), through the accumulation of symbolic capital, as well as the generative capacity that practical sense allows for new thoughts and actions to emerge. While Bourdieu's overall framework has been criticized as overly deterministic (Adams 2006, 515), the conceptual intersection of habitus, capital, and field is useful in reflecting the ways in which I broadly frame the self-representations observed among participants as a kind of responsiveness to, or participation in, their current social context.

Refugee Youth and Australian Multicultural Capital

Cultural capital is traditionally regarded as controlled and distributed in the domain of institutions like schools and used by parents and professionals to the advantage of certain groups over others (France, Bottrell and Haddon 2012). Attention to the "objectified nature of cultural capital" as it emerges through interaction in more informal settings however, can inform a sense of agency among young people (France et al. 2012). In the Australian context, discourses promoting the value of effective integration on the one hand, and those promoting tolerance and the notion of antiracism on the other, are prevalent. I consider such discourses as a form of capital in the Australian multicultural field. I use the term *multicultural capital* to refer to those discourses and the broad moral elements of multiculturalism in the Australian space. People from refugee and minority backgrounds may simultaneously be asked to develop fragmented identities for more effective assimilation or integration; treated as more or less one-dimensional in the name of tolerance; and both problematized and celebrated from both angles. Young people are aware of these dynamics and engage with the ideals and messages emerging from Australian multiculturalism in terms of their use of multicultural capital.

Through messages of integration and tolerance, multiculturalism that young people are exposed to in their lived experiences promotes both the irrelevance of skin color, and the celebration of racialized diversity. As I observed them, these messages alternated between a denial of "race" as a defining characteristic and the consequent emphasis on hybrid identities on one hand, and on the other, the promotion of diversity as distinguished by and essentialized through skin color and culture of origin. Young people's practice of inhabiting and evading racial and ethnic identity through hybridized and essentialized representations of themselves occurs in conjunction with those messages of integration and tolerance inherent to multicultural discourse.

By constituting themselves and their sense of belonging through what can be described as hybridized and essentialized representations, whereby they speak to their own sense of identity, young people effectively exercise their perception of, and response to, the multicultural capital that frames their lives. In doing so, they figure themselves into the dialogue and approach a sense of belonging in the Australian multicultural field. For example, despite the tenuousness with which participants' schools (and the broader community) often engaged with race through multicultural discourse, it was indeed one of the most salient aspects of their identities. Young people's essentialized representations of identity where skin color was made central emerged both in subtle opposition to messages promoting the ethos of integration and antirace rhetoric and in accordance with the ethic of tolerance and celebrating and accentuating their difference, both of which they regularly encountered in their schools and community environments (Moran 2016).

Conversely, the same participants also regularly represented themselves in hybridized ways in which they demonstrated both the insignificance of the restrictive descriptors of race and ethnicity as well as their ability to mix and merge with young people of different ethnic and racial backgrounds. Through their emphasis on hybridity in their processes of identification, young people aligned themselves with integration rhetoric based upon the value of overcoming difference, which was promoted at school and in the broader community (Moran 2016; see also Arkin 2009, Bourdieu 1984). At the same time, through their emphasis on hybridity young people subtly resist the school and community emphasis on tolerance which locates their ethnicity as central and worthy of celebration and accentuation.

But here is the rub. How are we to reconcile the fundamentally habituated and unconscious nature of people's engagement with social context, as represented in Bourdieu's conceptualization, and what I observed as the more deliberate hybridized and essentialized self reflections of young refugees in Australia? The notion of dynamic responsiveness helps us to do so. As people's sense of identity emerges in response to their social context, it is through some combination of both deliberate intention and less precise perception.

I principally maintain that the self-reflections or -representations I observed among these young people are the work of partially knowing social actors. What I explain largely in terms of a kind of participatory positioning in which young people's sense of identity reflects back on their perception of messages central to multicultural discourse points to both an internal reflection of those messages and a more deliberate engagement with them. These are not mutually exclusive phenomena—conscious self-representations are not free of structural constraints that shape and provoke them, just as more subconscious and habituated representations do not disallow any kind of reflexivity. A consideration of the agency inherent in self-representations, as well as the internalization of social messages, constraints and discourses that inform those representations at a less conscious level, help to broadly explain the processes through and conditions under which these young people perceive and pursue belonging in national space.

Responsive Identity and Multiculturalism

At the start of this chapter, I outlined my aim to explore the mechanisms through which young people's talk about race and the ways in which race is approached and managed in Australian multicultural discourse are linked. At the heart of this link, I explored how young people project an alternating sense of essentialized and hybridized racial and ethnic identity which acts as a form of capital. This allows young people from refugee backgrounds to respond to the multicultural discourses (of integration and tolerance) designed to address race and ethnicity that implicitly frame their lives. In their responsive identity work, these young people sought an oscillating sense of belonging—to one another, to the wider Australian society, and to symbolic connections with global networks.

I began by conceptualizing identity in terms of assertions of sameness and difference in the search for belonging to social context. I outlined the concepts of hybridity and essentialism as reflecting the complex and seemingly contradictory ways young people engage in this process. Their self-representations act as a form of capital which allows these young people to respond to and engage with the broad moral framework of Australian multiculturalism. They do so through the nuanced ways in which they claim belonging and "not-belonging" (Moore 2011, 63) to different elements of their lived multicultural context, in large part through references to race and ethnicity in their everyday interactions with one another.

Young people's mobilization of race and ethnicity is meaningfully connected to their awareness of and engagement with the multicultural discourses they encounter in their daily lives. Conversely, their racialized identity practices are not formulated exclusively or even predominately through their experiences with racism and exclusion, which multicultural discourses are implemented to address. Indeed, their responsiveness to the discourses of integration and tolerance demonstrates a kind of symbolic or multicultural capital (Bourdieu 1986) related to the implicit moral framework of the Australian multicultural context (Moore 2011, 61).

Young people's experiences with multiculturalism are revealing for a number of reasons particular to their generation. Not only do they encounter diversity and live with intercultural mixing at a rapidly accelerating rate, but they have also experienced an increasing backlash against multiculturalism (Harris 2013). The ways in which multiculturalism is enacted and managed in this context is intrinsically related to these young people's cultivation and projection of their sense of identity. However, their emphasis and denial of race does not emerge solely from their capacity (or lack of) to navigate interethnic "multicultural encounters" as established in the literature on "everyday multiculturalism" (Harris 2009; Werbner 2013; Wise and Velayutham 2009). Rather, such racialized identity work is also acutely related to the messages through which the moral fabric of multiculturalism itself is established within host communities of young people from refugee and migrant backgrounds.

The identities of these young people may indeed be described as "hybrid," "in-between," "fluid" (Bhabha 1994; Hall 1996), and "ambivalent" (Ngo 2010), but beneath this, it is not only their encounters with one another as well as the white Australian population which makes them so, but also their engagement with the messages designed to manage such diversity. Young people's alternating assertions and denial of the significance of skin color through hybridized and essentialized representations of identity critically engage discourses of integration and tolerance to which "race," however implicit and abstracted, is central.

Rather than conscious and deliberate strategies, a kind of subtle positioning or dynamic responsiveness better reflects the ways in which young people grapple with choice and constraints in their pursuit of a sense of themselves and their social place. These young people had recently experienced the movement, loss, and restructuring of their lives inherent to the refugee experience; they expressed a pervasive awareness that racism and ethnic tension were at least perceived to be significant issues in their lives; and they were confronted by the fact that they looked so obviously different from the broader population among whom they lived.

Throughout the remainder of the book I consider these complex dynamics. In doing so, I seek to demonstrate how young people may mobilize or present racialized depictions of their ethnicities in a kind of response which may echo, resist, or manipulate the ways in which they are implicitly racialized by the white majority in a multicultural framework. In the chapters that follow, I explore the identity-making processes of these young people in the context of the everyday as well as the more exceptional manifestations of multiculturalism they encounter, and how in this context they are drawn to represent themselves in racialized ways.

In doing so, I seek to distil the lines of comparison between young people's self-representations and the broad moral discourses that frame their lives within the social landscape of Australian multiculturalism. Their dynamic responsiveness to the external framing of their lives in their cultivation of identity and belonging allowed these young people to begin developing an enhanced sense of control and certainty in their social worlds. Through playful banter exhibited in their everyday lives, as well as in formal performative representations and their engagement with the political context of their lives, young people fixed one another in social place, asserted knowledge of who belongs where, and tested and manipulated these boundaries of belonging.

4

Everyday Identity

Self and Belonging through Friendship,
Fighting, and Dating

Social relationships, for these young people, were foundational to describing how they saw and understood themselves. Justifying and defining their friendships, arguably even more so than cultivating them, helped them to establish how they fit in social context. The social space outside of fixed ties to kinship groups and national territory is of marked relevance to young people from migrant and refugee backgrounds for whom these relationships and ties to place have been dismantled through the experience of (forced) migration. In the hyperdiversity of the current multicultural context and following the rupture caused by their migration experience, peer groups are central to formulating a sense of identity for these young people.

Moreover, the degree of creativity, flexibility, and choice in constructions of friendship justifies such social relationships as deeply relevant to anthropological inquiry. Several scholars point to the period of childhood and youth as a time when establishing friendships is significant for creating, exploring, and maintaining a sense of oneself (Back 1996; Chen, French and Schneider 2006; Cheney 2007; Chhuon and Hudley 2010; Chikkatur 2012; Dyson 2010, 483; Montgomery 2009; Wulff 1995b). For the young people with whom I worked, forming and justifying friendship bonds is a deeply important endeavor that provides an avenue through which they may respond to and find their place within dominant power structures.

Not surprisingly from what we have seen so far, race and ethnicity—in terms of their centrality or insignificance—were central to the ways in which these young people justified their relationships. Notice I refer to their *justifications* rather than their *choices* in social relationships as key to establishing a sense of self and belonging. The extent to which they were actually free to choose was influenced by a range of social factors including family expectations and the extent to which their school structure fostered certain connections over others.

More accurately, it was the ways in which they described and justified their friendships and romantic relationships, and indeed the extent to which they emphasized the role of choice in establishing them, that provided the scope through which these young people engaged with the broader multicultural context of which they were now a part. The everyday dynamics of young people's social relationships and how they talk about them, as well as how those relationships are tested and unsettled, is central to their everyday articulations of identity.

The particular ways in which these young people give reason for the who and why of their social relationships is itself a kind of social positioning through which they constitute themselves within, and in relationship to, the local context of the school, their home and family lives, and the broader Australian national space. The justifications they provided for who their friends were, and why, were not neutral. Instead, as in much of their identity making practices, the ways in which they describe their social relationships are intricately tied to the degree of significance they place on racial and ethnic background. The ways in which their friendships were pursued, forged, negotiated and upheld provides a clear example of how young people engage with and exhibit a kind of dynamic responsiveness to multicultural discourse in the context of their everyday lives.

What Makes a Friend?

At Paddington High, many of the young people referred to their group of friends as "the Africans" and often accounted for their exclusivity as based upon "being black." Samah, a fourteen-year-old Sudanese girl who had lived in Australia for four years, often answered my questions about others in her class by saying, "Is he white? Then I don't know him. If he's black, I know him." The background to her mobile phone featured a big red heart and the words "I love being black." She, with her close friend Vic, who was sixteen and also Sudanese, described how she made friends like this: "It's being black. If you don't know someone, someone introduces you and you're friends. It's easy to be friends with black people . . . for me it's hard to be friends with white people. I don't know why . . .'cause they're not black."

During another conversation which unfolded during lunch time at the Paddington High courtyard, Nine, a nineteen-year-old Sudanese boy who had been living in Australia for two years, offered his insight into how friendships were formed for himself and his peer group. In response to my questions about what he looks for in a friend he answered: "I don't like to . . . I don't know how to say it, but I don't like friends from one country. It's good to mix it up. You never know when you'll need someone. At the studio and in the city, I don't work with Africans. I don't always have to be friends with the black people."

Samah and Vic, who were both present for this conversation, shrugged and nodded in seeming agreement. A similar dichotomy existed among young people at Kedron Club in discussions of how friendships were formed. The various explanations young people provided for what constituted friendship and how friendships were formed can be boiled down to two main and opposing categories broadly represented by the statements provided above. In some instances and contexts, young people articulated that their friendships were based largely upon racial or ethnic affiliation, and in other instances and contexts they claimed that race and ethnicity had nothing to do with who they were friends with or why. The tension between these two categories was addressed in conflicting depictions of the amount of deliberate thought or choice that went into their social relationships. Moreover, the dichotomous justifications of their friendships, and the degree to which they articulated the relevance of race in establishing them, highlights the imprecision of a binary understanding of young people's social networks as either racist or inclusive. It also represents a useful entrée to analyzing their everyday engagement with broad multicultural discourse.

Sometimes young people depicted their friendships as based upon a mundane element of happenstance or as the consequence of ordinary and casual friendly interactions. In these instances, they downplayed the significance of race and ethnicity in forming friendships. At other times, they depicted their friendships as actively pursued based upon a shared conceptualization as culturally, ethnically or racially "other" than the wider, white Australian population. Most of the young people I spoke with about their social relationships had accounted for them at separate times in both of these manners. That is, ethnic identity was often evoked differently, from not at all, to very strongly, by the same young people in different instances. However, there was a marked difference in the ways in which young people at Paddington High talked about how they made friends versus those at Kedron Club. As young people described the ways in which they made friends based upon one or the other of these broad explanations they called upon hybridized and essentialized representations of themselves that emerged in response to the multicultural landscape of their daily experience.

"Friends Is Friends": Friendship Based on the Everyday

Atong, who was fifteen, Sudanese, and had only been in Australia for a year, told me her friends came from "Any country. Some from Africa. Some from this country. Some from other countries. . . . Some near my house. I just make friends with them. Talk to them. These girls. And other girls." Obama,[1] also fifteen and Sudanese, and who had lived in Australia for five years, stated, when asked how he makes friends, "Talk to them . . . mostly everyone. All countries. Meet them at school usually. People who like the same thing. Like sport." And Jessica, a thirteen-year-old Karen girl who had lived in Australia for three years, said she made friends, "Mostly at school. On weekends. Sometimes on the train. One is Australian, and one is from Sudan. I like funny people; anyone." Atong, Obama and Jessica all attended the same school, down the street from Kedron Club where I first met them.

Like those just described here, many young people, and particularly those who attended Kedron Club, accounted for their friendships as occurring out of the mundane, every day or matter-of-fact circumstances of their lives. This included being at the same school, being in the same year at school, and being of the same gender as their friends. In these explanations of how they made friends, young people deemphasized the centrality of their own choice. When friendships were described as emerging naturally out of the local context of school and grade, young people emphasized that they were not actively sought—that they do not "choose" friends; they simply "make" friends. In arguing that they did not actively choose their friends, young people usually referenced some element of ethnic identity, such as country of origin or language, in terms of how little it mattered to them, thereby implicitly downplaying the significance of ethnicity or race in the formation of friendships.

This proposed lack of choice in developing friendships allowed young people to imply that they did not have any ethnic requirement for the people with whom they socialized. As they explained, they were instead able to create a friendship bond, or "make" friends, with whomever they met in their local context, and whoever displayed desirable friendship or personality traits. For example, when I asked Catalina, a sixteen-year-old Karen girl who had been living in Australia for three years, at the after-school club, who her friends were and how she became friends with them, without any provocation on my part toward country or language on one hand, or her everyday environment on the other, she said, "Many friends. Same class at school . . . they are all different. All different country. It doesn't matter. They are all nice. Many are even English." Similar responses to the same questions also emphasized everyday circumstance as central to friendship making as they actively deemphasized choice or requirements for ethnic identity. I spent time talking to several young people during individual interviews about the following questions: "What do you look for in a friend?" and "How do you make friends?" Some of their responses are as follows:

The first day I was hanging out with them, they showed me around . . . my best friend Hugh, he showed me around that first day, now we've been friends since primary. He lives around here and we're still friends. He's Australian. I can be friends with Australia or all different places. (Mathew, 13, Burmese)

I don't look for anything. We help each other out, we become friend . . . It doesn't matter. Anybody. Anybody can be someone's friend. Doesn't matter if you can't speak English. Friends is friends. (Jessica, 13, Karen)

Just talking to them. I usually like the ones who are not too good, not too bad, in the middle. The ones that are not concentrating too much, not getting in trouble too much. Like they get in trouble like I do, but not too much. Not like going to jail. They can be from any country. I don't chose that. (Santino, 15, Sudanese)

I don't really pick. Like, we'll play sport on the same team and stuff. I got a lot friends and stuff. . . . It doesn't really matter [where they are from]. Lots of different places. But most are from Australia and stuff. If I go somewhere I meet some people. [Local park or shopping center], or a lot of people hang out in the city . . . I don't call first, I just go there and go to somewhere like [arcade] and just see them. (John, 15, Sudanese)

The first few weeks, few days, you don't know anyone. Then you get used to it. . . . I go up to one of them and ask, "What's your name?" Friends? They're always there when you need them. My best friends? One is Japanese, and one is Australia. There are others too. (Sam, 16, Sudanese)

Most of my cousins got other friends. They meet up with us and all of us become friends again. There are some from school, some from basketball, I got heaps. . . . Well, I actually . . . if we're almost doing the same thing a bit and get along together, stay happy together sometimes. . . . They're all mixed up. Not just the Africans. (Aliir, 16, Sudanese)

In these conversations I was careful not to probe concerning the relevance of culture, race, or ethnicity. Yet these young people, all of whom I first met at Kedron Club, were careful to emphasize that their friendships were not based on ethnicity, language or country of origin but rather on shared activities or friendly interactions (apart from some examples in which young people emphasized the Australian-ness of their friends). In these accounts young people emphasized that they can be friends with anyone from anywhere and that the act of friendship can be negotiated between any two, like-minded people. Lisa, when explaining how she makes friends, stated, "They can be from Africa, China. . . . I never pick friends. I just make friends. I like being friends with everyone. It's just the same."

By underlining circumstance as the key foundation upon which friendships were built, these young people reflected a hybrid element, capable of overcoming differences, of their own sense of themselves. They did so by highlighting that they could be friends with anyone with whom they shared a local daily context. In their proposed ability to identify with people of various backgrounds, they demonstrated that they did not have a restrictive, essentialized identity of their own, at least not in terms of racial or ethnic identity. Such hybridized representations of self emphasize young people's sameness with what they depicted as the mainstream, white Australian population. Their explanations reflected the multicultural ideal of integration and acted in opposition to the language of tolerance which serves to celebrate difference and evoke essentialized reflections of ethnicity.

On the other hand, some explanations young people provided for their friendships point explicitly to elements of ethnic and racial identity. In these justifications, young people evoked essentialized representations of themselves through which a sense of otherness was central. Here choice was emphasized and similarity to one another and difference from the broader population were strongly maintained.

"We Are Them": Friendship Based on Being "Other"

In reference to their friendships with young people who were not Australian, or who identified as members of their own racial, ethnic or cultural background, my participants explained their friendships as based on being other. When I asked some young people in the school courtyard the questions "What do you look for in a friend?" and "How do you make friends?" Nine, who argued in a statement above that he does not need to be friends with "the Africans" or "black people" and that he prefers to "mix it up," told me, "it's easier when they're from 'other' countries. If it's Australia it's harder. People not from Australia it's easier. We understand each other. We've been in the same situation." Similarly, Elijah, a fourteen-year-old boy from Uganda, responded, "Sometimes it doesn't matter where you're from. It's sometimes easier to get along with other people than Australians because they have some similar background to you or something you experience."

While young people sometimes expressed that aspects of ethnic identity didn't affect their friendships, the same young people also at times acknowledged that friendship was more immediate or easy when it occurred between two people who were not from Australia. In these instances, they projected an essentialized otherness through emphasizing similarity between one another, in a disassociation with the broader Australian population, without necessarily articulating that racial or ethnic affiliation with one another was necessary.

For example, Lisa, a Burmese Muslim, and many of the Karen girls were friends with one another despite the national conflict between their ethnic groups in their countries of origin. The girls regularly mentioned their differences based on ethnic and cultural background, but they did so as they also deemphasized those differences and forged a more united sense of identity in relationship to the broader Australian population. Around her Karen friends, who were all Christian, Lisa usually "forgot" to account for her school absences based on Muslim holy days, she often mentioned that her father was Karen, and although she identified as Burmese based on her mother's nationality, she regularly signaled that she was not born in Burma, but rather in Thailand.

Her friends obliged this plurality and similarly justified their friendship. Many of them made comments like Wah Wah's that, "Lisa is OK because her dad is Karen . . . she does not hate Karen people" and "Lisa is not from Burma." Sometimes those justifications fell short. As Jessica, a fifteen-year-old Karen girl in Lisa's circle of close friends, answered in a casual conversation with me about making friends, "It's hard to be friends with people from other countries. Because when it's Muslim and they're hungry and you give them food they can't eat. It easy to be friends with someone from your own country, you speak same language and you understand." Conflict occasionally erupted between Lisa, her friends and members of her family in relationship to a range of underlying factors including ethnic, religious and language differences. I explore one instance of this later. However, as Lisa emphasized her multiple identities (she is Burmese, but born in Thailand, her father is Karen, although her mother is Burmese, etc.), and as her friends similarly accentuated this plurality, they also mobilized an essentialized otherness to the broader population.

My participants from Sudan, Guinea, and Uganda also often accentuated an essentialized otherness which trumped their many differences in background. Within their friendship groups at Paddington High they argued and teased one another with insulting stereotypes based on their vast differences ranging from ethnicity and tribe, to the route they took into Australia, such as when Vic told Zi, "Shut up. I'm not a Dinka and I'm not a Sierra Leone so leave me alone!" However, they just as often represented themselves outwardly as a unified and cohesive group of "Africans" based on their identification as other than the broader population. As opposed to emphasizing the circumstantial elements of how they make friends, in these depictions they emphasized the role of choice in selecting friends that helped to cultivate their sense of racial or ethnic otherness. For example, the following responses were provided in one-on-one interviews when I asked a number of these young people, "Who are your friends?" "How did you first become friends with them?" and "Did it take a long time to make friends when you started at this school?"

> My good friends are Elijah, Alex . . . mostly the Africans, yeah. Mostly we get along at this school. The Africans get along . . . I talk to people . . . somebody to trust. A lot of times it's outside of school; [local] park, or African parties; basketball club. (Tino, 15, Sudanese)

> I came to school and met more friends. It wasn't that hard. It wasn't that easy. It was easy with the Africans. We see each other and say hello. Even

if we don't get to be closer friends, we still see each other, say hello. (Nine, 19, Sudanese)

Not long, it was very easy. They come up to me and talk to me. It was easy to meet friends because there are some Africans here . . . and it's easy to make friends with Africans. (Zi, 18, Sudanese)

Both [Australian and African young people] are kind. But sometimes . . . I go to the Africans. It's hard to explain, we're both the same. We are the same common. We are . . . we kind of . . . we have the same nationality. It's hard to explain. We all love the same kind of thing. We help each other. I don't know—it's like being African. Some of the stuff you do, you just can't do to other people. If it's something weird in African, we get that. But if I tried to do the same thing to someone else they would say, "what are you doing. I don't get it" . . . It's just what you fee [starts to say "feel" and trails off]. Sometimes you laugh, and you just keep laughing. We just enjoy each other's . . . how do you? . . . we are *them*. It's impossible for me to live without them. I need to be around them all the time. (Elijah, 16, Sudanese)

Elijah very clearly stated his sense of himself and his friendship group as other in relationship to the broader population in his statement "we are them." He tried to formulate a notion of what it is that holds them together with one another and apart from the wider population. Being "them," for Elijah, provides the basis for friendship. In this interview, he went on to articulate how friendship with people outside of his group of "them," particularly with white Australians, was useful in highlighting the exclusivity of his own friendship group. In describing what it was like to have Lauren, the only white Australian in his immediate friendship group, as a friend, he said, "We actually enjoy having someone like them around. She says we're more fun than other people. She says when you sit with them they just don't say anything."

In their articulation of a sense of similarity and groupness based on a loose and variable sense of ethnic identity, young people evoked essentialized representations of themselves as other through their descriptions and justifications of their social relationships. As differences were cast aside in the creation of a fixed, essentialized "non-Australian" or "African" sense of self, these young people approached and manipulated their sense of an us/them binary. Self-essentializing through young people's descriptions of how they made friends allowed them to emphasize a sense of similarity between those who identified as other, and as such allowed for a sense of community and solidarity in the context of the change they had experienced, as well as social conditions over which they had little control in their new environments.

Many young people from African backgrounds in Brisbane worked to carve out a space for this sense of community to thrive and flourish through their participation in a network of underground "African parties" initiated and attended exclusively by and for young people.

African Parties: Being Together and "Being African"

African parties were a big deal to a number of these young people. As Samah told me early in my fieldwork, "You want to get the good answers from me? Come to an African party, that's where it's gonna happen." These parties allowed young people to establish and maintain networks of African peers—and through moments of playful exchanges and social drama, to define and revise their sense of "being African."

African parties occurred approximately twice per month during my fieldwork and drew crowds of up to one hundred African young people. Most of my participants who attended these parties were students at Paddington High. News of the parties circulated throughout the city via text messages on mobile phones, and although Anglo young people were welcome and invited, their ethnic exclusivity was marked in their being commonly referred to as "African parties." Groups of African young people chipped in to rent halls in community centers or pubs for the parties, and they would select, hire and pay a DJ to play music at the event. Parties began anywhere between nine and eleven P.M., usually on a Saturday night, and continued into the early hours of the morning.

For African young people who described their group of friends as being the result of active choice based largely on ethnicity, rather than the result of circumstance, African parties provided a venue from which to actively strengthen those networks. Attendance at African parties also allowed young people to articulate the significance of being African to the formation of their friendship groups. When I asked Vic about her school formal she explained, "It was good because I went to an after party. An African after party so it was good. . . . No, no one from school, it was all Africans." In addition to adding substance to her school formal, Vic's description of the party displayed her distinction between her school life and her identification with an African community—and the higher significance she placed on the latter. While she attended the party with her African friends from school, including Zi and Nine, when asked if there were school friends at the party she responded, "no one from school, it was all Africans."

These parties were not, apparently, widely observed or noted by the broader community. They often occurred in out-of-the-way locations, such as in a community hall near a shopping center or on a side street surrounded by few houses, and they occurred late at night. Teachers did not mention the parties and during those that I attended, or were described to me during my fieldwork, there was no police presence or neighborhood complaints. According to the young people who organized and attended, it was essential that the parties remain unnoticed by the broader population. As they warned, when these parties drew attention from the broader community they were likely to be interpreted as signifying deviant behavior or possible gang activity. As Samah explained, "When they see us all together—any time they see a group of Africans together, police come to our stuff." That they occurred largely and purposefully outside of adult awareness reflects their import as places of resistance or refuge from broader social messages around the perceived danger of large groups of ethnic minority young people socializing exclusively with one another.

The main activity at the parties occurred inside the hall and in the parking lot. The parking lot was usually heavily populated by between nine and ten P.M. and young people filtered between here and the hall throughout the night. When an African young person arrived, they circulated throughout the guests that were already present and wordlessly shook everyone's hand. Sometimes a smile, nod, or brief introduction was offered. Music and dancing took place inside the hall and socializing, and some drinking occurred in the parking lot. Hip hop music could often be heard throughout the parking lot and immediate surrounds, and when an Arabic song was occasionally played much of the crowd erupted in applause, song, and dance.

Community and belonging were established at African parties for most young people in attendance out of a shared sense of identity as a singularly "African" group. While "being African" provided access and a sense of belonging, that phrase was contested and negotiated among the young people of a wide range of ethnic and cultural backgrounds who ascribed to it. Indeed, a central endeavor at these parties among the young people who attended was to make constant reference and amendments to their ascription to, and interpretation of, what "being African" meant.

For example, at the first party I attended several young people had thrown their first of many "fancy dress" parties, in which party goers were encouraged to dress up in a costume of their choosing. Most of the girls dressed in a style one would not be surprised to find at a Western costume party among young people of the same age—very skimpy and highly sexualized nurse, witch, and fairy costumes. When I met Vic and her cousin in the parking lot, they were both alternatively wearing long colorful sheaths of fabric wrapped around their bodies to form long dresses, small lacy hats, long lacy gloves, crosses around their necks, and both were carrying clutch purses under their arms. We walked through the parking lot and they greeted their friends. When we entered the party, another friend ran over to them and said, "Are you Japanese?! . . . What are you?!" The girls shrieked with laughter and responded, "We are African ladies!"

The very meaning of "being African" was itself appropriated and manipulated at African parties in an exploration of identity and African-ness. Parties provided a space in which to define being African that was removed from the direct social management of African-ness initiated and stipulated by others, such as at schools, where it might on the one hand be deemphasized, and on the other hand singled out and celebrated in specific, formalized settings (see also Forman 2005).

A sense of essentialized otherness that young people cultivated in their attendance at African parties serves to create a sense of belonging in the Australian context. A context through which these young people are confronted with various structural inequalities and the appeals to integrate and assimilate, as well as the complexities and realignments of national ties and kinship and social networks. However, as demonstrated in their engagement with the notion of "being African" at the fancy dress African party, the constitution of an essentialized otherness is hybrid in practice—the boundaries of belonging are permeable, and differences may be discarded or evoked in different contexts (see also Noble et al. 1999, 39). Likewise, Noble and Tabar (2002), in their study among a group of Lebanese young people in Sydney, illustrate how various essentialized identities may be articulated in different ways in different contexts as similarities and differences are highlighted and downplayed: "It's not that there aren't differences, or that they aren't important, but at this level of identification they aren't that important, just as, at another level, Lebanese-ness becomes less important than wog-ness . . . in opposition to 'Australian' students. . . . This Lebanese-ness . . . is a curious amalgam of essentializing and hybridizing elements. Essentializing in that it asserts a given-ness to Lebanese identity which naturalizes it; and hybridizing in that it throws together and subsumes at least momentarily often quite radical differences." (Noble and Tabar 2002, 134–135)

By positioning themselves as an essentialized, cohesive group through their attendance at African parties and in their descriptions of how and why they make friends, young people demonstrated a fluctuating notion of similarity to certain people and difference to others in relationship to various aspects of ethnic identity. In these instances differences were cast aside, and the role of choice was emphasized in the constitution of a unified sense of otherness to the broader population. Conversely, young people also presented themselves in terms of a kind of hybridity which allowed for the deemphasis of ethnic identity, and which was subtly articulated in accordance with an emphasis on easy integration with the broader population through the everyday circumstances of their lives.

While young people, in some instances, described friendship as being based on the mundane elements of their everyday lives and explicitly denied ethnicity as being relevant, in other instances they pointed to ethnicity as central. Their emphasis on hybridized and essentialized representations of themselves through how they made friends both echoed and resisted the messages inherent in the discourses of integration and tolerance emphasized in their schools and in the broader social environment.

Friendship and Identity Work

While their tendency to affirm or deny the significance of race or ethnicity cannot neatly be divided along these lines, whether or not young people emphasized skin color or country of origin in explanations of friendship making frequently differed in response to local context. Most students who attended Kedron Club were enrolled in a school where they were segregated from the broader student population in ELL-only classrooms. These young people projected a hybridized representation of their friendship making process and frequently argued that "skin color doesn't matter," that they do not chose their friends, and that they like to "mix it up" in accounting for how they made friends.

On the other hand, the young people who attended Paddington High were mainstreamed with the broader student population and more directly exposed to a strong integrationist rhetoric which emphasized the supposed insignificance of race. The majority of the young people who attended this school, as demonstrated by Samah in the earlier example, tended to distinguish themselves and their friendships choices as based almost exclusively upon an essentialized depiction of "being black." Here it can be observed that young people's affirmation and denial of the relevance of race was mobilized in dialogue with the predominant ways in which they encountered multicultural discourse based upon integration and tolerance in their daily lives.

In their hybridized self-representations, such as demonstrated largely among those who attended Kedron Club, young people reflected a kind of symbolic capital whereby they demonstrated an understanding of the value of overcoming difference emphasized in the rhetoric of integration (Bourdieu 1984). However, as they maintained the irrelevance of ethnicity to their sense of identity and belonging, young people spoke back to and subtly resisted a notion of tolerance that posits ethnic difference as something that should be accentuated and celebrated. In the emphasis of their capacity to merge and incorporate difference, assertions such as "I just don't think of it," "race stuff doesn't really matter to me" and "we like to mix it up" were frequently made in interviews with me when I asked them how they made friends.

These assertions may be explained in part by the interview context itself. Young people were more likely to banter back and forth about skin color while talking with one another than they were to openly discuss it with me in response to my follow up questions. Their reluctance to acknowledge the role of race in friendships again demonstrates an understanding that they were not supposed to see race as a relevant issue in their lives. While visiting with Santino and his brothers and sisters in their home, they were telling me who their friends were and describing them as "Aussie friends" versus "African friends." When I began to pursue this distinction and probe the significance to friendships of where people are from, the direction of the conversation changed quickly, and they parroted back, nearly in unison in a tone verging on sing-songy, "No, skin doesn't matter." The trajectory of this conversation is exemplary of many others in which young people accounted for their friendships in racialized terms and subsequently denied the relevance of race in response to further questions.

Emphasizing a lack of significance of racial categories in forging friendships allowed my informants to demonstrate their often legitimate inattention to skin color in their personal relationships, as well as to subvert perceived racial boundaries and inequalities. However, such hybridized self-representations also allowed young people to echo dominant discourse of how race ought not to matter to them. On the other hand, presenting their race and ethnic identity in essentialized ways allowed them to subtly challenge that claim and to forge a sense of community, solidarity and belonging.

"Being black," when actively claimed by young people, carried with it a positive feeling of inclusion based upon the cool and the resistance of a counter-white identity. Such self-conscious racial essentialism however, also emerged in a kind of subtle resistance to the integrationist discourse that was so heavily promoted at Paddington High. As I discussed in chapter 2, under the broad framework of multiculturalism, rhetoric at Paddington High sought to frame young people as devoid of any politically incorrect differences (such as skin color) that might threaten to distinguish them from the broader student body, thereby inhibiting integration.

When an announcement was made for "international students" during the school lunch period one afternoon, I was rhetorically asked by Vic, "Why aren't we 'international?'" She answered her own question, "We're not international because we're the multiculturals. We're not supposed to be all about black, but we're the multiculturals." Vic and her friends understood the subtle cues that they were not supposed to emphasize their black identities in favor of integration within the school environment outside of those occasions when they were called upon to do so. At the same time, in some aspects of their school experience, these young people were characterized as eliciting a sense of tolerance through the celebration of their cultural and ethnic difference. They demonstrated an awareness of the complex denial of race while embracing cultural difference in their representation and justification of their friendships. Sometimes they countered the integrationist push with racialized self-essentialism in the form of near constant references to race and skin color as central to their social relationships. And sometimes they did the opposite.

That is, in their descriptions of how they made friends young people emphasized hybridized and essentialized representations of themselves that both echoed and resisted the messages inherent in the discourses of integration and tolerance emphasized in their schools and in the broader social environment.

Furthermore, as they engaged with tensions of belonging, essentializing and hybridizing representations of themselves often merged, overlapped, and sometimes contradicted one another. As they oscillated emphasis between these dual explanations for how they constituted social relationships they drew upon different implications for their sense of self-understanding and social belonging.

The various ways in which young people sought and discussed boyfriends and girlfriends was similarly instrumental to their identity work. Opposed to the ways in which they at times justified their friendships as based on circumstance, however, dating was more explicitly about choice, and most often with particular reference to skin color. While they did "mix it up" by dating people of different racial and ethnic backgrounds, in the course of my fieldwork I never heard these young people argue that "skin color doesn't matter" when it came to dating. Instead, they seemed to choose and justify their dating relationships with explicit and unapologetic consideration for skin color or other associations with race and ethnicity.

Ethnicity, Race and Romantic Relationships

For the Burmese, Chin, and Karen girls at Kedron Club, boyfriends were an increasingly common and charged topic of conversation over the course of my fieldwork. These girls especially referred to skin color and ethnic background in terms of who they "liked," "loved" or wanted to date. There was great variance of racial and ethnic dating preferences, both between the girls and among individuals over time.

Eh Eh, was Karen and thirteen years old when we first met. She was from Burma but had spent the majority of her life in Tham Hin refugee camp in Thailand, before relocating to Australia only one year prior. Her current boyfriend, whom she was keeping secret from her mother, was Karen as well. Jessica, also thirteen, Karen, and relocated from the same refugee camp two years prior explained, "It's so funny, Eh Eh said 'no Karen boy.' But after a few months she has a Karen boyfriend! She thought she'd have Australian [thinking], no, Indonesian boy." When I ask what "type" of boyfriend she and her sixteen-year-old sister Catalina, would like, Catalina joined the conversation and explained, "Me, only one. Karen boy. Just one." She looked at Jessica laughing and went on, "She told me the other day . . . she wants many." Both girls continued laughing as Jess explained, "I want one Australia, one from another, then last one, Karen . . . I want five!" Catalina added, "But last one, Karen. Last one."

One day after school at Kedron Club, Wah Wah, a fourteen-year-old Karen girl originally from Burma and most recently from the Tham Hin refugee camp was playing a fortune-telling game with Jessica. They traced their hand onto a piece of paper and labeled a different category for each of their five fingers: profession, wealth, transport, house, and marriage. In the center of the hand, different options for each of the categories were listed, such as, for the category of wealth: "rich, poor, not rich but a little bit of money;" for marriage: "married, promise, boyfriend, lied to," and so forth. The marriage category generated the most enthusiasm.

Wah Wah started to clap her hands and jump up and down upon learning of her results. She exclaimed, "It said I will marry an English! I like English, not Asian boy . . . this one is Australian." Jessica too was excited because according to her fortune, she will "marry Karen boy." Wah Wah explained, "Jess likes Karen boy! Yay! Cat like only Karen boy too!" They played this game for some time and continued to get excited about their own and one another's results. Their preferences in marriage partner were always articulated based on skin color or some other signifier of ethnic background, and while these preferences differed between the girls they were aware and supportive of these differences and of the specific preferences of one another.

Approximately ten months after this game was recorded in my field notes most of these girls had boyfriends for the first time—the topic of dating became ever more contentious and complicated, with race and ethnicity still discussed as central to their dating choices. Many of the girls, including Eh Eh and Wah Wah as well as Ce Ce and Jenna, both thirteen, Karen, and from Burma, had white Australian boyfriends, who at this time also began to regularly attend Kedron Club. This was the first time any white Australian young people had attended.

Over a two-month period the girls continually broke up with and traded these boyfriends between one another. Wah Wah began dating Jenna's previous boyfriend and Ce Ce began dating the boy Wah Wah dated prior to Jenna's boyfriend. This boyfriend swapping did not appear to affect their friendships with one another—instead they continued to excitedly and playfully discuss dating options based on ever changing racial and ethnic preferences. During this period, the girls oscillated between their preferences for Karen or white Australian boys but giggled at the prospect of dating "African" boys. When her friends asked if she would choose an "Australian" boyfriend, Lisa responded that she did not know and provided the same response when asked if she would choose a Burmese boyfriend. However, when I followed up this line of questioning and asked if she would pick an African boyfriend, Lisa laughed, looked surprised and said, "African?" When I questioned this shocked reaction Jenna too laughed at the prospect and claimed that while there were "no rules" about dating African boys, she personally would not.

Toward the end of this two-month period in which the girls showed the most interest in dating "Aussie boys," a shift occurred, and many of them, including Jenna, began to express an interest in dating "African" or "black" boys. The girls started breaking up more permanently with their white Australian boyfriends and these boys stopped attending Kedron Club. Ce Ce explained why she ended her relationship with an Australian boyfriend. She said, "I saw him do something. I saw him do things like a girl. Squeal like a girl. And he can't dance. I saw this, and I just thought, 'Awwwe.' I was so disappointed. I don't like this. Now I will go out with African boyfriend."

Ce Ce later explained that at her church she and some of her friends had been criticized for having Australian boyfriends rather than being interested in Karen boys and that this influenced her decision to date people of many different ethnic backgrounds and skin colors. She said, "Everyone at church said we [Ce Ce, Jenna, Eh Eh and Wah Wah] don't love Karen, so now I'm gonna go out with black people! I'll go to New York city where they can dance!"

The African boys at Kedron Club were not as vocal or direct around me, nor do I suspect with one another, about whom they wanted to date. They did, however, regularly make more indirect comments about how unattainable or unlikely it might be to date "white girls" or "Australian girls." Stephen, a sixteen-year-old Sudanese boy, commented to Santino while discussing dating one day, "it would be funny if an African gets an Australian for a girlfriend. . . . No, it doesn't really happen man." And Santino equated whiteness with beauty while watching a movie in which the two main characters were white, but the man was depicted to be less physically attractive than the woman. He said, "She's white and beautiful; he's fat and ugly. How's he ever gonna get her? Fat guy can't get hot white girl! Girls don't all like nice. They like face, body, arms. At my school the fat people are nice, and they get nothing." Conversely, at Paddington High, the African boys lamented the fact that there were not enough "hot African girls" for them to date. As Tino quite regularly expressed, "There aren't heaps of African girls at this school! We need African girls!"

"Next I Will Go Out with African Boy": Dating and Identity

All of the young people, with whom I spent time throughout the course of my fieldwork, frequently discussed skin color or other signifiers of ethnic background in accordance with dating. Many spoke directly to their own and their friend's personal preferences for the ethnic background and skin color of the people they wanted to date. For some, the preference was to date a person of the same background and skin color as themselves. For others, it was to date a person of a different and specific ethnic background and skin color than their own, which often changed over time. Moreover, there was an apparent gendered element to young people's choices around dating and racial preference with girls acting more explicitly as consumers of the racial elements of their romantic partners.

While young people at least some of the time argued that skin color was not relevant in their friendship choices, they almost never made this argument when describing their preferences in romantic relationships. Although these descriptions of sexual and romantic preferences have racist undertones and effects, these young people did not appear to understand their social worlds in such terms in all realms of their lives or, indeed, in all of their social relationships. This variability demonstrates what Herron (2018) describes as a "perverse cosmopolitanism," in which young people can use racist terms to frame some domains of their lives and demonstrate inclusiveness in others.

By seeking boyfriends and girlfriends of the same ethnic background as themselves they could maintain a sense of group solidarity and cohesion as well as appease parental pressures, while by seeking someone of a different ethnic background to themselves they could challenge those norms. An expressed preference for dating people perceived as ethnically or racially "different" may be employed by young people to express a flexible and hybridized sense of self through association, while the desire to date people perceived as ethnically or racially "same" may be conversely mobilized in order to express an imagined essentialized sense of self and connectedness to a particular group.

I'm not suggesting that these young people invariably choose who they want to date (or, for that matter, be friends with) for specifically self-conscious or strategic reasons having to do with some sense of who they are or who and how they want to be. More likely, like everyone else, they develop preferences and attractions to people they meet and spend time with. Perhaps, as Ce Ce expressed, she really did just want to date someone who was a good dancer and was not as interested in someone who was not. Instead my interest here is in the ways in which these young people discuss, justify, and constantly refer to their relationships in terms of skin color and ethnic identity. Such explanations not only demonstrate their interest in and attention to ethnicity and race, but also allow these young people to speak back to structural influences or limitations to which they are exposed in their larger social environment.

Familial expectations, for the majority of these young people, dictated a strong preference for them to date someone of their own cultural and ethnic background. There were, of course, some exceptions, where parents expressed a desire for their children to socialize with white Australian young people for several reasons, such as to foster integration, to enhance English language skills, and to avoid the negative social stigma of ethnic minority youth association with "gangs." Young people as well sought to assimilate and integrate into the dominant culture and were aware of messages to do so at the school, community and national level. Dating provided a means for these young people both to assert their own desires and to indirectly respond to those messages.

Ce Ce initially wanted to date only white European or Australian boys and outwardly rejected boys of both Asian and African backgrounds. Conceivably, this preference was rooted in some level of desire to fit in with or become more a part of the perceived white majority population. While she did not apparently achieve this sense of inclusion within the white majority in the school context and was teased for her accent and her imperfect spoken English, she was also later rejected by members of her own ethnic background at the Karen church for not dating within that community. It was after communicating this latter sense of rejection that she began to articulate an abandonment of her earlier desire to fit in with the what she perceived as the mainstream majority population and the desire to seek a sense of belonging elsewhere. For Ce Ce, rebellion took the form of expressing a desire to date from another group that she perceived, based on skin color, as equally or even more marginalized than herself.

These young people experience the social pressures of defining how and where they fit both within their own familial and ethnic groups, and within the broad national context in which they live—an environment wherein they look different to most of the population and where they perceive themselves to be directly and indirectly singled out, based on their skin color, and through the discourses of integration and tolerance to which they are regularly exposed. As they seek and define their dating relationships, they explore their own curiosity and interest in skin color. In doing so, they may honor and reject the various pressures around ethnic affiliation to which they are exposed as they define a sense of self and social belonging in relation to their peers. After having explored the ways in which young people's descriptions of their friendships and their dating preferences are reflected in their complex and emergent sense of themselves, let me now turn to the role of conflict and what it means for such relationships.

Conflict and Resolution among Friends

I present here, three conflict situations that occurred over the course of my fieldwork. These periodic episodes usually manifested in an emotional outbreak, followed by a period in which participants generally settled into the same friendship roles as prior to the conflict. Such moments seemingly allowed young people to voice similarities and differences to one another, which were sometimes masked in the outward projection of both an essentialized sense of groupness and the hybridized ability to get along despite cultural and ethnic difference. Moreover, the investment in the resolution of the conflict, among young people not directly involved in the conflict itself, demonstrates the significance of a sense of group solidarity.

Nine and Tino

In the Paddington High courtyard during one lunch hour, a group of African boys were playing a betting game that involved rolling change toward a cement wall. Zi and Nine were involved in the game peripherally but as far as I could tell they were mostly just lingering by the wall and taking the money that others threw. Samah was sitting with Tino and said to him, "Nine and Zi, they're bad people man." Tino agreed, "Yeah, they have no respect." Their comments surprised me. Not only were Tino and Nine cousins, but as far as I had observed up to this point, both Samah and Tino were friends with Nine and Zi. Together, they called themselves "the Africans." They sat together at "the African table," spent lunch times joking and hanging out, and attended African parties together.

After a time Nine gave up his wall lingering and walked over to where Samah, Tino and I were sitting and watching the game when Tino said something to him about cheating. Nine looked upset and confused. He said, "Was I even over there?! Was I playing?! Why are you being like this to me man? What's wrong with you?" Tino, quickly moving from mumbling and dismissive, to very angry and agitated, shouted back at him, "Because you owe me money!" He then turned toward Samah, gestured toward Nine and said, "he took what is mine. It was $160, and it's been three months! I don't take what's yours! You took what's mine!" Zi, who at this point was standing with Nine and the others attempted to lighten the mood. He said to me, motioning toward Tino, "This guy is on drugs. I've never seen this guy act like this."

Reconstructing the issue based on the accusations that were made and the answers to questions I later asked Tino, Nine and Samah, this is what I gathered. Nine borrowed a new microphone that Tino bought three months prior and failed to return it or reimburse Tino. During the fight, Nine initially argued back, addressing me, Samah, Zi, Tino, and others in close proximity, "I told him I lost it!" To this Tino responded, "Then pay me back!" They argued back and forth like this, with Nine saying that he would pay Tino back and Tino doubting this claim and urging Nine to make it happen. Throughout their heated conversation, Nine kept bringing up that he really was not cheating in the game, as Tino had originally accused him when the argument started and ignoring the microphone issue. Tino only responded by restating the microphone issue and ignoring the initial game cheating accusation. Nine acted bewildered as he stood above Tino. Shaking his head, he repeated, "Why are you being like this to me. What's wrong with you?" Tino, also very upset and emotional, kept responding, "I don't give a fuck; you owe me money."

During the argument, Zi had slipped away and was sitting nearby at their mutual table of friends. The group was aware of what was happening and tentatively and repeatedly looked over but did not interject. Samah tried to mediate and eventually Vic came over to join her. They addressed the different topics Nine and Tino were arguing over and concluded that Nine may not have been cheating at the game, but that he did owe Tino for the microphone. When Tino and Nine began arguing over whether the microphone was $150 or $160, Vic told them to agree on $150 and work on that basis, and Tino would only lose $10. Then Vic said, "You guys are family, don't be like this over money." Tino responded to this comment with renewed heightened emotion: "I don't want to be family with you anymore! I don't care about you! You took what's mine!" Nine responded that he would pay Tino back soon and the subject was dropped. Vic and Samah began talking about something else and the boys continued to sit next to each other but did not speak for the short remainder of the lunch period. The whole episode lasted for about fifteen minutes.

Later that night, Nine and Tino were hanging out near each other in a group at a school function and there was no evidence of any tension between them. They posed for photos with their arms around each other and laughed at the same jokes. I asked Vic if they made up and she said, "Yeah, they're fine now . . . I don't know. They worked it out." The next day when I asked Nine if they made up he said, "Nah, all I have to do is pay him back and I'm fine. Maybe he was not having a good day." Later I asked Tino if he thought Nine would pay him back and he said no. When I asked if he was still mad he looked away, smiled and quietly said, "Yeah, until I get my money." To my knowledge Nine never paid Tino back and they never fought about the issue again. Their relationship remains intact.

Jenna, Ce Ce, and Atong

This conflict occurred between three girls at Kedron Club, and rather than being acted out in a brief upheaval, it lasted for several weeks before the relationship between the main players was eventually stabilized. Two friends, Ce Ce, Karen and in eighth grade, and Jenna, Chin and in eighth grade, had a fight. When Atong, Sudanese and in ninth grade, took Jenna's side, Ce Ce and Atong began to fight. As Ce Ce explained, the fight began when Jenna allegedly offered to read something aloud in class for Ce Ce's friend Wah Wah because Wah Wah's reading was slow. When Ce Ce got angry at Jenna for "making fun" of her friend's reading, the fight began. As Ce Ce explained:

> I told her shut up. I told her shut up and now she mad at me. I don't care. OK, Wah Wah was reading and Jenna said, "Can I read that for her?" so I said shut up to her. See, sometime when we read we have broken English. So, when Wah Wah read, she make fun and I told her shut up. And then she get mad and she tell me I'm selfish. She tell me that she learned it that October people are selfish. My birthday is October. Selfish mean you only care about yourself. When someone say something like this to me I don't forgive it. I get very angry. I never forgive it.

She went on to explain how Atong got involved:

> I would be friend with Jenna again but not if she friend with Atong. She think she is the best! She told Jenna not to give it up if I don't say sorry. Why should I say sorry! She told me she'd kill me! She told me if she was in Africa she just bring a knife to school and she'd kill me! I said let's try! If she kill me, I say thank you. Then I'd be a ghost. It doesn't matter because

if you die all your pain and problem just move on. It doesn't stay. She said she'd kill me and I tell her let's try! I'm not scared of her.

At the point when this conflict occurred two distinct groups were forming at Kedron Club: one consisted of Jenna, Atong, and Lisa, Burmese and in grade eight; and the other consisted of Wah Wah, and Ce Ce who were cousins as well as friends. Four other Karen girls, Jessica, Catalina, Paw Wah, and Eh Eh, floated between the groups. These four girls were present when Ce Ce told me the story. They advocated for the fight to end and encouraged Ce Ce that her relationship with Jenna could easily be salvaged. They did not mention Atong. Wah Wah, whose reading Ce Ce originally defended at the start of the fight, said, "They will be friend again at camp. I know it. They will be best friend." Ce Ce repeated that this would not happen as long as Jenna stayed friends with Atong. Catalina added, "Yeah, I told her they will be friends again. I know because I fight with people before and now we are friends."

Ce Ce and Mathew

This final example is of a conflict that arose at a shopping mall between Mathew, Lisa's younger brother, and Ce Ce. Mathew and Lisa are Burmese, Muslim, and primarily speak Burmese, and Ce Ce is Karen, Christian, and primarily speaks Karen. Although these differences did not apparently interfere in Lisa's friendship with Ce Ce, in this instance they erupted in conflict between Ce Ce and Lisa's brother, Mathew. Besides Ce Ce, Mathew, and Lisa, Wah Wah, Catalina, and her sister Jessica were at the mall when the conflict arose.

The fight began at the food court when Lisa and I went to buy food for the others. When we returned, Mathew was crying with his head turned away from the group. Everyone looked uncomfortable and no one spoke. Lisa talked to Mathew in Burmese and no one else said anything or would answer my questions. Everyone looked away and said they didn't know what happened. Lisa and Mathew privately bickered as Lisa tried to ascertain what happened. Eventually Mathew told me that Ce Ce spit in his face twice. He was glaring at her when he told me. Ce Ce said it was an accident and Mathew said it was on purpose. Lisa rolled her eyes and looked frustrated. Finally, Ce Ce glared at Mathew and said, "I know all about you."

When we left the food court, Lisa walked with me behind the others and told me that Ce Ce swore at her brother but that she is saying he swore at her first. She went on to say, "I can't be mad because I don't know the truth. . . . But why does she say, 'I know about him.' . . . She knows about him?! She doesn't know anything about my brother; she doesn't know my brother; she just met my brother one time!" She then revealed that she "doesn't always like" Ce Ce, although they hang out together in the same group, and that Ce Ce can be mean and lies sometimes. Lisa reflected that maybe this is so because "She doesn't have a mommy and daddy." Lisa and Mathew walked together and held hands, and Ce Ce, Wah Wah, Jessica and Catalina walked together.

Later, after Lisa talked to the others, she and Catalina told me that Ce Ce got mad at Mathew because he was "speaking in Burmese language" and Ce Ce didn't understand it and thought he was "saying something naughty." Lisa said, "He wasn't saying something naughty though, they just don't understand Burmese language." When Lisa and Mathew left, Lisa hugged everyone good-bye, including Ce Ce. Lisa, Mathew, and Ce Ce didn't speak of the issue again. When Mathew and Ce Ce were next together in a group they did not interact with one another directly and no further conflict episodes arose. Similarly, no explicit conflicts arose between Lisa and Ce Ce, although their relationship with one another did not appear to be as close as each of them with the other girls.

On the way home from the mall on the day of the fight, in the parking lot, Catalina and Jess told me their version of the story. Catalina explained:

> I'll tell you a secret. Mathew is very naughty. He was talking in Burmese language and Wah Wah and Ce Ce don't understand it, but I know a little bit of Burmese language, so I know what he said. . . . Oh, I don't want to say it; it's too bad. . . . He said that her parents don't take care of her or something like that. She didn't understand it, but she knew he was saying bad things, so she get mad at him. Wah Wah told him to shut up and he said, "I hate Christian." And she is a Christian. But I am a Christian too. He said that in English. He said it twice. He said "I hate Christian. I hate Christian."

When I asked who they thought was at fault they replied in unison, "both." They explained that Ce Ce was also at fault because, although Mathew said things that place some of the blame on him, as Catalina explained, "She says things that are mean and doesn't think not to hurt your feelings." Jessica said that she thought Wah Wah started the fight because as soon as Mathew began to speak Burmese she said, "Shut up."

Identity at Work in Conflicts

In analyzing the implications of these moments of conflict I'll first point out the obvious. Sometimes a fight is just that—a fight. And conflict is no more significant or unique to the relationships between these young people than it is for any other. However, within the heated exchanges illustrated above, moments in which young people negotiated, revised and reinforced a sense of themselves and where they fit in relationship to one another were brought to life, often with clear reference to signifiers of ethnic background, religion and language.

These examples demonstrate how young people's emphasis on their similarity to one another, in relationship to the wider population, may be called into question, allowing for the articulation of difference within friendship groups. In other instances, these fights demonstrate how young people's emphasis on their ability to merge differences of cultural and ethnic background may also sometimes be compromised. The conflicts represent moments when young people's outward projection of an essentialized sense of groupness, or a hybridized capacity to "mix it up" is momentarily disrupted, and when differences between young people which are often downplayed are directly engaged.

Ce Ce, Jenna, Atong, and Wah Wah, all attended Kedron Club together and were enrolled in ELL classes separate from the larger student body. Ce Ce's initial anger at what she saw as Jenna's transgression in highlighting Wah Wah's insufficient reading abilities, points to the fragility of these young people's sense of place and belonging, as well as the ferocity with which they might safeguard what standing they have. All of these girls described their friendships as based largely upon circumstance rather than deliberate choice, and all regularly emphasized how little racial or ethnic background mattered to the making and maintaining of their friendships. When they fought, despite their regular claims of the insignificance of ethnicity, they fell back on culturally ascribed and stereotypical differences in fighting styles. When Atong threatened what she would do if she were "in Africa," Ce Ce countered by arguing that it would not matter because she would be a ghost. Atong later relayed to me in her description of the conflict that, "here we fight, but we fight with words not fighting." As they established where they fit in the social context, their varied claims of similarity and difference to one another were continually renegotiated through momentary episodes of upheaval.

In their brief but intense argument, Ce Ce and Mathew addressed differences in language and religion which were often brushed aside in their daily lives and in their outward representation of the insignificance of background and their ability to merge difference. Although many of these young people regularly emphasized the irrelevance of differences based on aspects of ethnicity, in the heated moments when conflict arose they differentiated themselves by drawing on the very differences which they downplayed or denied in other contexts. Conflicts allowed for the articulation of those heavily laden differences between friends which were most often articulated as hardly relevant to their relationships with one another.

While the conflicts of Ce Ce, Mathew, Jenna, and Atong were all among those who attended Kedron Club and outwardly reflected the ability to merge and overcome difference through the description of their social relationships, the conflict that arose between Nine and Tino emerged from a different foundation. Nine and Tino and their friendship group of "the Africans" all attended Paddington High where they were mainstreamed, and where they regularly articulated their differences from the broader student body and an essentialized sense of groupness with one another. Momentary conflict allowed them to address disagreements or ruptures in their relationships while maintaining their outward projection of an essentialized affiliation with one another.

These conflicts, at least briefly, deconstructed a sense of essentialized group similarity or hybridized ability to disregard difference. When this happened, other people in the friendship group often stepped in to ensure that those in conflict eventually resumed their usual relationships and roles. Vic and Samah actively mediated to reach resolution between Nine and Tino, while the table of boys disengaged but kept close tabs as the situation unfolded. Similarly, when Ce Ce and Jenna fought, Wah Wah and Catalina promised the continuity of their friendship.

The role of mediation here demonstrates the importance of friendship and connectedness in these young people's lives. This is also evidenced in their tendency to voice issues or differences in moments of heightened emotional intensity and subsequently allow the friendships and a sense of normalcy to resume, often despite the lack of an outcome which offers any clear resolution to the conflict. The importance of a sense of group connectedness is evidenced in these conflicts, sometimes even over personal preferences. While Samah could observe in a casual and detached way that Nine and Zi were "bad people," her friendship and affiliation with them was not affected or questioned despite this opinion.

While young people may describe and justify their relationships in ways which allow them to represent themselves in multiple and sometimes seemingly contradictory ways, such moments of escalated emotion and tension can reveal a fragility in those justifications—justifications which emerge in intimate relationship to the outward projection or denial of ethnic difference. The relevance of the wider group in resolving, moving beyond, or downplaying conflict demonstrates a sense of collective investment in those justifications insofar as they help to maintain a sense of group belonging and the established projection of the degree to which ethnic and racial background is relevant to friendships.

Relationships and Responsiveness in Context

Everyday social relationships, particularly for these young people who have been through forced migration, relocation. and the breakdown and realignment of various kin and social networks that the process entails, are essential in the constitution of a sense of self understanding and social belonging. Both friendship and romantic relationships provided a platform from which young people were able to assert or deny a sense of racial and ethnic identity, through the ways in which they justified how and why they were drawn to one another. An active emphasis on choice allowed them to embrace their sense of racial and ethnic identity while a passive emphasis on circumstance helped them to subvert the limitations of those categories. Their emphasis on socializing outside their group versus inside, and whether that was determined by choice, circumstance or some form of coercion, provided a way to affect their sense of self and belonging in the everyday landscape of multiculturalism. The ways in which they described friendships and chose romantic partners reflects and rejects the language of the multicultural ideal as they encountered it in their daily lives. Moreover, an analysis of the multiple lines along which young people connect to, and differentiate themselves from, one another serves to highlight their diverse practices of both inclusion and exclusion in multicultural context (Harris and Herron 2017).

Young people portrayed hybridized representations of themselves and their ability to "mix it up" and forge friendships with others from "any country" through their explicit denial of the consequence of ethnic signifiers such as country of origin or language. In other contexts, they presented essentialized representations of themselves through the justification of their friendships largely based on being "African" or being "other" than what they perceived as the mainstream population. Furthermore, they actively sought romantic relationships with others on the explicit basis of skin color. This allowed them to articulate a sense of affiliation and solidarity along with a cohesive and bounded group, drawn from markers of race or ethnicity, or, alternatively, to rebel against such limiting associations. In moments of conflict, the claims of sameness and difference to one another that young people asserted in justifications of their social and romantic relationships were momentarily called into question.

Young people's relationships with one another are constituted, maintained and redefined in the context of, and in dynamic response to, a range of outside and often conflicting social pressures. In this context, such social pressures range from the more intimate familial expectations, to the wider messages emerging from Australian multicultural discourse to conform and to integrate, or conversely, to celebrate ethnic difference. But does their emphasis on "mixing it up," versus mostly hanging out with "people other than Australians" or "the Africans," really reflect the multicultural discourse to which they were regularly exposed, or is it just a preference?

To my observations it was a little bit of both. While the establishment of their relationships is certainly in large part related to those indefinable nuances of affinity and circumstance, the ways in which they described them reflects a subtle engagement with the framing constructs of their lives. The justification and maintenance of their social relationships can act as a form of resistance or response to both social marginalization and to the popular discourses used to confront it. Justifications of their relationships provides a foundation for sociopolitical responsiveness by allowing young people to perpetuate a sense of self-understanding based on skin color and ethnic identification, on the one hand, and providing a basis from which to articulate its lack of relevance and import to their lives, on the other.

The focus of this chapter has been on the everyday activities through which young people from refugee backgrounds define a sense of self. Central to their everyday identity processes is the making and unmaking of social relationships. In the next chapter I will step away from the everyday nuances of identity work and explore the more explicitly self-conscious and performative aspects of how these young people define a sense of self and belonging. In their performative representations of identity young people engage ethnic capital to constitute a sense of affiliation with racial and ethnic groups, and to speak to the multicultural discourses of integration and tolerance.

5

Performing Identity

Capital and Connecting in Multicultural Context

Opportunities were ample for these young refugees in Australia to display, or more formally articulate, a sense of themselves in circumstances which I broadly describe as performative—those that stood apart from the mundane dynamics of everyday life. Social performance, as it emerged from several platforms including activities initiated at Paddington High and Kedron Club, allowed for a more explicitly self-conscious engagement among young people with how they conceived of and sought to represent themselves. Through performance drawn from the intersections between memory, lived experience, and their personal imaginary, these young people cultivated alignments and affiliations with cultural, ethnic, and racial groups. Doing so allowed them to respond to the multicultural discourses that framed their everyday lives in creative and sometimes paradoxical ways.

As avid consumers of commodities and ideas from resources that traverse national borders, young people's performative acts occur locally but increasingly derive meaning from global resources (Correa-Velez et al. 2010; see also Laura Moran 2016). Indeed, intimate relationships among young people no longer emerge solely from within the bounds of the community in which they live, but increasingly develop through social media in the form of what Chambers (2013) describes as "mediated intimacies." Such mediated intimacies act as a kind of social capital and provoke public demonstrations of social connection which have arguably altered the meaning and experience of intimacy for young people (Chambers 2013). These virtual, transnational connections also aid in young people's exposure to and use of a range of transnational cultural commodities. However, the development of virtual personal bonds and the creative mobilization of global resources that are often the result of such relationships emerges in relation to local narrative contexts and aids in the process of cultivating belonging therein. In their assertions of belonging in local context, the flexibility through which young people cultivated a sense of themselves through diverse cultural resources was sometimes deemphasized in their performative projection of fixed and immutable identities.

Performance provides an avenue for an especially deliberate engagement with multicultural context. While their everyday interactions demonstrate an oscillating affirmation and denial of the relevance of racial and ethnic identity in different circumstances, performing identity represents a unique moment of particularly heightened, self-conscious intercultural exchange. Removed from the delicacy, nuance, and savvy so useful in everyday multicultural context, performance permits more pointed representations of identity. In performative moments, young people engaged with what I describe as symbolic ethnic capital in ways that tended to represent a sense of their racial and ethnic identity in primarily essentialized ways.

In making these claims I draw on Bourdieu's (1986) conceptual framework of symbolic capital as well as Modood's (2004) and Tabar, Noble and Poynting's (2010) work on ethnic capital to outline a concept of symbolic ethnic capital observed in young people's performative identity practices. Through performance, these young people used textual resources (Dimitriadis [2001] 2009) as capital in the construction of a shared and favorable sense of place and ethnic association around which a sense of belonging might develop. I frame their resourcefulness in this endeavor as a form of symbolic ethnic capital through which young people negotiate the competing drives of cultivating racial and ethnic identity in conjunction with a sense of local and national belonging (see also Tabar et al. 2010, 11).

My analysis of youth performative identity first requires the establishment of an analytic category of symbolic ethnic capital and its relevance to the Australian multicultural context. From here, I explore the various forms of capital through which these young people engaged in their performative representations of self. Formal performances of what is broadly couched as "cultural identity," as they were elicited in the school context, and a hip hop song written and performed by a small group of Sudanese young people who attended Kedron Club allow for my analysis of the relevance of performance in establishing identity in multicultural context.

I consider young people's performative acts beyond simple mimicry or adaptation, but rather as indicative of agency and participation in globally relevant mediums that help them to define a sense of self and belonging in local context (see also Moore 2011, 62). The use of capital in performance helped these young people to construct a shared and favorable sense of place, to create positive associations with their own black or "nonwhite" identities, and to negotiate and create meaning out of the displacement and marginalization they experienced in their lives.

Capital and Performance in Multicultural Australia

In the opening vignette of the book, I observed Tino teasing Samah about "free-stylin'" in reference to her merging of English, Dinka, and Swahili languages, while listening to hip hop music and wearing "African clothes." This scene unfolded as they waited outside of the school auditorium for their African dance performance to begin. The dynamic I sought to illustrate in sharing it—the merging and overlapping of various cultural resources and ethnic symbols—was commonplace among my research participants. Playing with cultural signifiers in this way allowed them to communicate; to differentiate themselves from and to find common ground with, one another. They engaged in such playful banter over various and sometimes conflicting cultural symbols as together they answered the call to perform elements of a collective cultural identity.

As Tino demonstrated in his exchange with Samah, in their self-conscious projections of identity, the authenticity of these young people's use of ethnic symbols and cultural resources was routinely scrutinized in their playful interactions with one another. What I describe as symbolic ethnic capital captures young people's performative adaptation of global resources as they were mobilized in projections of identity. Symbolic ethnic capital allowed young people to articulate a sense of self and belonging with one another, and through that endeavor to also engage and respond to the multicultural context in which their daily lives unfolded.

Capital or symbolic cultural resources, and particularly those that involve pop culture, are central to young people's performance of identity. In their performative representations of self, these young people utilized various cultural resources, concepts, and associations from local and global arenas in ways that were not always obvious or straightforward. They mobilized cultural resources as a kind of symbolic ethnic capital in performance as they sought to define a sense of where they came from, sometimes in alignment with an imagined Western other, in their projects of self and belonging in local context.

Symbolic Ethnic Capital

The relationship between ethnicity and social and cultural capital has been taken up by many scholars as a kind of negative capital (Bourdieu 1986; Hage 1998). As briefly described in chapter 3, cultural and social capital in Bourdieu's formulation refers to elements of personal characteristics and material goods that enable a sense of belonging in a particular group or social context (Bourdieu 1986, 243–248). Fundamentally, people achieve status based on economic, cultural, and social capital. Bourdieu's concept of symbolic capital represents the process by which capital is recognized and given meaning in social context (Bourdieu 1986, 102; see also Hage 1998, 53). From this formulation, it was argued that a lack of capital among ethnic minority groups resulted in various forms of social exclusion and an uneven distribution of wealth and resources.

The concept of "ethnic capital" instead highlights a productive relationship between ethnicity and the accumulation of capital for the purposes of educational achievement and social mobility (Modood 2004; Shah, Dwyer and Modood 2010; see also Collins et al. 2000; Nayak 2009; Reynolds 2010; Tabar et al. 2010; Weller 2010). As Modood explained in his conceptualization, young people of nonwhite ethnic minority backgrounds in Britain demonstrated higher levels of educational achievement then their white working-class counterparts. He attributed this to a kind of ethnic capital whereby an ethos of high educational aspiration was transferred from parents to children of ethnic minority backgrounds (Modood 2004).

In the context of Australian cultural politics, ethnic capital has been defined as the resources and capacities, validated by the state, which are utilized by migrants and their children to settle in Australia (Tabar et al. 2010, 16). As I employ the concept, "symbolic ethnic capital" emerges. not through familial parent-child relations, but through the transmission of attitudes, norms. and aspirations that emerge from young people's diasporic connections which are "self-fashioned" based on a highly racialized sense of ethnicity (see also Tsolidis and Pollard 2009). The mobilization of race and ethnicity as symbolic ethnic capital is particularly evident in the critical and often tense practices of identity making engaged by young people as they mobilized what I have described in terms of their hybridized and essentialized representations of self.

As I have described, hybridity and essentialism are modes of self-representation that allow a kind of dynamic responsiveness to the ways in which these young people are represented in the Australian national context (see also Moore 2011, 61). As I demonstrate it here, symbolic ethnic capital is mobilized by young people in the performative representation of a kind of self-racialized identity which serves as a rallying point for solidarity and a sense of belonging in the moral and political context of Australian multiculturalism (Moran 2016). In addition to enabling a sense of belonging with one another, symbolic ethnic capital allows young people to engage with the ideals of multiculturalism as they encounter them in their everyday lives.

Their strategic use of capital in highly racialized and essentialized self-representations demonstrates young people's identity work at times as somewhat subversive. Rather than inserting themselves into the Australian multicultural context in terms of either assimilation with white Australian peers or demonstrating their ethnic heritage in ways that adhere to Australia's multicultural agenda (Anthony Moran, 2011), young people borrow from a range of cultural signifiers to define their ethnicity also in terms of a broadly conceived Western other, or in terms of being black or not white (see also Warren and Evitt 2010).

Just as whiteness emerges as a form of symbolic capital in the Australian multicultural field, these young people may mobilize ethnicity as a distinct form of symbolic capital in the context of multiculturalism. In the school context, those who conform to the norms of integration by downplaying their racial and ethnic identity and alternately, when asked to do so, perform their ethnic identities within the celebratory language of tolerance are held up as exemplars of what a "good" refugee can be. Symbolic ethnic capital captures the specific enabling capacities of young people's explicitly racialized ethnic resources in aligning themselves with others in the context of Australian multiculturalism. By representing themselves in overtly racialized ways, young people reflect essentialism in ways that respond to discourses of integration and tolerance encountered in multicultural context.

The ethnographic detail that follows demonstrate young people's use of symbolic ethnic capital in the construction of both an imagined Western other and an abstracted sense of their cultural backgrounds. Following this, I demonstrate how such cultural resources aid in performative representations of home and belonging to place. I explore how one group of young people forged alignments with an Americanized or African American other using hip hop culture and symbolism, and how others performed essentialized representations of their cultural and ethnic backgrounds as they were called upon to do in the school environment. Their use of symbolic ethnic capital in the performative cultivation of home and belonging, often through presenting racially essentialized depictions of themselves, allowed these young people to engage and respond to the multiculturalism they encountered in their daily lives in the Australian context.

America, Africa, and Cultivating the Other

In a shopping mall with Catalina and Lisa, Karen and Burmese research participants respectively, Catalina enthusiastically grabbed Lisa's arm and said, "I took another picture last night!" She pulled out her phone and showed Lisa a picture of herself leaning against a wall with her hair down, a serious expression on her face and wearing cut off denim shorts and a bikini top. Lisa squealed, "Oooh!" when she saw it. They began to analyze the photograph. Catalina pressed, "How old do I look in this one? Do you think I'm looking twenty? I wanted to look twenty in this one? Twenty and America [sic]." After some continued discussion of this photo, who took it, whose clothes she was wearing, and so on, Catalina asked Lisa, "You taking many pictures, yeah?" to which Lisa said that she was and pulled her mobile phone out of her pocket.

All of the young women involved in my research, and especially those with Karen and Burmese backgrounds, used photographs taken with mobile phone cameras to create and share images of themselves with one another. For these girls, taking pictures of themselves usually posing alone, often in sexually suggestive positions while wearing Western style clothes and makeup, and then later scrutinizing the results with one another, was an everyday practice. As Catalina explained to me, "Karen are always taking pictures. They like to. I don't know why. We did it in camp too. But not with camera like this. Simple." The girls took pictures with their mobile phones, shared them with one another and uploaded them onto social networking websites, such as, initially, Bebo and Hi5, and increasingly, Facebook. This practice, as Hjorth argues, allows people "the ability to document, re-represent and perform the everyday" (2007, 227). And particularly for young women, mobile phone cameras allow them to "'perform' conventional gender roles with a twist" (Hjorth 2007, 235).

Such self-representations often occurred in accordance with Western styles and imagery, and in particular, with the American hip hop culture and musical scene. All of the young people with whom I worked asserted some sort of claims of knowledge about or association with American and hip hop culture. I interpret their constant engagement with all things American and hip hop as a form of symbolic ethnic capital. Young people with African backgrounds played with and asserted claims of knowledge and belonging to various elements of African culture which also reveal the role of symbolic ethnic capital. Similarly, Karen young people participated in cultural events through which they portrayed what it means to be Karen, often in juxtaposition to the benefits of now being a part of the Australian multicultural tapestry. Their use of cultural references to an abstracted notion of America or to their own cultural backgrounds act as a form of symbolic ethnic capital in that they elicit essentialized, highly racialized projections of identity which young people mobilize in their varied assertions of belonging.

Young people's use of symbolic ethnic capital in self-conscious, performative ways carves out a space for a more deliberate engagement and a responsiveness to their social context that exists alongside the dynamics of everyday life. Moreover, the use of symbolic ethnic capital in performance allows for an avenue through which young people might negotiate the vulnerability and marginalization that is a part of their lives in complex and unpredictable ways (Dimitriadis [2001] 2009).

Claiming Culture: "You Don't Even Know America Man"

An abstract idea of America forged an association to hip hop culture, and indeed a sense of opportunity and material wealth for many of these young people. In addition to their constant references to and expressions based upon the hip hop music scene, American cultural references also emerged around young people's style of dress, their use of English and American colloquial language, and their assertions of their own and policing of one another's knowledge about and connections to America. Going to the United States was expressed as a deeply entrenched desire for many of these young people.

America as an abstract identifying reference point was reinforced by the fact that most of them had some family members who had been resettled in the United States. Because of this, many had visited America or were planning to visit at some point in the near future. Moreover, checking the authenticity of one another's claims to go, or have been to America, was a common theme. Upon learning that I'm from New York State, Gabe insistently and incredulously asked, "So you're from the neighborhood of New York?! Are you telling me you're from the neighborhood of New York?!" And when Vic "discovered" that Gabe's claims to have been to America were false, she excitedly reported to the rest of the group, "Ha! I proved Gabe didn't go to America. I asked his sister. That's the biggest lie of all!"

In addition to regularly and persistently asserting their connections with and desires to go to America, these young people also drew upon a style of colloquial language and dress commonly associated with American hip hop culture. One day, Catalina greeted Ce Ce upon her arrival at Kedron Club with the phrase "sup" (American slang for "what's up"). Ce Ce, somewhat satirically, shook Catalina's hand and responded with an overexaggerated "Suuuuup Maaaan!" Both girls laughed, and they never looked back. After that first seemingly sudden, "sup," I rarely heard these girls, or their friends greet one another in any other way. Similarly, and around the time of the "sup" launch, they made increasingly regular use of the word "man" to punctuate their sentences.

Many girls represented in the book experimented with Western makeup and dress, and many of the boys preferred clothing with prominently displayed American logos and brand names—sometimes in accordance with stereotypical associations such as criminal activity and material wealth or the lack thereof. Gabe, when attending Kedron Club, dressed in jeans slung low around his waist and a thick black belt with a large, gun-shaped rhinestone buckle, a baseball cap worn sideways, a white tank top and a lot of big silver jewelry, asked rhetorically, "Just because I dress all gangsta does that mean I'll whip out a gun and steal something?" In his creation of an Americanized "gangsta" image and its stereotypical association with criminal activity, Gabe made frequent reference to the police even though he had apparently not ever been in trouble with them. In a typical interaction, at Paddington High one lunch time he approached a table of his friends who were engaged in some school assignment related conversation and asked them, "What are we talking about? Police?"

In their projection of a sense of American-ness young people referenced African American people with whom they associated in playful, performative ways. For example, Obama, who claimed to have had this nickname long before he ever heard of the U.S. president, was called "black Obama," in opposition to the then-president, whom he and his friends had nicknamed "half-black Obama." Obama's friends constantly referenced his nickname in association with the concept of "America," material wealth, and the president, such as when Santino teased, "You're rich, Obama, go back to America, go to your wife and kids."

While such language and symbolic action demonstrates a playful and seemingly inconsequential engagement with American colloquialisms and hip hop style, young people's interest in and use of "America" as a reference point for their sense of self was significant and entrenched. The most prominent and wide spread example of the mobilization of America as a form of symbolic ethnic capital emerged through young people's engagement with the hip hop music scene itself.

The Centrality of Hip Hop

A music genre born out of disadvantaged urban neighborhoods of New York City during the 1970s, the use of hip hop music for a sense of belonging and identification among minority young people is a widely documented and increasingly global phenomenon (Aidi 2014; Forman 2002; Warren and Evitt 2010). The global uptake of hip hop music demonstrates an evolving "transnational black culture" positioned around ideas of brotherhood and resistance which provides scope for interpretation and the infusion of local experience (Patterson and Fosse 2015; Warren and Evitt 2010). "The progressive politics of rap," as Moore describes it, engages with social exclusion, racism, urban violence, poverty and issues of power and dominance (2011, 65).

As Warren and Evitt have argued in the context of Indigenous Australian young people's adaptation of hip hop music, disenfranchised groups relate to hip hop because it encompasses a "fusion between the traditional (language, cultural stories, histories and dance) and contemporary (equipment, software and technologies)" and is "appropriated through transnational black networks, across diverse locations" (Warren and Evitt 2010, 156). As a medium of expression which is explicitly designed to respond to localized identity politics in urban contexts, hip hop music provides an ideal platform from which young people can consciously engage issues of race and ethnicity as they emerge within the political and social climate of their own lives.

In reference to Sudanese refugees in Cairo, Forcier (2008) argues that rather than a simple adaptation of American hip hop style, young people's mobilization of hip hop cultural references can be interpreted as the emphasis on themes of wealth over the abject poverty of being a refugee (see also Moore 2011, 64). He writes that this manifestation is not an attempt to mimic African American culture, but rather is a rejection of the proscribed refugee identity characterized by poverty and lack of opportunity in favor of an identity that emphasizes material wealth and financial success.

The young people represented here, in addition to certain aspects of style and colloquial language, expressed an affiliation with hip hop cultural references. They did so through their alignment with symbolic urban spaces such as "the 'hood" and "the ghetto," and through their constant policing of the authenticity of what is "real" in terms of their own and one another's connection to these spaces (Forman 2002, xviii). Associations with place, as well as the notion of "the real," are treated with great consequence in hip hop culture, which deals explicitly with issues of locality and authenticity (Dimitriadis [2001] 2009, 66; Warren and Evitt 2010).

The young people in my study sought to identify with "real" black experience in terms of the cool, the resistance, and the counter whiteness of an African American identity (Laura Moran 2016). They forged these alignments through essentialized, highly racialized representations of their identity and sense of belonging which drew on American and hip hop cultural references as a form of symbolic ethnic capital. While many of the young women represented here appropriated elements of American hip hop style and colloquialism, it was predominately the boys who more explicitly engaged with the messages of power, police and toughness emerging from hip hop. Their use of hip hop cultural references allowed young men to use their masculinity, which, as young migrant men, often acts to stigmatize and work against them (Pruitt et al. 2018), toward more positive associations. hip hop culture offered a nonwhite identity associated with power and belonging for these young people, and rap music provided a medium through which to constitute and represent their own self-understanding and to engage with the everyday politics of their lived experiences.

In informal interactions and formal performances at their schools, young people also utilized symbolic ethnic capital that they defined as emerging from their cultures of origin in defining a sense of self in multicultural context. African participants established their sense of association with Africa through their assertion of knowledge and talk of things decidedly "African" such as the tribe to which they belonged, the language they spoke and elements of a self-conscious and decidedly African image and sense of style.

Everyday Africanness: Tribe, Language, and Style

African participants engaged in assertions of what constitutes "being African," as they emphasized their sense of Africanness and guided one another to do the same. They did so through teasing one another in a kind of playful, animated bravado. Just as in relation to American and hip hop cultural symbols, young people were interested in asserting claims of knowledge about and alignments to their countries and cultures of origin. Tribes were of relevance as symbolic ethnic capital in asserting young people's connections to, and knowledge of, Africa.

Through playful teasing, young people critiqued either the characteristics of one another's tribe or their lack of knowledge about their own or others' tribes. When Vic and Samah were discussing a friend of a friend, Samah's first question was, "Is he Nuba, Dinka, Nuer?" to which Vic replied "No, he's Nuer and Logbara." When Samah asked, "What's Logbara?" Vic replied, "It's an African tribe! What the heck. Don't you know your African tribes?" On another occasion, Joseph similarly scolded Vic for her lack of knowledge about her own tribe. During lunch hour at Paddington High, Joseph told me that the Nuba were the first known tribe in Egypt. When I confirmed with Vic that she is Nuba, and as she said yes, Joseph interjected, "She doesn't even know the history of her own people."

African young people also teasingly insulted one another about their respective tribal affiliations, and less frequently, their countries of origin. On one occasion Samah was teasing Vic because Vic kept grabbing things out of Samah's bag. Vic was the only Nuba person hanging out with all her Dinka friends. Samah slapped Vic's hand away and said, "What's the matter, you Nuba people can't keep your hands to yourself!" Another day, when Nine and Zi were obviously and mockingly talking about Vic and laughing from one table away from where she was sitting, Vic shouted, "Don't say anything about me! I am not Dinka and I'm not Sierra Leone so shut up!" And later, on the same day, Samah was teasing Zi about something and said, "You Sierra Leone." They both laughed, and he asked her "What did you mean by that?" Vic didn't answer Zi's question and he let it go without saying more. Later, I asked Vic why she called him a Sierra Leone and she said, "That's his place!" Zi then explained to me, "She's just making a stupid. She doesn't know what she's talking about." Again, they both laughed.

Tribal and sometimes national affiliation provided a platform from which young people asserted knowledge about being African that allowed them to both identify and disassociate with one another in different moments. Through assertions of knowledge about tribes as a form of capital, young people both fully inhabited and vacated their sense of Africanness. Tribal identity was most often mobilized by African young people for creating playful distinctions and one upping each other in their performative demonstrations of Africanness. When asked directly about tribes and their significance, however, they often said that tribes were not very important now that they are living in Australia. As Samah explained, "I don't think the tribal thing is a big deal. Just in Africa. It's weird how Australians don't have tribes. They are just one people. . . . That's so boring."

In their projection of a sense of African identity, young people also playfully teased one another about their proficiency in African languages. The use of regional dialects indeed served a practical purpose—participants reported using Arabic, Dinka, or other languages than English in the classroom to comment about the teacher or other students without their understanding, and English with siblings and friends at home to have conversations without their parents understanding. However, language use also provided a means through which young people asserted their superior sense of Africanness in comparison to one another. On numerous occasions, participants teased one another about their lack of proficiency in African languages, usually in front of a group of other young people, such as when Vic teased Samah, "You don't understand him?! He's speaking your language—how do you not understand!"; when Santino accused AJ, "This kid doesn't even know how to speak!"; and when Tino jokingly mocked a new student, "And this guy calls himself an African. Let me say it in African for you!"

In a final example of asserting Africanness as symbolic ethnic capital, African young people regularly assessed and critiqued how African one another looked depending on hair and clothing style. When Vic explained to her friends, during the school lunch hour that her straight hair look that day was not her real hair she said, "It's not mine. No good African girl would have this hair." Similarly, when an Australian student approached wearing a hat tilted to the side, Vic told him, "You look like an African coming over here with that hat on," and everyone laughed. On another occasion, Zi approached Vic and Samah one afternoon, pulled out a blue tie, and said he was going for a job interview. Vic and Samah burst out laughing and told him the tie was too big and in the wrong color. Vic said, "Since when did you start wearing colors like this anyway? You should be wearing yellow, or orange, or red. That's what we wear! Give this thing to a business man! It looks like you're a little kid wearing a grown up's clothes."

Young people engaged in teasing insults based on being African by critiquing one another's Africanness in style and dress and asserting knowledge about Africa through tribal references and language use. This allowed them to police the boundaries of who belonged where and to constitute their own sense of themselves through identification and disassociation with one another. Symbolic ethnic capital, both in claims of Americanness and Africanness, was central to these young people's sense of themselves and engagement with their local context. In the section that follows, I will explore how such capital was mobilized in formalized performances for the purposes of cultivating identity and belonging, and in engagement with the multicultural context in which these young people were immersed.

Performative Constructions of Place and Home

American cultural capital, and particularly that gleaned from the hip hop music scene, was utilized in the constitution of self and group identity for many of the young people represented here. In a primary example of this, an interest in hip hop music translated into a project in which I assisted a group of seven Sudanese participants to write and record a hip hop song during my fieldwork. By strategically mobilizing American cultural resources as symbolic ethnic capital, the song the young people wrote helped them to articulate and negotiate their sense of place within the various racial constructions they inhabit in multicultural Australia. As I'll describe, young people participated in equally noteworthy performative representations of their own cultures of origin, through which they also used symbolic ethnic capital in the cultivation of a sense of identity and in responsive relationship to their local context.

Africa as "the 'Hood"

The writing and recording of their own hip hop song helped this small group of Sudanese young people to articulate and negotiate their sense of place in terms of their journey from Africa to Australia and their experiences as black people in Australia today. The participants in this project were Santino, his sister Lola and brother Omar, as well as Obama, Gabe, Omot, and Aher. I met with them at Kedron Club on Saturday afternoons and during the summer break over approximately three months to work on the song. The result provides an exploration of home, race, and racism through associations with common American hip hop references to poverty, crime, power, and toughness, primarily through their use of the terms "the 'hood" and "the ghetto." In doing so, they reveal the complex ways in which young people utilized certain themes emerging in hip hop music and culture—in their song lyrics and in the interactions that ensued in the process through which they were constructed—to make sense of and represent their own lives.

The group constructed the lyrics to the song on their own with minimal grammatical help from me, and with some adjustments by the studio's recording engineer to fit their lyrics with an audio track. They structured the song so that each had an individual verse and all seven sang and wrote the chorus collectively. Throughout the course of writing the song, references to "America" were constant. In the usual fashion, they regularly claimed they were going to America soon while their peers would accuse them of lying. They danced wildly to Michael Jackson songs which they played from their mobile phones, and they went into the yard to play "American ball" during impromptu breaks.

When the group brainstormed ideas around what the song should be about, they came up with the following: "the 'hood," "Africa," "Sudan," "basketball," "President Obama," "marijuana," "MTV," and "yourself." They narrowed it down to "the 'hood," "Africa," "basketball," and "President Obama." From this initial brainstorming session, the American and hip hop references to "the 'hood," "basketball," "President Obama," "marijuana," and "MTV" were utilized in accordance with participants' references to experiences that were most salient and personal to their own lives: "Africa," "Sudan," and "yourself."

When they began brainstorming lyrics, after an initial period of silence, the first line was called out by Santino: "We're poor!" In response to this, everyone shrieked with laughter and shouted things like, "You, not me! Don't write that!" Following this, everyone joined in and came up with a series of lines including: "The hood in Africa was pretty hard," "In order to survive we had to sell drugs."

and "Moving with da thugs. Rollin' faster than slugs." The juxtaposition between their real experiences of poverty and living in Africa with associations of power and toughness through selling drugs and hanging out with "thugs" allowed participants to subtly shift their self-representation toward a sense of empowerment rather than poverty. The associations they claim to draw such links is based on a constructed and racialized sense of ethnic identity. In these instances, "being black" carries value that transcends other cultural and ethnic alignments. I interpret the conceptual link these young people make between their own experiences of being young, black, African refugees with the power and the cool of the American hip hop scene as indicative of their creative employment of symbolic ethnic capital.

In another proposed verse, which Aher teasingly directed at Obama, he sang, "Obama is a refugee. Refugee. Refugee," and everyone, including Obama, laughed. Throughout the song-writing process, young people engaged with what they saw as negative stereotypes about themselves (poor, refugees) and reconstituted these to create a more positive and tough image associated with "gangstas," "the 'hood," and "the ghetto." I explore this process through an analysis of specific verses of the song.

The chorus of the song, which all participants sang together, is as follows:

We were born in Africa, Born young
Walking everyday in the ghetto place
We were born in Africa, Hot sun
Walking everyday in the ghetto place
Came to Australia, Left the 'hood
Came to Australia, When we could
Now we wanna go back, To a better place
Make it all good, Make it all good

In this verse, Africa is referred to as "the ghetto place" and "the 'hood"—both references used frequently in hip hop music and American slang to describe poor urban areas in U.S cities. The terms "the 'hood" and "the ghetto" in their usage in hip hop music evoke racist stereotypes of crime, poverty, and drugs, as well as images of power, masculinity, and toughness. For my informants, these terms are associated most acutely with a sense of belonging. An abbreviation of the term "neighborhood," Forman similarly describes the use of the term "the 'hood' in hip hop music as signifying, 'quite simply . . . a 'home' environment" (2002, xix).

When I asked the young people what the terms "ghetto" and "the 'hood" meant to them, they described them primarily as references to home and a sense of community belonging with family and friends. As Tino explained about the terms, "You hear it in songs, rap songs, it's a good place—it's family, friends, where I belong—it's a cool place where we all hang out, just hang out"; and Lola,

"It means you live in the poorest population . . . but it's alright because it's easier to find more friends"; Gabe, "It's a place to go back to see family and all that . . . it's kind of anywhere"; and Aher, "I think it's just leaving home and coming to a new place . . . it's a place where you live." The terms "the ghetto" and "the 'hood," represented finding a place of home, community and belonging, despite various obstacles related to poverty. By using these terms, young people were able to create meaning in their own experiences of displacement through an alignment with an image of blackness that in its pop cultural association reflects power and toughness as it depicts poverty and disadvantage. Obama's verse reveals tension in a conceptualization of Africa as "the 'hood":

> I know this place hurts, but you can go back, back to the hood.
> Where I live right now, it's all good. All good.

Obama reflects a positive association with Africa in terms of home and belonging in his verse while acknowledging that the place he's living now, although it does not provide such a sense of belonging, is in some ways a good place. Similarly, Gabe lamented the loss of Africa in an early version of his verse in the song, "I used to roll in the 'hood but now I can only roll in the suburbs." The sense of loss experienced by participants in their transition from life in Africa to life in Australia was reflected throughout the song. Aher's verse engaged this theme of leaving:

> I never thought that I would leave this place.
> Sitting in the plane, thinking about my fate.
> The first school that I went to was so gay.
> As they say, do the right thing and stay safe.
> I got a detention for saying one thing.
> I got all the attention that I need.
> It's a big wide nation, the next generation
> Follow the operation or end up on probation.

In addition to his experience of leaving Africa, Aher's verse provides an account of what happened to him when he arrived in Australia. It reflects the difficulties young people in his position have, despite the notion of increased safety, in adjusting to Australian school systems, as well as the outcome (detention and probation) that they frequently experience. However, when I questioned Aher about this experience he responded, "It's just a song, Miss!" Lola's verse provides further commentary on the movement from Africa to Australia:

> My name's Little Moon Man
> Man, in the moon
> Came to Australia because of the war
> Ran for my life

Not too soon
Got on that plane
Had to survive
Tried to keep safe but I lost my faith.

In Lola's verse about leaving Africa she evoked an image of survival with phrases like "ran for my life," "not too soon," and "had to survive." Lola was five when she arrived in Australia after a period living in Egypt as a Sudanese refugee. When describing her migration in an interview context she said, "I don't know why, school, studying, education maybe." Her depiction of Africa in the song did not involve the more positive associations with "the 'hood" of belonging and power, but instead evoked a sense of war, danger, and flight, which were not reflected in her lived experience as expressed in an interview context. The performative nature of the song-writing process instead allowed Lola to engage in a reconstruction of her experience of leaving that did not reflect the same sense of loss as in the others' verses.

Santino's verse is a departure from the previous verses which engaged explicitly with leaving Africa. He uses American and hip hop imagery in a reflection on the complexity of his experience in Australia:

Basketball is my favorite sport
I'm rolling with the President on the court
I got arrested and went to jail
They didn't give me any bail
So many nets it was a crime
Too many points in my time
See Obama in my court
Aussie girls messed me up
So, I just wanna go play ball
Kawaja, Africa

Santino relies on American cultural imagery in a depiction of his current life in Australia and in juxtaposition to the hip hop imagery of criminal activity and going to jail. He describes playing basketball with President Obama in response to his experiences with "Aussie girls." His final line points to a sense of the inherent juxtaposition of American hip hop symbolic representations, and a sense of identification with Africa, reflected throughout the song, but in this case in an explicit racial construction. *Kawaja* means white person in Sudanese Dinka. The juxtaposition of African and American symbolic references in the song was not always a straightforward association for all members of the group and sometimes caused controversy. In the construction of this verse, for example, Gabe argued that he did not want to use the word *Kawaja* because, he said, "It doesn't go. It's not in English." The others liked it, so it stayed.

In his verse, Omot explicitly engaged his experiences with race and racism as a black person in Australia:

I came from Africa, I'm too black.
I see people white but I'm too black.
They eat Octopus and I eat vegetables
They eat *fortude,* but I eat fruit.[1]
They say my place is where I live today.
But some day my place is where I used to live.
So many special memories
I bring along with me
and together they make my place.

Omot highlights the overt distinctions he notices between himself and the wider population upon arrival in Australia. Skin color was one of the most prominent references in constructing the song. When the group sang the chorus together they would interchange, "We were born in Africa, born young," with "We were born in Africa, born black," further highlighting the overlap between ethnic identity and race as defined by skin color. Similarly, the group decided to name themselves "B Unit," short for "Black Unit." The other names they came up with, including "the blackies" and "the fabulous black boys" further demonstrate the salience of their sense of themselves as black people in Australia.

In reference to the proceeding line of his verse, Omot explained the word *fortude* to mean "morning tea." His description of differences in diet, in conjunction with skin color, illuminates the sense of alienation that his first line portrays. Moreover, Omot's verse demonstrates an acknowledgment and acceptance of the pervasive implication that Australia is a "safe" place. His line about "place" being constructed "together" out of the different environments in which he has lived was initially written at his previous school and reflects the sense of luck and opportunity in his migration promoted in the school context.

Omot alludes to his sense of alienation in juxtaposition to racial and ethnic references. Beyond this though, he is not only providing commentary on his experience of social division based on his skin color, but this sentiment sits in direct dialogue with the integrationist push to which he is regularly subject as he negotiates what "they say" in comparison to what he feels in terms of his "place." Omot's awareness of race as central to his sense of self and indeed his perception by others, is evident in the first two lines of this verse. Yet he was equally aware of multicultural rhetoric that denies the relevance of race in its promotion of integration. As he states, "they say my place is where I live today," despite feeling a sense of belonging in the place where he "used to live." This tension between what was broadly expected and what was actually experienced in terms of cultivating a sense of belonging was evident throughout the development of the song.

Gabe, who had prior recording experience, took his role as a rapper in the song very seriously. For this reason, and, it eventually became apparent, because he could not read written verses proficiently he chose to "freestyle" and rap slightly different lyrics each time he performed. He would argue, "I don't write it, I don't read it, I'm all freestyle" and the others would become frustrated when each time it was his turn he would stand at the microphone for ten minutes and say, "I got nothing" before starting to rap.

During one such confrontation between Gabe and the others, Gabe struggled with the dichotomy between positive associations with Africa and American hip hop symbolic representations. While standing at the microphone preparing for his verse he said, "I got nothing . . . I only got gangsta stuff. I don't have Africa stuff. It doesn't go in this song. This song is about safe places. I only have gangsta stuff." For Gabe, the relationship between Africa and hip hop associations of "the 'hood" and "the ghetto" did not always match up. The other participants who were not as immersed in rap and hip hop culture were looser with their associations, while for Gabe the distinction between gangster associations and Africa or Australia as "safe places" was important. In the end result, Gabe conveyed a similar message to the other verses—that while he has experienced "the 'hood" in many places, he wants to go back to the hood in Africa where he might experience a greater sense of belonging. His verse is as follows:

> I've been a lot of places, seen a lot of 'hoods
> But I've never seen a 'hood just like this.
> My homies in the back, my homies in the back.
> I never wanna see them
> Never wanna be them
> I never wanna click, clack, bang
> I've been to different 'hoods
> But I wanna go back to the 'hood.

The minor confrontation between Gabe and the others illustrates the flexible use of pop cultural references as a form of symbolic ethnic capital in young people's self-representation. Such references were not simply adapted by young people but reflected their individual imaginary as well as broader social discourses. As such, inconsistencies were reflected in the range of ways young people used hip hop symbolism to make sense of their lives. "Africa" was often represented positively through associations with power and toughness portrayed in imagery of "the 'hood" and "the ghetto," while for Gabe, Africa represented a "safe place" which was incompatible with his interpretation of the hip hop imagery of "gangsta." Despite different interpretations of specific symbolic images, in its overriding messages, American hip hop associations were used in the verses of the song to construct an image of home and belonging in association with Africa. The final verse, which the whole group sang together in a call and answer fashion demonstrates this:

We got the 'hood in this place,
But Africa's the best.

In this verse, "the 'hood," as it represented a sense of home and belonging for these participants, could be detected in their current social environment, but was argued to be stronger in association with Africa. The mobilization of images of "the ghetto" and "the 'hood," through symbols gleaned from the global arena, allowed for a positive and empowering negotiation of these young people's experiences with displacement and marginalization, through which they asserted their sense of identification with Africa.

In the song they wrote, which in the end they decided to name "Born in Africa," hip hop associations with power, belonging, and toughness were particularly instrumental in constructing a positive image of Africa as home. Moreover, through the medium of hip hop, young people were able to express their sense of loss over leaving Africa, as well as the difficulties and advantages associated with their migration to Australia. Using symbolic ethnic capital in the cultivation of their hip hop song, my informants sought to cultivate an oscillating sense of belonging—to one another, to the wider Australian society, and to symbolic connections with global networks.

In addition to their use of symbolic ethnic capital related to American culture and the hip hop music scene, the young people represented here mobilized cultural resources from their home countries as a form of capital. In doing so, they also sought to define a sense of self and belonging in engagement with the everyday dynamics which framed their lives in multicultural context. Below, I explore formal cultural performances as they were elicited through school. In these examples of African and Karen cultural performances, both authenticity and flexibility were emphasized in articulations of belonging to a sense of home that existed in young people's memories and in their personal imaginaries.

"What if an African Comes to This": Multicultural Night and Navigating Authenticity

Both Karen and African young people participated in formal cultural performances at schools, articulated a sense of immense pride in these productions, and commonly sought to make them as "authentic" as possible. "Multicultural Night" was a highlight of the year at Paddington High for my African informants who each year performed African dancing on stage for the student body. After anticipation that began early in the school year, when the time for their performance came in the spring, young people began to discuss and plan what they would do at length and critique the performances of previous years. In their discussions, it was made apparent that dance performances produced through "mixing" dance styles from different cultural backgrounds were perceived to upset the preservation of authenticity and therefore deemed unsatisfactory. In previous years, a white Australian student dance group that called themselves "The Bring it on Dancers" utilized dance styles from many different cultural groups in their performances. In one of their lunch hour planning discussions, Elijah expressed the opinion of many: "Bring it on Dancers are lame because they're a mix of everything."

A group of eighteen African research participants at Paddington High danced to the song "Karolina," by Congolese musician Awilo Longomba at Multicultural Night. They practiced and choreographed their dance together during their lunch hour for weeks prior to the event. In the making of their African dance, despite their distaste for obvious "mixing" of different cultural dances, my participants merged a number of distinct dance styles from the many tribes, regions, and nations from which they came into one generalized "African" style with the help of videos found on the internet. During this process, they worried about authenticity. While we were sitting in the school court yard the day before their performance, Samah commented to Vic, "We're going to look so stupid, what if some Africans come to this, they'll be like, 'that's not how we dance, you're embarrassing us.'" Samah's reference to "real Africans" demonstrates Africanness for these young people as a performative, constructive process rather than a fixed trait. Her worry about the legitimacy of their performance is indicative of the flexibility with which young people mobilize symbolic ethnic capital and the insecurity such flexibility can sometimes induce.

The same group of students performed a more traditional dance, which they referred to as a "Boro" dance, at a subsequent school event. Similarly, to their performance at Multicultural Night, in this dance the young people merged different tribal dances from the many different regions from which they came and negotiated with one another about who would do what. In the process they laughed, teased and played with different ideas; as Joseph told Aliir, "You do the Nuba mountain part. I'll do the other." Tino, when critiquing a new student's pronunciation of an African word, launched excitedly into the question, "Do you like African dance!? You should see us all do Boro dance! Next year we'll bring spears!"

Participants' constant concern with authenticity in formal performances points to a tension between their own desires for self-representation and that which was imposed by others. They were concerned with what was "real," what "real Africans" would think of their performance, and they occasionally struggled with feelings of inadequacy in achieving the desired authenticity. That these performances happened in school when they were invited by others in positions of authority to "perform" their culture, and simultaneously encouraged to merge and mix with other "cultural groups," in the name of both tolerance and integration, indicates some inherent constraints on young people's quest for authenticity. Moreover, while they sought to outwardly depict themselves in these formal representations as an authentic but cohesive African group, these young people had to exercise flexibility in their boundaries.

I was able to also observe formal cultural performances among Karen and Burmese research participants on a few occasions. During one such performance at their school seven Karen participants and one Burmese participant performed two songs together. One song was about Australia—how lucky they were to be there and how Australia had helped them—and the other was called "We are Karen" and was sung mainly in Karen. As in African cultural performances, the young people were proud to participate—they practiced all day at Kedron Club the day before their performance. However, these young people were less outwardly concerned with authenticity then African participants.

Participants initially told me that they wrote the first song about Australia themselves but were guided by the question from their teacher, "How has Australia helped you?" When I asked what they would have written about without this prompt Lisa said, "Friendship" and Jessica said, "Yeah, or friendship and Christian . . . friendship, Christian and Country." When I asked which country, Lisa yelled out "Australia!" Jessica said, "Yeah, Australia and Karen . . . but not Burma." Lisa quietly nodded. The second song, "We Are Karen" was performed by mostly Karen participants but included Lisa, my Burmese participant, who did not normally identify as Karen. Participants were unconcerned about this apparent distinction and willingly included Lisa, as their friend, in this performance.

These participants were outwardly inclusive in their cultural performances and were malleable to influences from the school they attended which framed their performance in terms of opportunity in Australia. Nonetheless, as this example of performance demonstrates, while cultural performances in formal settings provide an opportunity for self-representation in which young people often take great pride, such performances are often initiated and framed through relationships of power and dominance (see also Forman 2005; Van Meijl 2006). Cultural performances in this context emphasized the dominant national, cultural ideal of diversity central to the moral and political framework of multiculturalism. And in so doing such performance points to the critical distinction between those who are empowered to impose and enjoy ethnic cultural diversity, through their endowment with "the code, into which it is encoded" (Bourdieu 1984, 2), and those who provide it (Hage 1998, 204).

Young people's demonstrations of flexibility as well as their policing of the boundaries of authenticity in performance indicates the intersections between self-representation, the cultivation of belonging, and an awareness of social context. African participants' quest for authenticity in cultural performance allowed for the outward projection of a cohesive, exclusively African group. In their projections of Africanness young people sought to blur distinctions between different ethnic groups and they worried about the accuracy of their representations. Karen participants' alternate reliance on flexibility permitted a sense of inclusion which subtly shifted the focus of their performance from their own cultural backgrounds to the desirability of being a part of Australia. Both Karen singing and African dance performances, which occurred at different schools, were decidedly rooted in a multicultural context where the ideals of Australian inclusiveness and tolerance for diversity were highlighted alongside the cultures that young people were called upon to portray. Whether they emphasized a strong concern with authenticity, or more openly demonstrated flexibility, cultural performances allowed the young people to make use of symbolic ethnic capital for participation in their own self-representations and engagement with dominant discourses and relations of power.

Symbolic Ethnic Capital and Multicultural Belonging

To summarize, young people approach a sense of belonging within the context of Australian multiculturalism through their use of symbolic ethnic capital—a process reflective of Bourdieu's conceptual framework of cultural and social capital and Modood's subsequent work on ethnic capital (Bourdieu 1986; Hage 1998; Modood 2004). American style, slang, and hip hop cultural references, in addition to a range of cultural symbols from their own countries of origin, acted as forms of symbolic ethnic capital which these young people utilized in various demonstrations of self-conscious cultural performance. At the heart of their representations, young people negotiated messages they regularly encountered in their school and community environments related to the complex ways in which their lives are framed in the Australian multicultural context. Most prominently, young people's highly essentialized, and often racialized, representations of self in performance reflect their perception and accumulation of capital which emerges in dynamic response to the ideals of multicultural tolerance and inclusion.

School multicultural performances, initiated by and performed in young people's schools, are reflective of how young people mobilize performative representations of identity in juxtaposition to the messages of multicultural inclusion and tolerance that they regularly encounter. The schools these young people attended called for inclusive cultural performances and referenced Australia as a superior nation-state, but such performances were also premised on the impetus to celebrate difference. In subtle engagement with these messages, young people couched their cultural performances through a range of concerns and priorities. In their African dance performance, a group of young people used hybridizing strategies to draw upon a catalogue of cultural resources that allowed them to present an essentialized and cohesive African identity (see also Noble and Tabar 2002; Tabar et al. 2010). As they sought authenticity they projected essentialized self-representations based on an overriding notion of being African through local webs of relationships and with symbols gleaned from an array of global resources. Their fretting over the authenticity of their performance in the process demonstrates the inherent power dynamic through which they are called upon to perform, against a pervasive backdrop created by an ethic of tolerance.

The cultural performance of a group of Karen young people (plus one youth who was Burmese) similarly demonstrates how cultural representations are often engaged within or alongside representations of Australia as a symbol of the inclusive multicultural ideal. These young people emphasized the flexibility and adaptability inherent in their capacity for inclusion through which modes of belonging were also eventually asserted. Their performance of the song "We Are Karen" was developed across ethnic, cultural, and religious divides, and significantly, in juxtaposition with a song praising the Australian multicultural ideals of inclusion and tolerance. While it does present some evidence of awareness of multicultural ideals, their performance of "We Are Karen," was something of an anomaly. While this performance allowed for flexibility, the much more common dynamic was that young people asserted essentialized representations of themselves in performance through the hybridizing strategies of adapting global references for specific, localized contexts and meanings.

To further clarify the connection between youth performances of identity and multicultural context, I will focus my analysis on the hip hop song written by Santino, Lola, Omar, Obama, Gabe, Omot, and Aher. This example of performance bears one critical difference to the others that emerged through school multicultural programs—the ideas for what the song would be about, the lyrics for the song, the song structure, the decision to write and record a song at all, were entirely theirs. Emerging more independently, the song provides a useful example of how the self-conscious nature of performance allows for a particularly deliberate engagement with social context.

As coordinator of Kedron Club at the time the song was written and recorded, my instigating role was solely to inform the young people that we had some extra funding and could do with it what they chose. I suggested a field trip, they informed me they'd rather record a song. At the start of the project I told them that the song could take whatever form they chose and that it could be about anything they wanted. I gave them no further guidance. Through their own words and ideas, as playful, light, and silly as they were at the start, participants were able to comment on their sense of loss at leaving Africa, the fear they experienced on their journey to Australia, and the complexity of their feelings of both exclusion and opportunity in making a new home, or a new 'hood, for themselves in Australia.

Not only do the lyrics of the song engage with the discourses of integration and tolerance to which young people were regularly exposed, but they were treated by the young people themselves as being in some ways subversive. Their song lyrics did not provide a foundation for integration with what they perceived as the mainstream, white population, nor did they represent traditional African culture as they were often called upon to do in cultural performance. Instead, young people's use of symbolic ethnic capital in this example allowed for them to reach further afield as they aligned themselves with African American notions of the 'hood and the ghetto in their representations of Africa as home. In doing so, they aligned themselves with one another through images and references to a broader social context entrenched with agency, dominance and community. In addition, their association with a hip hop ethic of power and dominance allowed for participation in the broad cultural values of moral authority and material wealth (Patterson and Fosse 2015).

In addition to enabling them to adapt certain ideals of hip hop culture, the writing of their song allowed these young people to respond to messages that both celebrate and deny the relevance of race in multicultural discourse. When they initially discussed ideas for the song, Omot said, "Let's make it about different colors. We're not all the same colors so color doesn't matter. Paint yourself. Spray paint. Blue." Lola echoed this broad sentiment of inclusion when she said, "yeah, let's make it about the world." While their gestures toward the trivial nature of skin color in their brainstorming session indicate an awareness of a kind of multicultural moral code to deny the impact of race, on the other hand they also demonstrated an understanding of race as central to their perception by others. For example, when discussing with the group my own research, and the possibility of writing about their rap in one of our song-writing meetings, one of the young people described my research to another as, "It's about Australia stuff. You're poor, you're black, why'd you move here."

Their occasional claims of skin color as insignificant, juxtaposed to their alternate highlighting of skin color as central and defining to their sense of themselves, reflect the symbolic capital through which young people demonstrate their awareness of both the centrality of race and the distaste of racism in relation to popular multicultural discourse (Bourdieu 1984; see also Arkin 2009, 725). This is evident in the complex ways in which young people grappled with the supposed irrelevance of race in the song-writing process, but ultimately embraced its centrality in the final outcome of the song. Their explicitly racialized ethnic resources in forging certain alignments demonstrates an engagement with symbolic ethnic capital as a resource in cultivating a sense of belonging in the broad social and political backdrop of their experience (Modood 2004; Tabar et al. 2010; Weller 2010).

Hybrid Youth and Essentializing Selves as Performative Multicultural Identity

In their more ordinary, everyday interactions, young people's presentations and descriptions of their own sense of identity oscillated between flexibility and hybridity in certain moments, and rigidity and essentialism in others. The highly self-conscious nature of performance, however, allowed for their unapologetic effort to depict largely essentialized, often racialized, representations of ethnic identity. Hybridizing strategies are evident in the ways performative interactions unfold within the global web of music and technology—my informants listened to Arabic, Karen, and American hip hop and pop music; they connected with other young people from across the globe via Bebo, MySpace, and Facebook; and they visited websites, looked at pictures and listened to music emerging from the refugee camps where they used to live. Hybridity allows young people to emphasize or deny both authenticity in their essentialized representations of self, and the inherent flexibility through which such representations are often constituted. Through their performative engagement with symbolic ethnic capital, young people from refugee backgrounds can complicate popular perceptions of the modern, hybridized youth (see also Arkin 2009).

However, young people's performative representations cannot be explained away as easily fitting within the conceptual categories of hybridity or essentialism. As Moore argues, "it is not just a matter of appropriating images from elsewhere, of mimicry, hybridity or even of resistance, but rather an active means of participation, a form of agency" (2011, 61). That is, young people's use of cultural texts and symbolic ethnic capital suggests an active participation in global trends and self-representations. For example, hip hop as a medium of communication is a tool through which people critique and respond to certain social conditions—research participants are no more adapting, hybridizing, borrowing than anyone else. They are using tools and resources available, as do we all, to reflect the whole of their lived experiences. The performative use of symbolic ethnic capital for these young people, especially considering the range of cultural influences and social perspectives they have encountered throughout their lives, enables dynamic responsiveness to the multicultural context of which they are now a part. Through both informal performative interactions and literal cultural performances, young people sought to fix one another in social place—a process through which certainty in belonging was asserted, sometimes challenged, and then reasserted.

Participants' negotiation of a sense of belonging with and to one another in their performative acts and interactions was entangled with their constitution of racialized selves and their awareness of race and racism as prevalent issues in their broader social environment. In the following and final ethnographic chapter I explore young people's dynamic responsiveness in national context as they negotiate issues of racism, citizenship and national belonging. This chapter illustrates their constant referencing of skin color as it emerges against the backdrop of their experiences and awareness of the treatment of "race" within the broader community. As they encounter issues around citizenship and nationality, rather than seeking to bind one another to categories, young people are explicit in their allowance of flexibility.

6

Politicizing Identity

Engaging Racism, Citizenship, and the Nation

Much of the identity work undertaken by these young people emerges with reference to some element of their sociopolitical positioning. They regularly framed themselves with reference to race and ethnicity in terms of how much it does or doesn't matter. As they described the elements that for them constituted friendship, they demonstrated the importance of being black, not white, or African in their essentialized projections of identity. On the other hand, young people sometimes rejected those claims in hybridized depictions of the irrelevance of race and their capacity to "mix it up" in terms of racial and ethnic backgrounds in friendship groups. In their more formal performative demonstrations of identity they largely favored essentialized self-representations which blurred differences between ethnic backgrounds in the presentation of a cohesive and racialized whole.

At the core of what I'm interested in exploring in this chapter, is why sociopolitical context plays such a foundational role in these young people's projections and negotiations of identity. I hope to demonstrate that they engage with sociopolitical context, particularly in terms of race and ethnicity, because their lives as refugees and as minorities, are overtly politicized according to these categories in the Australian multicultural context. Whiteness, for them, is a political construct through which "being white" functions as the default (majority) racial position. Falling outside of this construct, as these young people do, means that their race needs to be managed or at least addressed through calls for tolerance or integration in multicultural context.

I argue that their capacity for national belonging is both fostered and restrained through a kind of political representation or governance of their difference (Moore 2011) that emerges in response to their status as refugees, as young people, and as racial minorities. I seek to demonstrate their lives as overtly politicized by exploring a range of defining categories in terms of both how they emerge and are treated in public discourse, as well the numerous ways in which they are engaged and perceived by young people. The categories of representation I explore here include citizenship, national identity, refugee status, definitions of home, and the treatment and management of racism. Among the strategies for confronting the elements of power inherent to multicultural discourse was the flexibility young people allowed one another in their representations of national identity, including the extent to which they identified as refugees and how and where they defined a sense of home. Such flexibility, I argue, acts as a form of responsiveness to the governance of their difference.

Governing Difference, Identity, and the Politics of Representation

Henrietta Moore (2011) describes the recognition and governance of cultural difference as a form of "politics of representation." Cultural difference is governed by the ways in which differences are categorized and represented in political discourses and for what purposes. The governance of difference has been integrated into government policy and institutionalized in many parts of the world, most notably from the 1970s on, in policies of multiculturalism (Moore 2011, 32). I interpret both the management of racism and the ways in which citizenship is protected and attained as at the core of how difference is governed, managed, and represented in multicultural context.

As Moore notes, difference as a form of governmentality has emerged and is implemented in government policy, law, the media, through nongovernmental organizations (NGOs), and through a wide range of social practices and rights movements. The governance of difference effects political and economic life as struggles over the representation of group identities and needs are implicated in the allocation of resources and entitlements (Moore 2011, 33). One consequence of the governance of difference is the eruption of the notion of cultural diversity through which cultural claims to citizenship and national identity emerge in relation to cultural identity.

Defining citizenship and nationality in the Australian context has posed unique challenges and contradictions throughout its complex immigration history. Its relatively recent history as a nation-state, the diverse origins of its population, its largely symbolic ties to a foreign monarch and the lack of any historical event to mark its autonomy (Zappala and Castles 1999, 273–276), underpin the vulnerabilities through which a sense of Australian national identity and consequent ideas around citizenship and belonging are imagined. As discussed in chapter 2, claims of belonging in the Australian national field emerge in large part in relation to one's ability to demonstrate their Anglo-Celtic heritage as a form of symbolic capital (Bourdieu 1986; Hage 1998; Kapferer 1998). Official multicultural policy and discourse, although premised to do the opposite, can serve to further distinguish those who do not belong to this majority population. Indeed, the term "multiculturalism" itself is most often reserved for those from non-English-speaking minority backgrounds (Gunew 1990, III). Given the relevance of race in dictating degrees of belonging in multicultural context, both the ways in which citizenship is implemented and the ways in which racism is acknowledged and managed serve as ways of governing difference.

In the Australian context, as struggles over the interpretation and representation of racism and citizenship are engaged at a political level, these categories are perceived by young people as coming from the wider world. Consequently, as I explore and analyze here, the degree to which these concepts resonated in young people's own sense of their identity was variable. Central to this variability are the ways in which the notion of racism is framed as an obstacle to national belonging.

Experiencing and Interpreting Racism

When Vic missed the first half of lunch period at Paddington High one day, she explained upon her return, "They asked me about racism again. They asked if I've ever experienced racism. Again! I said it happened once. . . . Not here. Not at school." To say that these young people experience research saturation about the racism they experience is an understatement. It was commonplace for various government agencies or university researchers, like myself, to visit the schools these young people attended with questionnaires about their experiences with racism. The complex ways in which young people both vacated and inhabited (Back 1996) a sense of racialized identity in their everyday practices and in performative moments (explored in chapters 4 and 5, respectively), is mirrored in the way racism as a significant issue is both affirmed and denied in popular multicultural discourse. All of my research participants reported having experienced racism to some degree, and they had complex understandings and awareness of racist discourses across community and national contexts.

In my observations and conversations with them, young people described their experiences and understanding of racism as primarily class specific and often conflated skin color with socioeconomic status. They were acutely aware of the structural limitations placed on them, which emerged largely in relationship to their economic vulnerability (see also Hage 2002a, 15) and they described their consequent perception of themselves as social outsiders in terms of their skin color. When a group of Sudanese participants listened to a radio interview about their hip hop song described in the previous chapter, and the interviewer referred to them as having "difficult backgrounds." Santino, in a typical explanation said, "Hey, is she calling us poor! Because we're black? That's what difficult background means! It means you're black!" Everyone in the group laughed.

Though they apparently perceived this common assessment that they are black and therefore poor and understood that racism was believed to be a significant issue in their lives, most of my participants maintained that they did not experience racism in the contexts of their school environments and friend-ship groups. In their descriptions of racism they often merged accounts of their own experiences with indications of a public perception of the role of racism in their lives. An awareness of racist attitudes was regularly evoked and enacted in mock demonstrations of racism and teasing accusations, exchanged between young people, of being "a racist." In such exchanges, young people essentialized black identities in humorous interactions through which they exposed the con-tent of various racist stereotypes to mock and critically comment upon them (see also Back 1996, 161). In doing so, young people sought to elicit reactions and nod-ded to the perception that racism looms large in their lives.

"I'm a Black Man and I'm Being Mugged": Demonstrations and Accusations of Racism

I observed mock displays and playful accusations of racism through comments such as, "Don't do that, you're such a racist" or "Stop being such a racist and give me the ball" regularly throughout the course of my fieldwork. Young people engaged in such exchanges with humor as they traded accusations of racism back and forth. The practice of playfully deliberating over what was racist and why was also pervasive. I once observed a group of four boys, two white and two black, laughing and jokingly discussing whether the word "boy" was racist. A group of four black young people on their way out of school at the end of the day were laughing later that day, pushing each other and shouting, "I'm not racist! I'm not racist!" Accusations of racism were often aimed at one another in a teasing and mildly ironic tone, as if to indicate that being racist was not so much an option for them.

To provide just a brief sampling of mock demonstrations and accusations of racism over a range of circumstances: Obama argued with Santino over the computer at Kedron Club, pleading with me, "He can't go first, he's a racist;" Vic playfully slapped one of the dancers who did not know her steps during African dance practice and said, "You're such a racist! Do it right;" Samah informed me that Vic didn't give her a ride to her formal by saying, "No, she didn't bring me. She's a racist. Racist, I tell you;" and Gabe yelled to me while laughing and wres-tling with some friends at school, "Miss, miss! I'm being mugged. I'm being mugged by two white men. I'm a black man, I shouldn't get mugged!"

In addition to their mock accusations of racism, young people engaged in the constant use of derogatory, racist terms. One afternoon at Kedron Club a vol-unteer was talking about Arnold Schwarzenegger, oblivious to the four African boys cracking up with laughter over the sound of that name. They thought the "negger" in "Schwarzenegger" sounded like that most nefarious of slurs and were coaxing each other to "say it out loud if you're a man." Through their near con-stant use of this term young people were able to assert that they knew the nega-tive and deeply racist sentiment it entailed, but they were able to use it themselves,

and thereby subtly negate its problematic association. They did so for the purpose of engaging racist attitudes, or in this case it seemed, for their simple
amusement as teenage boys. On two other occasions, Nine pointed out his
friends to me by gesturing toward Aliir and saying, "My best friends are this
monkey and that monkey," and Samah explained to Joseph why my baby was crying when he held her by saying, "She just doesn't like monkeys."

Through their easy use of racist terms and their joking accusations of
racism, young people demonstrated their awareness of racism and indeed its
perception as a significant issue in their lives, while at the same time they were
able to slightly invalidate racist stereotypes by making fun of them. In this way,
their exchanges around racism created a sort of caricature in which the absurd
content of racism was highlighted, and young people postured that they were
not so deeply affected by it. I interpret young people's playful use of racist stereotypes and accusations of racism in terms of what Back describes as "parody-
ing" racism (1996, 161). Through their joking engagement with constructions
of racism, and as Back also observed among young people from minority backgrounds, "'race' ideologies were subverted and 'commonsense' racism publicly
ridiculed" by my informants (1996, 173). Furthermore, as Back also describes,
young black people regularly engaged with racist name calling and racist terms
and they did so not to hurt one another, but rather as a means of "exposing the
content of [the] stereotype and ridiculing its meaning" (1996, 177).

That is, through their teasing use of racist discourse young people were able
to strip such discourse of any real meaning. In addition to hinting at the fallacy
of racist thinking and ideology and allowing young people to demonstrate that
they were perhaps not so profoundly affected by it, they also demonstrated their
ability to invoke racist discourse to their own advantage in particular and occasional situations. For example, Zi explained to another African student how he
might get away with wearing beads in his hair against school policy. As Zi
explained, "All you have to do is say, 'How dare you tell me not to wear these,
this is my culture, that's racist.'" At Kedron Club Santino claimed to Obama, both
African participants, that racism was the reason for his low exam grade. He said,
"She gave me a B-, she's racist. Racist to me only. She wasn't racist to you . . . you
deserve your grade." And when I asked Vic why she left her previous school, she
responded "It was boring Miss . . . [and as an afterthought] they are racist." In
some instances, "racism" was used as the simplest explanation for a range of
complaints which may or may not have been based in experiences with racism.

When an incident was perceived as having racist undertones but did not
appear to demonstrate this decisively enough, it was also common for young
people to enhance the racist content in their retelling. In one prominent example, a group of girls who attended Kedron Club were at their school hanging out
in a classroom and straightening one another's hair during the lunch hour. I was
there too as their teacher stormed into the classroom and started yelling at the

students that they should not be straightening their hair during the lunch hour. The teacher told them they would have to pay for the electricity they used in doing so and the girls were clearly confused and did not realize that they were breaking any rules. They didn't argue and immediately started packing up their hair things to leave the room. As they did so, they mumbled quietly in Arabic to one another. The teacher's agitation escalated, and she yelled, "Don't you use that lang- [starts to say language] Arabic in my classroom!"

The girls left and as they debriefed and related the incident to the others outside, the main girl involved said, "She's a racist! She's so racist! She told me 'Don't speak in your dingo languages!'" While this incident clearly had racist elements, such as the teacher's refusal to let the girls use their languages and her stumbling over what to call it, and quite possibly her general contemptuous attitude toward them, the story was retold with statements that were never made. While racist foundations were likely present in and affecting the encounter, the girls used their own experiences and interpretations of racism to more emphatically illustrate what they felt to be a racist attack.

This incident illustrates the juxtaposition of racism as an actual and prevalent experience in young people's lives, with the self-conscious pervasive awareness that racism is also perceived to be a significant issue in their lives—the latter a reality that can be utilized and tapped into for various purposes and to make various points. By deconstructing their experiences of racism and engaging racist stereotypes in playful verbal interaction or in exaggerated ways to make a point, young people may become active participants in racist discourse and thereby affect its weight in their lives.

Racism and Belonging in Multicultural Discourse

In the context of Australian multiculturalism, Anglo cultural privilege, and ethnic minority disadvantage (in terms of, for example, public sector employment and media representation) exist in juxtaposition to the denial of racism in social and political discourse (Dunn and Nelson 2011, 588). This complexity is evident in the social practices of young people represented here. These young people recounted experiences of racism mostly in abstractions and sometimes claimed not to have experienced it at all, but nonetheless demonstrated a pervasive awareness of its significance as a social issue. They did so in their frequent depictions of racist encounters and their sarcastic accusations of racism among one another. To interpret my informants' engagement with racism more fully I now look to perceptions and treatment of racism as they emerge in broad public discourse.

Research on racism in Brisbane, and Australia more broadly, demonstrates a complexity of societal beliefs that both acknowledge and deny the existence of racism. Survey data collected for the Challenging Racism Project (Dunn and Nelson 2011; Forrest and Dunn 2011), previously described in chapter 2, was conducted in Brisbane and its outer suburbs via telephone interviews. People were asked whether it was good for society to be made up of different cultures; whether and to what extent they felt a sense of security in the context of cultural difference; and (to gauge their position on multiculturalism) whether Australia is weakened by people from different ethnic backgrounds maintaining their cultural traditions (Forrest and Dunn 2011). The results of this data were that Brisbane is "tolerant" but that the "acceptance" of ethnic diversity was accompanied by pro-assimilation views (Forrest and Dunn 2011:446). That is, people were accepting of cultural diversity to the extent that ethnic groups largely adapted the cultural practices of the majority population—findings were similar across Australia as a whole.

According to Dunn and his colleagues' research, intolerant attitudes manifest through media representations of ethnic minority groups in outlets such as tabloid news and talk back radio (Forrest and Dunn 2011, 450). Despite evidence of intolerance, much public discourse denies the prevalence of racism. Dunn argues that the denial, deflection, and justification of racism as inevitable manifests in the Australian context in a range of ways and is a prominent aspect of "contemporary racism," or "new racism," which, as Dunn describes, "is typified by denial politics, and discourses of deflection and absence" (Dunn and Nelson 2011, 589). The denial of racism manifests most strongly among political leaders, according to Dunn's research, while there is a much higher level of acknowledgment of racism among the Australian public (Dunn and Nelson 2011, 589).

The deflection and denial of racism finds scope to manifest in the social context of current discourses of multiculturalism, which position racism as something that exists outside of or opposed to multicultural social policy. Indeed, a principal impetus for multicultural social policy is its potential to overcome the pitfalls of racism in an ethnically diverse society (Hage 1998). However multicultural "tolerance" allows for the subtle acknowledgment of privilege in the context of belonging to a nation, while indirectly subsuming issues of race.

Moreover, as Dunn's research outlines, there is a positive association between reported experiences of racism and its denial which is closely tied to the degree to which people from minority backgrounds perceive a sense of national belonging. That is, when people perceive a sense of belonging to national space they are positively empowered to critique it (see also Hage 1998). As Dunn illustrates, when minority groups perceive a "lesser claim to citizenship" this may manifest in "a reticence to state that there is racism in Australian society" (Dunn and Nelson 2011, 597). Indigenous Australians are more likely to acknowledge their experiences of racism and perceptions of Anglo privilege than other non-Anglo minority or migrant groups because, as Dunn contends, "their [Indigenous Australians] belonging is less contestable, and therefore their right to make claims and sense of entitlement is stronger" (Dunn and Nelson 2011, 598).

Likewise, the occasional lack of public acknowledgment around issues of racism may leave these young people from refugee backgrounds disempowered to assert their own experiences with it. Conversely, their sense of belonging may be hindered precisely because of the ways in which they are framed as affected by racist experiences, despite their claims that such experiences are not pervasive or significant. The slippage between discourses of multiculturalism that deny racism and those that acknowledge, and even insist upon it as an issue in the lives of young people from minority backgrounds, mirrors the duality of young people's intermittent denial, and playful depictions of their own experiences of racism. While young people's acknowledgment of racism in their lives was inconsistent, their humorous engagement with it was a constant. This allowed for them to participate in the ways in which their lives were framed around issues of racism in a sociopolitical context that simultaneously denied racism and warned of its prevalence.

That their experiences with racism are absolutely real, and in many cases, pervasive, is not in question. Rather, what I seek to tease out by demonstrating a relationship between young people's creative engagement with racism and the contradictory ways in which it is treated in public discourse, is how the treatment and management of the concept of racism itself can act as a tool in the political representation of these young people's lives. The identity practices through which young people both project and abandon racialized self-representations emerges in part as a kind of responsiveness to the political representation through which they are implicated in the management of racism. The various ways in which young people's lives are framed through public discourse around citizenship and nationality can also be examined as central to the governance of young people's difference. Their engagement with these categories reflects a flexibility that similarly acts as a form of responsiveness to the political representation of their lives.

Belonging to the Nation: Citizenship, Nationality, and Inclusion

Citizenship and nationality carry specific and contextualized meanings and reflect a sense of belonging (and not belonging) to place. In the Australian context these categories are engaged most acutely, and perhaps paradoxically (Castles 2000, 130), through the current political and broad social framework of multiculturalism. My participants conceptions of nationality and citizenship demonstrate how they perceive and engage the various connotations these categories invoke in ways that often delimit their sense of social belonging. Their engagement with citizenship and nationality demonstrates a perception of the often racialized power dynamics inherent to multicultural discourse through their conflation of immigration status and skin color. For these young people, categories of nationality and citizenship acted in part as externally imposed devices related to the treatment and management of difference in multicultural discourse.

There is a congruence between what I have labeled as the discourses of integration and tolerance related to multiculturalism and multiculturalism as official immigration policy dictated through the categories of citizenship and nationality. It is through the process of designating and attaining Australian nationality and citizenship that the discourses of integration and tolerance take on broad social and cultural significance at the scale of the polity and the nation. The process of recognition or representation of who belongs in national context serves to reinforce the superiority of the recognizers and thereby reproduce the social context in which such is required (Dalsheim 2013; Povinelli 2002).

In my interactions with them, young people acknowledged the social organizing categories of nationality and citizenship in two primary ways. First, they talked about Australian citizenship and national identity as being practically beneficial in terms of designating a status that enabled travel, especially to their countries of origin. Second, however, they understood and discussed citizenship and nationality as indicative of barriers to inclusion in the Australian national space which they often explained in terms of skin color.

Young people grappled with citizenship through paperwork, tests and ceremonies and they were confronted by articulations of national belonging regularly in their school context. Below I examine the complexities reflected in the extent to which my informants implicated themselves in the discourses of citizenship and nationality, and why. In doing so, I'll present two key ethnographic examples. One details Vic's internal conflict in taking up Australian citizenship, and the other explores Tino's response to the everyday politics of nationality with which he was confronted at school.

Acquiring Citizenship: Reconciling the "Real Stuff" with the "Fake Stuff"

The process of applying for Australian citizenship has been revised with changes implemented in April and June of 2017 (Webster 2017). Among these changes, the residency requirement for applying for citizenship increased from twelve months to four years, a formal English language test was implemented, and changes were made to both the "pledge of citizenship" and the citizenship test (Webster 2017). The citizenship test was changed to include more questions to assess "good character" and to weed out religious extremism (Benson and Baxendale 2017). Specifically, questions were designed to assess attitudes about violence against women, forced marriage, and genital mutilation. In addition, applicants for Australian citizenship are now asked to provide "evidence of integration," including employment records, tax payments and children's school payments (Benson and Baxendale 2017).

The citizenship test is "designed to assess whether you have an adequate knowledge of Australia and the responsibilities and privileges of Australian citizenship" (Australian Department of Immigration and Citizenship [DIAC], n.d.-a). The test asks various questions relating to the historical, political and cultural knowledge inherent in an Australian national identity, such as: "What do we remember on Anzac Day?," "Which official symbol of Australia identifies Commonwealth property?," and "Which of these statements about government in Australia is correct" (DIAC, n.d.-b). Upon obtaining Australian citizenship through the completion of the citizenship test and other application materials, new citizens must attend a citizenship ceremony wherein they make a "pledge of commitment" to Australia. The current pledge reads: "From this time forward, under God [optional], I pledge my loyalty to Australia and its people, whose democratic beliefs I share, whose rights and liberties I respect, and whose laws I will uphold and obey" (DIAC, n.d.-c).

To fully adhere to the logistical procedures and paperwork requirements of the citizenship process, young people sometimes had to compromise aspects of their own sense of identity. They did so not always to achieve a sense of belonging in the Australian context (although this was sometimes a primary motivation), but also for the more practical purpose of subverting structural barriers which allowed for the maintenance of connections to their countries of origin. During one lunch hour at Paddington High I helped Vic, along with her friend Samah, to fill out the initial paperwork in the process of obtaining Australian citizenship.

When she came to the questions about her family background Vic asked, "Do we have to have real stuff on here or can it be fake stuff?" When we asked her what she meant, Vic became agitated and said, "I mean real or fake?!" Samah and Vic went back and forth like this for a while before Vic explained that she wrote the name of her "real" mother's name, who is still in Africa, on the citizenship form. But on her paperwork utilized upon entry to Australia her "stepmother," with whom she currently lived, was listed as her mother. I offered that the form says, "real or adoptive," and Vic responded that her step mother did not adopt her. Samah then urged Vic that for her citizenship to go through she had to fill out the paperwork with her familiar relationships exactly as they were on the paper work she used upon entry, or alternatively, she could change that information first and then apply for her citizenship. Vic, at that point very agitated, yelled, "I want to write my real mother! Because I just want real stuff! My real mother! I don't want to have fake stuff!" Samah restated her argument and Vic responded, "Shut up Samah! You're annoying me now. Just shut up," before leaving the room.

A few days later I asked Vic if she finished with the citizenship paperwork and she responded, "No. I quit that. I don't want to be Australian. Not now." A few weeks following this Vic approached me and excitedly told me, "I'm getting my citizenship on Tuesday! Because it was easy. My mom just said let's go down to immigration. Then they asked me a few questions and said, 'You have your citizenship.'" Vic attended the citizenship ceremony in a formal dress, and her "stepbrother" and two friends from school came to watch. After the ceremony she told me, "It was so cool! For my family, it felt good" and that she felt "a little bit Australian." I didn't ask her how she handled the discrepancy of how to define her mother on her citizenship paperwork.

During my fieldwork Vic struggled with various immigration officers and lawyers to work out a way to bring her "real" mother, residing in Africa, to Australia. She described this as essential to feeling at home and frequently said that she wanted to live in Africa but, "if my mom comes here I'm gonna stay here." She would alternate between calling the mother she lived with in Australia her "mom" and her "stepmom" depending on the state of their often volatile relationship. In the process of filling out her citizenship form, Vic needed to compromise her deeply held feelings of familial ties to conform to the categories and definitions required. She did so, however, not necessarily to deepen her feelings of belonging to the Australian national space, but more immediately to close a gap of belonging to her country of origin by furthering the possibility of bringing her mother to Australia.

Vic's desire for Australian citizenship, her adherence to the familial labels required for acquiring citizenship, and the extent to which her Australian citizenship contributed to a sense of "being Australian," were unstable and continually revised and changed. The process and outcome of becoming an Australian citizen, while ultimately a positive experience that allowed Vic to feel "a little bit Australian," served to maintain a feeling of being slightly outside of the bounds of social belonging in the Australian context. Moreover, many young people recounted that, regardless of formal citizenship, skin color remained an obstacle to a complete sense of national belonging. In one telling comment, when I asked him if he considers himself Australian, Mathew, a Karen participant laughed, "Nah . . . it's skin color, not citizen. . . . My family, my grandpa and grandma."

Not all of my research participants experienced this sense of conflict over citizenship choices as intensely as Vic. For many, the idea of citizenship was primarily embraced as a form of practicality. When I asked them about acquiring citizenship, common responses included "If I want to apply to anything, like Uni or anything, it's better if you get it," "I want to get it, so I can travel around the world for soccer," and "I could travel and go overseas with that." However, for those who were intensely entrenched in personal conflict over the acquisition of Australian citizenship, like Vic, their lack of belonging in the Australian national space was emphasized through the very process of becoming citizens.

As Hage argues, for many who have experienced migration, the intensity of emotion with which they negotiate the dynamics of national identity represent "guilt-ridden moves within a general moral economy of social belonging" (2002b, 203). Vic's internal struggle over becoming an Australian citizen reflects her attempts to repay a symbolic moral debt to the country she left behind, and the mother she left behind, as well as to the country that offers her the hope for a better future (see also Hage 2002b). Moreover, the complexity involved in young people's personal choices regarding discourses of representation, such as citizenship, was broadly understood by their peers. As such, they often supported one another, as Samah did Vic, in the sometimes fraught task of navigating structural frameworks while maintaining their sense of authenticity. Young people similarly encountered, and worked to manipulate, resist and sometimes substantiate political representations around notions of national identity. In doing so, they were able to speak to their experiences of social belonging in Australia.

Defining Nationality: Flexibility and the Implications of Multiple Belongings

While young people grappled with an abstracted notion of national belonging as they negotiated the citizenship process, they were more explicitly confronted with the task of "being Australian" in their daily lives, and particularly in the school context. There was an annual competition at Paddington High in which students were given a topic or concept they were challenged to depict using chocolate crackle (a sticky concoction made of rice cereal, marshmallow and cocoa powder) and other sweets in a sort of diorama. Most students and staff participated in and looked forward to this event. The topic for the competition during my field research was to create an image of an "Aussie summer." Most students made dioramas of beach scenes, picnics, barbecues, and other typical Australian summer scenes, as did most of my research participants who attended Paddington High.

Tino, and three other of my African participants who attended Paddington High, worked together in the competition. They constructed a giant hill-shaped mound of chocolate crackle, with little men made from biscuits strewn about as though dead and surrounded by lashings of red gummy sweets which appeared to depict blood. They called their entry "Somertime [sic] War." Judges of the competition walked around the entries with a clipboard discussing and noting the "Aussie-ness" of various entries. They ignored Tino and his friend's entry without comment. Their ELL teacher complimented another African student's entry while I was standing with him and exclaimed, "What was Tino thinking? He did war!? What was he thinking?" And then to me, sarcastically, "You'll have to write about this; you better take a picture."

When I talked to Tino about the project the next day he said he didn't remember what his project was. I asked him if it was called "Somertime War" and he said, "Yeah, something like that I think . . . because people think of summer and they think of happy. But in some people's lives it's not as happy as in our lives." While aligning himself with other Australians in his use of the phrase "our" lives, Tino critiqued the value and relevance for himself, and a portion of the students participating, of such a nationalistic topic. Their "Somertime War" entry resisted the sharedness of identification with the tradition of "an Aussie summer."

Like citizenship, young people's encounters with the externally defined category of Australian national identity sometimes served to highlight their lack of belonging in the Australian national space. In these moments, young people expressed an inhibition to fully participate in, or an inclination to speak back to, nation building projects at their schools and in other social settings. However, embracing Australian national identity also enabled, for these young people, a straightforward way of identifying themselves which helped them to evade the more nuanced and complex range of national identities they might otherwise inhabit or portray. That is, while in some circumstances, and for some young people, the oversimplification inherent to various politics of representation led to frustration and turmoil, for others this oversimplification was precisely the draw. As Wah Wah exclaimed when I asked her what she considered to be her national identity, "Australia! Then if the person asks you where you're from you can say, 'I'm Australia too.' Just like that! And you can go to Thailand like that too."

Moreover, young people strategically chose to emphasize different national identities in different contexts and for a range of purposes. Lisa described her nationality as Australian during one interview with me. She explained, "Because when I live in Thailand nobody said I'm Thailand. In Australia if you have citizenship you are Australian. I want to be Australian because I don't want to go to Thailand anymore because it is my new life in Australia." However, on another occasion while discussing her Burmese background, from which she often tried to distance herself, Lisa stated, "I'm with Thailand. And if they don't believe me and ask me more questions I can answer everything. . . . It's not Burmese; I've never been to Burma." As Lisa's differing emphases on national identity demonstrate, categories of national identity do not necessarily evoke a sense of belonging but can instead reflect an inherent sense of not belonging, as they are often mobilized in response to the perception of needing to provide answers to the question about where they belong.

With each other my informants knew and understood the flexibility with which they might define themselves through one or another nationality. As such, they allowed each other to identify differently to one another and flexibility was normalized and supported. In a group interview I asked siblings Santino, Omar, and Lola whether they felt at all Australian (or Sudanese, African, both, neither, etc.); Santino immediately responded "No" while his brother Omar said "Yep." Santino responded to Omar by saying, "No we're not, we don't do anything like Australians. We don't eat the same thing. All different." Omar responded, "We eat pizza, ham, lettuce." Santino thought and responded, "No, I don't feel like Australian," and Omar said, "I do." Santino and Omar were close in age, attended the same school, and moved within the same circle of peers. Yet they often defined their sense of national identity in different terms. And significantly, they allowed one another to do so. While young people often sought to fix themselves and one another to particular racial and ethnic categories, when asked to define themselves in terms of citizenship and nationality they allowed one another to diverge, consider, change, and manipulate.

Having lived at the borders of national identity for much of their lives, citizenship and nationality as markers of identity were neither bounded nor fixed for these young people. And they were deeply aware of the complexity of ways in which their lives were framed in public discourse with relation to these categories. Through the emphasis of citizenship status and Australian national belonging each as something to achieve and work toward, these categories of governance highlighted participants' social belonging as something in progress.

The categories of citizenship and nationality, in their establishment and maintenance, served to subtly propose that young people could and should be full participating members of Australian society, but that they were not quite there yet—and that they would therefore indeed benefit from accelerated integration as well as the tolerance of the broader community. Refugee status as another aspect of political representation in these young people's lives similarly evoked the messages of integration and tolerance implicit in multicultural discourse. Young people perceived refugee status as something that was treated by the broader population as problematic in some way. And their identification as refugees was tenuous.

The Double-Bind of Refugee Status

Unlike discourses of citizenship and nationality intended to highlight who belongs and provide an avenue to extend that belonging to others, the political representation of refugee status explicitly distinguishes those who identify as such to be social and national outsiders. The notion of being a refugee didn't appear to manifest in the everyday lives of my informants with the same frequency and clarity as concepts of citizenship and nationality. Instead, "refugee" remained an elusive concept understood vaguely as something negative and something that hindered belonging to the broader Australian population. Moreover, their status as young people from refugee backgrounds calls into question a matrix of further considerations around defining notions of home and belonging.

I conceptualize their classification as refugees as a form of political representation insofar as young people's personal identification as refugees was weak and variable, while the label carries political implications—which, as I explore below, young people apparently perceived—that yield negative associations in the Australian context. The lives of these young people are regularly represented in broad sociopolitical context with both positive and negative connotations. As young people from refugee backgrounds they are framed by the predominant discourses of "dysfunction and failure" or "resilience and success," as well as by the binary division of a generational culture clash which leaves them torn between cultures (Ngo 2010, 3). In addition they are perceived as lucky to have resettled in Australia but unlucky in their experiences prior; they are survivors, victims and sometimes freeloaders; they are both vulnerable and in need of protection, as well as dangerous and in need of correction. The reality, of course, is infinitely more nuanced than these binaries can capture. And like in their engagement of citizenship status and national identity, young people allowed one another flexibility in whether or not they identified as refugees.

Rather than intensely arguing over their refugee status, or perceived lack thereof, even siblings debated the issue in a decidedly dispassionate way and settled on one side or the other seemingly without a great deal of angst or deliberation. Significantly, in negotiating refugee status they engaged with various externally applied identifying categories through the language and conceptualization of a dichotomy of "good" versus "bad" perceptions about their lives and experiences. Through their direct consideration of whether refugee status may be easily conceptualized as "a good thing" or "a bad thing," it is evident that their categorization as such gains meaning externally as a political and popular discourse of representation which emerges through the governance of difference.

Defining the Good and the Bad Things

Young people were aware of the broad implications of their status as refugees and citizens as potentially contentious and publicly perceived through conflicting positive and negative associations. Their perception of positive and negative connotations in association with their refugee status was particularly evident when I asked them open-ended interview questions based on their broad life experiences (e.g., "What is important or significant to you in your life?"). Before responding they would regularly seek clarification by asking if I was after something "good or bad."

For example, when I asked Elijah what the word "refugee" meant to him, he answered, "Is it in a bad way or in a good way? I don't think it's bad to be a refugee because it's just a situation they're in." When I asked Shalla, a fourteen-year-old Karen girl, "what is important in your life?" she answered, "Like what kind? Is it something bad or something good?" And in an interview with Santino and his brother, Ben, and sister Lola, I asked them to describe something important about their lives and Santino answered, "You want something bad? I don't get it . . . I'm different, I'm from somewhere else." To this Ben clarified, "Santino is lucky to be here because some people don't get the chance," and Santino answered back, "Why are you just saying my name, you're lucky too?!"

My question, which was intended to allow Santino and his siblings to define for themselves what was significant in their lives, immediately led to their engagement with the idea of being outsiders. What is noteworthy is that they did so in direct association with a scale of public perception (of which I, as the interviewer, for them embodied) by initially asking if I wanted "something bad." Perhaps this sense of internalizing is best captured by Mathew who would constantly, teasingly and provocatively use words associated with elements of his status as a refugee youth to anything and everything—while riding in the car with him, his cousin and his friend one afternoon, he said, "Who names these streets? If it were up to us we'd name this one 'Vulnerable Street' and that one 'Violent Street.'"

Many of my informants associated refugee status most readily with poverty and needing financial assistance, or with living in a refugee camp. In Elijah's interpretation of refugee status, he described it as "just a situation they're in." Following his statement I asked Elijah directly whether he considered himself a refugee. He responded, "Probably. I didn't actually have any trouble there. But it's hard because I don't want to say like, 'I'm not a refugee,' but I didn't have any trouble." Elijah states that technically he is "probably" a refugee but maintains a distinction between his situation and his understanding of "them" as drawn from associations in media representations and his perception of public understanding. He expresses simultaneously his reluctance to fully separate himself from the category, indicating that he feels that at least on some level it is one which technically applies to his life.

From his brief statement two key factors may be drawn—both pointing to the broad perception, observed among most of these young people, of themselves as outsiders in association with their representation as refugees. The first, the term *refugee* is associated with trouble of some form, and the second, young people feel a sense of obligation to define themselves as refugees. In other words, they have not all experienced the difficulties typically portrayed as defining the refugee experience—not all have lived in camps or experienced a harrowing journey. But they do understand themselves to be on the outside of what they recognize as mainstream society, and they do understand that their lives are portrayed in association with the term refugee often enough, so that they believe they are most likely defined by it in some way.

The category of being a refugee, then, carried more meaning externally than it did to the young people who were labeled as refugees. Nonetheless, their broad perception of their association with the term *refugee* led young people to debate and engage with one another to define the term and their relationship to it. When Santino and his brother and sister discussed whether they were refugees, an argument about what constitutes being a refugee ensued. In a group interview I asked them what the word refugee meant, and Santino answered, "That means. . . . Yeah, I know it. It's a camp like. A place they help you before you come here. I think I am one." Omar thought this was absurd and said, "No you're not!" to which Santino answered, "Yes I am. Who give you the chance to come here and fill out those forms? Refugee people." Omar reflected and offered no further comment.

Young people would sometimes distance themselves from the term refugee by describing their situation of living in refugee camps or fleeing their country of origin in terms of being "like a refugee," as though being a refugee were some indefinable experience they could approximate but were not quite classified by. As Wah Wah, who had spent much of her life in Tham Hin refugee camp described it, "Refugee is the people who don't have a country. It's when you leave, and the UN gives you food and a teddy bear at Christmas." Moreover, many young people who didn't spend time in refugee camps expressed greater ambivalence about their status as refugees. Obama, who had not spent any of his life in a refugee camp, was tenuous in his self-identification with the label *refugee*. As he explained, "That's people, when government treat them bad they leave to come to a camp. I didn't go to a camp. I went to Egypt then straight to Australia. I don't know if I'm one."

Other Sudanese young people, all of whom had refugee status in Australia, reflected similar ambiguity in their identification with the term refugee. When I asked him the meaning of being a refugee and whether he defined himself as such, Gabe stated, "It's people who come out of a place that's wrecked already. Like kids who are in war. There's a lot of trouble in the town. I'm not really one. Well I guess . . . I think I am." Samah stated, "I don't really know. I am a refugee, but I don't know that much. I don't really care about it. I don't know why I came here. I reckon it was fun there." And Vic similarly offered, "Refugee, refugee . . . I don't know. People say you're a refugee, but I never really lived in a camp. But most of the kids in my school lived in a camp in Africa. I don't know if I am. I don't think so."

While in some of their accounts a sense of wanting to evade negative categorizations with which they don't seek to identify was evident, young people also expressed a sense that they genuinely didn't fully understand the term but believed that they were implicated in it in some way. Bound up in this implication is the perception of opportunity and safety afforded to refugees. Indeed, young people often externalized their experiences and understood the label of "refugee" to be for others who they perceived to have had a worse experience than themselves. During a casual conversation at a shopping center in response to my question about why she thought some of the African students who also attended Kedron Club came to Australia, Catalina, a Karen participant who had spent most of her life in the Tham Hin refugee camp, explained: "They came here because they are poor like us—but more poor. Like they have no water. I know because I've seen shows on TV. But in Santino places [I ask where and she says Africa] more people help them. I've seen it; all people go and help them. Not where we come from."

In her account Catalina distanced her own experience from Santino's whom she described as having lived through "a more difficult situation" than herself.

Prompted by a question about refugee status, Catalina constructed a definition of "refugee" as somehow other than herself and her own experience. While Catalina pointed out that her struggle was indeed as severe as Santino's, she simultaneously evaded the external definition of "refugee." These young people were generally aware of the associations with the term refugee as being a "bad" thing. As such they avoided defining themselves by it to the extent that they could, but also portrayed their awareness that the negative connotation of refugee in some way applied to them. This may be explained in part with the extent to which refugee issues, in the Australian context, are focused around "boat people" or those who enter Australian shores unauthorized (see chapter 2), while most of my informants arrived in Australia as approved humanitarian entrants. But I believe there is more to it.

By identifying with the classification of refugee young people aligned themselves with something they perceived as broadly and vaguely negative. However, their tendency not to identify as refugees seemed to evidence not only the reluctance of identification with a category about which they perceived negative associations, but also a genuine disparity between the way in which they were externally framed as refugees and the extent to which that label carried meaning in their own lives and experiences.

Similarly to the variability with which they negotiated their citizenship and nationality, the degree to which young people felt implicated in discourse around refugee status may be partially accounted for in their experiences of social belonging. While status as a refugee reflects a sense of being other than the dominant Australian society of which they are a part, some of my informants, by not identifying as having refugee status as shown in the statement from Elijah mentioned earlier, perceived themselves as not demonstrating a sense of belonging with one another. In this sense, identifying as refugees leaves young people in a double bind. If they do not represent themselves as refugees they risk disassociating with one another in their broad perception as outsiders and, if they do, they risk alienation with the wider population. This sense of alienation from broader Australian society, in relation to their refugee status, is related in part to the political and popular discourse of being "torn between two cultures" with which young people from refugee backgrounds are often represented.

Where Is Home: Political Discourse of the Culture Clash

The discourse of a "clash of cultures" or "being torn between two worlds," manifests in relation to the resettlement of young people from refugee backgrounds and depicts intergenerational conflict and a struggle to define home (Ngo 2010, 5). For the young people with whom I worked, the theory of a culture clash should be all the more prevalent, according to the narrative of struggle between modern versus traditional or first world versus third world (Ngo 2010, 5). They had recently been through the process of forced migration and resettlement in

Australia, and as such had much of their immediate family still living in their country of origin or in neighboring refugee camps. However, rather than experiencing a "clash" between two distinct cultures or being "torn between two worlds," as they negotiated belonging, my informants expressed a sense of home in both the countries from which they were displaced and in their place of resettlement. And they did so in ways that appeared relatively unproblematic.

There was a great degree of flexibility and nuance based on individual circumstances and choice in the ways in which young people characterized home, and this was understood and supported within peer groups. Thakin, a twelve-year-old Karen boy, responded to my question about where home is by saying, "I don't really think about that. I just think of where I am right now. What I'm doing right now." Gabe said, "Home is first my house. Then Sudan. I don't really know if I miss there. I've never really lived a life there," and Elijah offered, "Australia is good. And if not Australia, Africa. Back to my village."

Significantly, the ability of these young people to oscillate between different conceptualizations of home did not appear to emerge out of confusion, frustration, angst, or even a sense of nostalgia. Rather, it was apparently related to more practical considerations such as where "a good job place" might be. Based on their depictions and stated opinions about their lives both past and present, neither were characterized as entirely good or bad. These young people seem to have a sophisticated awareness of the positive and negatives of each, as well as a nuanced understanding of the inconsistencies between how aspects of their lives are popularly depicted and how they emerge in lived experience.

For example, I didn't ask Nine about violence in his previous home when he stated, "I was young when I was there. I couldn't capture the violence. It's bad and good. That's what I always say. But I was used to it. People say it's bad now because they've seen something different." Nine's comment captures the unconflicted feeling with which these young people often spoke about notions of home in their country of origin. At the same time, it captures an awareness of the perception of difficulty through which their lives are often publicly managed and represented. Contrary to this public representation, as young people considered their feelings of where and what home was, tension, confusion and frustration were observed only very minimally.

The concepts of home and familial belonging are not without complexity for these young people. A degree of culture and generational clash and frustration may, of course, have been evident in ways that I did not capture in my participant observation–based fieldwork. "Culture clash," along with the trauma young people from refugee backgrounds often experience in the process of relocation and resettlement, often leads to serious mental health concerns (Gifford et al. 2009; Correa-Velez et al. 2010, 1400). I accept that feelings of nostalgia and longing for another home do occur and that these feelings may lend themselves to conflicting emotions and turmoil. However, this experience appears not to be nearly as dominant as the "torn between two worlds" discourse seems to suggest.

In the political framing of these young people as refugees, as in the process of becoming citizens and becoming Australian nationals, the notion that they were away from home was emphasized and the task of creating a new home was urged. Popular media accounts detail familiar stories of refugee and migrant young people confronted with wildly different and conflicting cultures and struggling to reconcile the traditional cultural expectations of their parents' and grandparents' generation, with what it means to be a young person in Australia today. Such illustrations help to distil and advance understanding of the momentous changes and challenges faced by young people of refugee and migrant backgrounds (Ngo 2010, 7).

However, by framing their cultural influences in binary and conflicting categories, participants' cultures of origin were invariably framed as somehow developmentally behind their modern Australian counterpart, if romantically exotic. Such binary distinctions in popular and political discourse relate to the governance of difference in the Australian national space and contribute to the push for migrants and refugees to redefine a notion of home in relationship to Australia. Young people's perception that the fact of their refugee status is pervasive and problematic is at least in part rooted in the discourse of culture clash. In the process of defining home they were regularly exposed to pressures at school, home, and from the wider community to acknowledge the country from which they were displaced, or another element of their refugee experience.

At Kedron Club one afternoon Wah Wah was holding my baby and cooed, "Hello. My name is Wah Wah, I come from [provided name of] School." A staff member at Kedron Club then commented pointedly, "And *where else* do you come from?" Wah Wah's looked puzzled and her friend Jessica answered for her, "I know! She's like me, she come from the camp." The staff member looked at Wah Wah and said, motioning toward the baby, "Then tell her that." Wah Wah, with a confused look on her face complied and told the baby that she came from "the camp." As this somewhat bizarre interaction illustrates, the tenuousness with which a notion of these young people's "home" was treated among the broader community was not necessarily reflected in their own sense of their life experiences. It is within these social portrayals of cultural conflict and turmoil about home that young people encounter the perception of their refugee status as an obstacle to belonging.

How young people implicate themselves (or do not) in discourses of cultural clash, in defining the terms of their citizenship and nationality, or in their experiences with racism, reflects their perception of those categories as framing constructs in their lives. Indeed, I propose it was through the treatment of racism, citizenship, nationality and refugee status that young people were most explicitly confronted with a kind of outsider status and the broad public marking of their difference. And, I argue, their identity work engaged with the ways in which their lives were framed in political and public discourse.

Let me illustrate the tentative sense of belonging discourse around citizenship, nationality and refugee status often evoked in participants with a final ethnographic anecdote. Omot could briefly shift his status as outsider to that of insider when he felt he had more claim on the Australian national space than I had. When he realized that he had lived in Australia for a longer period of time than I, Omot soon gave me a card to commemorate my first year of work at Kedron Club, which he signed at the bottom "P.S. Welcome to Australia."

Politics of Representation, Processes of Implication, and Dynamic Responsiveness

Discourses drawn out of the politics of cultural diversity around citizenship and nationality, refugee status, the management of racism and how to define home emerge in and have come to impact upon the lives of these young people. Through the governance of difference in the Australian context, young people from refugee backgrounds are presumably offered a better future as Australian citizens, refuge from their country of origin and the chance to create a new home; and they are also presumed to be subjected to racism. These dynamics, I would venture, emerge similarly in other settler nations where discourses of opportunity rub uneasily against current political trends toward protection and isolationism. Young people in such contexts often engage with the broad political discourse that seeks to frame and manage their lives, highlighting the prevalence of youth as social actors in contexts of migration. In doing so they are apt to make allowances for themselves and one another regarding how and to what extent they implicate themselves in those discursive frameworks. As Ngo (2010, 11) states: "Identity thus involves a double action, where in one movement we are put in subject positions by others who draw on available, powerful discourses to identify us; and in another movement we take up subject positions by drawing on available discourses ourselves."

So as Ngo (2010) argues, young people respond to the discourses and structures that frame their lives by manipulating, resisting, or reproducing them in their own sense of identity. The extent to which political and popular discourses around racism, citizenship and national belonging affected my informants certainly differed in intensity. As Hage (2002b) explains, the intensity of an experience has to do with "the extent to which a reality is involving and affecting" (2002b, 193).

The analytic tools of implication and intensity are useful in considering the degree to which these young people are affected by the conceptual categories I have outlined here that frame their lives in popular and political discourse. Hage (2002b, 201) links this notion of implication to Bourdieu's concept of *illusio*, which demonstrates the ways in which people invest themselves in particular social realities in order to import meaning into their lives, and how this process masks the fact that life is not intrinsically meaningful but rather meaning is derived through such investments (Bourdieu 2000, 11). One's implication in a particular social reality is dependent upon their sharing in the illusio of that reality. Following Hage, I interpret the degree to which some young people implicate themselves within the dominant discourses around racism, citizenship and refugee status in terms of social belonging.

As Hage argues, migration is often "a guilt-inducing process" (2002b, 203). For young people who have left their country of origin at a relatively young age, the debt of belonging to their new community is likely to be felt as much as or even more strongly than their debt to the one they have left. By obtaining citizenship the moral debts to each country might be illuminated while both are only partially reconciled. The intensity through which my informants implicated themselves in the discourses of opportunity reflected in the representation of Australian citizenship, in the notion that they are outsiders in the representation of their experiences of racism and as refugees, and in the idea that they have complex relationships to multiple symbolic homes, reflects their sense of social belonging, or lack thereof, in the Australian context.

I do not want to overstate young people's resistance to belonging in the Australian national space—they desired it for a variety of instrumental purposes such as securing jobs upon graduation from secondary school, and more generally in terms of valuing aspects of Australian life and culture to which they sometimes sought a sense of belonging. Instead, I have intended to demonstrate how these young people engaged the multicultural discourses they encountered in complex ways that often reflected a subtle resistance to the power dynamics to which they contributed. Multicultural citizens in the current Australian context absorb the competing push toward integration and national belonging and the pull toward various forms of transnationalism and maintaining and forging diasporic connection. Such hybridities, as Carruthers (2013) argues, challenge the capacity of modern multicultural nations to adequately recognize and engage these new multicultural subjects. The negotiations of identity captured through young people's engagement with the dynamics of representation explored here help to distil a relationship between their experiences and interpretations of the world, and the discursive frameworks to which their lives are subject.

The very ways in which young people engaged, manipulated or denied the relevance of such discursive frameworks reflects their awareness of and responsiveness to the politics of representation. Lisa explained how she handles, or indeed stops, questions and challenges to her identity in terms of citizenship, nationality, refugee status and home. She said, "If they ask me . . . I just say I have a strange life in Thailand. But now I'm OK to live myself forward—to be who I am today." Friends present nodded in approval. Lisa's recognition of the ways in which her life experiences might be framed around particular categories of political representation, and her reluctance to be defined in this way, resonated.

Indeed, my attempts during interviews to ask open-ended questions about the broad defining features of their life experiences often resulted in responses that seemed to implicitly deny the relevance of those categories that take on such major significance in public perception. For example, Catalina and Jessica were nearly constantly engaged with one another in discussions about being Karen (or Australian, or even African) and seemingly sought to define themselves accordingly. When I asked what they saw as the most important thing about themselves, Jessica answered, "It's that I have straight hair. But a little bit wavy," and Catalina responded, "I have curly hair." And when I asked the same question of Gabe, for whom his association with Africa, African Americans, and "being black" appeared central to his sense of identity, he responded: "It's just that I'm a trouble maker. I like to start trouble, but I don't finish it. To some people it's bad. To me it's not bad or good. My life story is good I guess. Because I'm living a good life. I got my ma with me, my sisters with me. My brothers and aunties are overseas in America and I'm going there this year or something. I've played basketball my whole life. I love music. That's about it really. There is nothing else."

Gabe's response simultaneously acknowledges the dichotomy of good versus bad connotations he perceives in externally imposed defining categories, while it challenges any pressure to adhere to or define himself by those categories. An awareness of their political representation is indeed reflected in young people's tendency to resist definition through externally imposed categories related to the governance of their difference. Just as significantly, however, the self-definitions these young people do more readily adhere to, namely their sense of racial and ethnic difference, speak to the ways in which their lives are overtly politicized as refugees and as minorities in the Australian multicultural context.

Viewed through the lens of dynamic responsiveness, young people's identity work demonstrates an awareness of the political context through which their lives are framed, as well as a sophisticated engagement with the messages implemented by government bodies and other authoritative entities which ultimately emerge to adjust and affect that context. The complex processes through which the politics of representation and personal identity mirror one another indeed highlight the interrelatedness between broad social narratives and self-understanding.

7

Self, Belonging, and Multicultural Morality

I began this book with a description of how my own assumptions about the young people with whom I conducted research were challenged as I embarked upon my fieldwork. Recent youth scholarship demonstrates young people breaking down racial and ethnic barriers through their everyday practices and increased exposure to multicultural contexts (Harris 2013; Harris and Herron 2017). This research stands in contrast to other studies of youth, which situate young people as immersed in racial and ethnic conflict in contexts of diversity. It was the notion of youth everyday exposure to diversity resulting in progress and a sense of hope for the future of multiculturalism that most strongly influenced my thinking. It still does.

However, my bent toward conceptualizing youth as agents of change and progress presented one core dilemma: why were they so preoccupied with categories of racial and ethnic difference? The more immersed I became, the more I could see it. Race and ethnic background played a central role in how these young people from refugee backgrounds defined themselves. Race was central to how they accounted for the everyday dynamics of their social relationships, it informed the ways in which they presented themselves in more formalized cultural performances, and it affected the ways in which they constituted a sense of national belonging.

I was also made more aware, through the course of my research, of the centrality of race and ethnicity in managing and maintaining the moral landscape of multiculturalism. These young people were constantly framed as racial and ethnic beings, in both the celebration of their race and ethnicity and the denial of its relevance, through the messages they encountered in their everyday lives. Their constant engagement with a sense of their own racial and ethnic backgrounds, I came to understand, developed at least in large part through a kind of responsiveness to the messages that framed their lives in multicultural context. This notion of responsiveness became the central premise for how I made sense of what I was observing in the complex dynamics of how these young people defined themselves.

Through placing dynamic responsiveness at the center of how young people formulate and present their own sense of identity, a relationship between personal identity and broad social narratives of belonging and inclusion becomes explicit. It is this relationship which provides perspective beyond *what* young people from diverse backgrounds are doing in contexts of diversity—for example, whether they are breaking down barriers or building them—but *why*. The implications for the "why" of youth identity in multicultural context are vast. Dynamic responsiveness as a lens for interpreting identity allows us, in essence, to push beyond identity.

In the current world context, nationalist ideology and the moral condemnation of racism butt up against one another through the management of increasing migration and displaced peoples. Debates concerning race and whiteness, immigration and border control, globalization, multiculturalism, and assimilation are of paramount concern internationally. Central to these concerns are the lives of young people, who are influencing and being influenced by all of these issues. My hope is for this research to shed light upon both the young people represented here (and others like them) who must negotiate a sense of themselves in a fraught and complex social environment, as well as the future of living with diversity and multicultural inclusion more broadly. My aim in presenting the identity work of these young people through the lens of dynamic responsiveness is to provide a framework that allows us to explore how we formulate a sense of who we are in engagement with influences from our social environment, and how this fosters a sense of affinity and connection. Also of paramount importance to me in presenting this research is to illuminate why such identity work matters in terms of what might be necessary to advance and address the current crisis of multiculturalism.

My overriding concern, in other words, has been how young people pursue and foster belonging, and in what ways belonging is, or is not, made available to them in the Australian national space. Indeed, the discursive frameworks that render national spaces visible (in this case, multiculturalism) are both implicated in and impact upon processes of identity making. Through the prism of youth, self-conscious and increasingly immersed in diversity as it is, identity work in relation to social context is pronounced.

Before drawing together some of the major themes of the book in attempt to further elucidate the relationship between the range of identity-making practices I observed among these young people and the broader narrative frameworks in which they are situated, I wish to add a final caveat. While it has been my aim to highlight the relationship between young people's self-representations and the social contexts in which those identities emerge, I have tried not to overstate the relationship. While the ways in which young people racialize themselves in their intimate relationships with one another emerge in dialogue with public discourses concerning race, their racialization is not born from those discourses. Their responsiveness does not reduce their actions to a mere form of mimicry, and we can, of course, still trust and take seriously both their experiences of racism and the value they place on their racial and ethnic backgrounds in contributing to their own sense of identity.

Identities indeed emerge from a constellation of preferences and predilections too vast to even begin to resolve here; and of course, equally relevant in defining a sense of oneself, to the themes of race and ethnicity that have emerged as central in this context are gender, class, religion, sexuality, language, family, peers, and so forth. The ways in which people articulate their identities, however, is most revealing. By isolating responsiveness, the intention in the ways in which these young people describe their place in the broader social landscape is made apparent. That intention helps to highlight certain social dynamics and deemphasize others. Young people's dynamic responsiveness plays a central role in defining elements of social context, and in so doing may be conceptualized as allowing for their participation in the politics of belonging.

Responsive Identity and Why It's So Dynamic

I have spent a lot of time throughout the book exploring how the work of making and remaking identities is undertaken as people respond to their social environments and the political context of their lives. But why do I describe this responsiveness as dynamic? By qualifying responsiveness in this way, I mean to capture an element of change. What emerges in local context, around which a kind of self-definition is elicited, is not static. In other words, people constitute a sense of themselves, at least in part, in response to something—but the something is not the same for everyone, and what it is changes. The young people represented here are exposed to a kind of sociopolitical management of their lives in multicultural context. Their racial and ethnic backgrounds in relationship to their status as minorities and as refugees—even their youth—are part of the formula through which their lives are framed and managed. That sociopolitical management of their lives in relation to being refugees, to their race, and to their ethnicity is the something through which these young people define a sense of identity.

As they perceive the centrality of race to the multicultural context in which they live, young people absorb, reframe, and engage this premise in their identity work. And as they encountered messages of multiculturalism in particularly constant and incessant ways, the specific cultural minutiae to which they responded through their identity work was realized. This demonstrates that our understanding of young people's self-representations must be pitched at the local level, but must also consider what is significant, prominent, or pervasive in their broad sociopolitical landscapes. These young people's engagement with popular and political discourses concerning race, diversity, and inclusion, which were expressed most potently in their often humorous exchanges with one another, allowed them to have a voice in the broad social framing of their lives. To the sense of identity that they outwardly portrayed, and as reflected through the multicultural messages they regularly encountered, race was relevant.

Perceptions of Inclusion and Exclusion: What's Race Got to Do with It?

Race and ethnicity, as they were called upon by these young people, served largely as a means of inclusion. The ways in which they represented themselves through sameness and difference to one another, to the broader population and to networks outside of national context, often occurred through their emphasis and deemphasis of racialized characteristics and ethnicity. Through their varied and complex "ethnic choices" (Song 2003), they associated and disassociated with people whom they described as having the same or different ethnic backgrounds or racialized characteristics to themselves.

By representing themselves in racialized ways and alternately "inhabiting" or "vacating" their racial and ethnic backgrounds (Back 1996), young people enabled a multiplicity of options for how and to whom they might assert a sense of belonging. Race and ethnicity provided them with a range of contexts through which to assert belonging, in part because of the global diasporic connections it enabled for them. However, the ways in which young people called upon a sense of belonging in relation to their wider connections to Africa, the Karen community, or sometimes America, were interpreted and invoked in relationship to perceptions and discursive frameworks they encountered in local context. Africanness, for example, was articulated and formally performed when young people were called upon to do so in school performances which framed such celebrations of ethnic diversity in terms of the triumphs of multiculturalism (Hage 1998, 204, 2003, 17). Whether emphasized or denied, racial, and ethnic signifiers were well integrated into meaningful narratives for these young people.

In contrast to the ways in which race and ethnicity enabled a multiplicity of assertions of belonging in different social contexts, categories of citizenship, refugee status, and nationality rather highlighted the ways in which participants did not quite or entirely belong to their national space. As such, these categories were not strongly integrated into young people's self-understandings or articulations of belonging to others. Significantly, the stipulations for being popularly and politically deemed to be citizens, refugees or nationals inherently emphasize a kind of processes through which one might pursue and achieve belonging. By emphasizing belonging as in flux or in process, these categories were imposed and perceived as primarily defining the terms of exclusion rather than allowing for a sense of inclusion.

Central to how articulations of race and ethnicity were made meaningful to them, young people presented themselves in hybridized and essentialized ways that engaged with broad social discourses. There is a narrative overlap between young people's articulations of belonging and the broader discursive frameworks that dictate its viability in their daily, lived social contexts. It is largely from within this overlap that I locate the multiplicity of self-representations I observed among young people in terms of their participation in the broad social management of their difference.

Integrated Narratives, Hybridity, and Essentialism

As I argued in chapter 3, the theoretically fraught concept of hybridity is useful here, not precisely in its popular current formulation to describe a kind of mixing, merging, or mimicry of cultural references in the formation of new identities. Rather, for my purposes, hybridity captures the ways in which young people justified and described their formulations of identity in terms of their denial of the limiting capacity of difference. As I use it here, *hybridity* refers to young people's articulations of their capacity for flexibility made apparent in their ability to overlook difference, to "mix it up," and to embody, encompass or include different cultural frameworks in various aspects of their lives. I conceptualize young people's emphasis on their own capacity for multiplicity (and the ways in which I have endeavored to capture it through the concept of hybridity) as responding to a broad narrative context central to the social fabric of Australian multiculturalism.

As Moore has acknowledged, the concept of hybridity carries explanatory power and is theoretically valid when demonstrated as emerging from and "embedded in popular culture and celebrated through various mediations, and cultural and institutional forms" (2011, 209). I have endeavored to demonstrate the conceptualization of hybridity through which I have framed my observations of young people's representations of identity, as emerging from and enacted within the narrative framework of multiculturalism in the Australian context. As discussed throughout the book, the popular narrative framework of multiculturalism urges the celebration of difference, often in terms of ethnic and cultural background, while it insists upon the ultimate irrelevance of cultural and ethnic difference for formulating relationships, for constituting a sense of self-together, and for being together harmoniously in community.

As young people emphasized their ability to "integrate" with the broader population despite those differences which were simultaneously framed as noteworthy, they both paralleled and contradicted various attempts to govern cultural difference that emerged through the social and policy framework of multiculturalism. The concept of hybridity captures the ways in which young people asserted a sense of identity through their ability to overcome difference, which allowed for articulations of belonging to what they perceived as the mainstream Australian community. And while messages emerging from the broad narrative framework of multiculturalism fueled young people's position that difference was of little significance to them in their hybridized representations of self on the one hand, their essentialized representations of self ran counter to these claims.

When they expressed their sense of identity in terms of being explicitly, exclusively, and unwaveringly African or Karen for example, they represented themselves in essentialized ways. I have sought to demonstrate essentialized self-representations also in relationship to multicultural discourse, through the language of "tolerance," wherein difference is upheld and revered. Through self-essentializing young people emphasized characteristics that created a sense of belonging between one another in local friendship groups, and in relation to global networks of young people or pop cultural icons representative of the diasporic communities to which they also sought a sense of belonging.

Young people engaged the contradictory messages emerging from multicultural discourse in a sometimes paradoxical relationship to how they framed their own experiences and identity making practices. That is, hybridized and essentialized representations of identity for these young people were enacted, in different moments and contexts, in ways that both reinforced and contradicted messages of integration and tolerance that emerged and framed their lives in their daily social environments. Moreover, their emphasis on sameness and difference through hybridized and essentialized representations was not static. As they engaged with tensions of belonging, their essentialized and hybridized representations often merged, overlapped, and occasionally contradicted one another. And in their use of a range of cultural preferences in the presentation of themselves as a cohesive, essentialized group, these young people were at the same time engaging in hybridizing practices.

Evoking hybridized and essentialized representations of self allowed young people to create a sense of belonging through asserting sameness to certain groups and difference to others. Hybridized self-representations allowed for young people to demonstrate sameness across differences in an attempt to overcome essentializing perceptions of their marginality. In their emphasis on sameness in hybridized representations they acknowledged inherent differences while emphasizing their ability to overcome them and thus assimilate into what they saw as the mainstream population. Alternatively, in their emphasis on sameness in essentialized representations they denied inherent differences and thereby asserted a sense of belonging and solidarity with a group of insiders designated from a perceived position of marginality, in opposition to the broader population, and in a kind of resistance to assimilation or integration. This allowed young people to emphasize stereotypical and racialized representations of ethnicity on the one hand and a lack of concern for or acknowledgment of racial or ethnic difference on the other (Noble et al. 1999, 40).

Although hybrid and essentialized representations may not likely or usually be invoked so deliberately as to warrant their description as strategies, they allow for a subtle yet certain positioning through which young people may call upon different representations of themselves in relation to the varied messages, frameworks, and influences they encounter. As such, hybridized and essentialized representations of self may be interpreted as a kind of symbolic capital in the Australian national field (Bourdieu 1986; Bourdieu and Wacquant 1992). Such self-representations may be leveraged as capital in terms of valorizing both flexibility in demonstrating one's ability to integrate on the one hand, and the celebratory aspect of difference on the other. As they constructed a sense of self and identification with others and played with the discourses that came to frame their lives, they did so as partially knowing social actors. They were not absently framed by external narratives, nor were they always consciously or explicitly strategic in their response to them.

The result of their oscillating racialized identities, and indeed the diverse contexts in which their everyday lives unfold, reflect diverse intercultural social bonds. As Harris and Herron's (2017) work on everyday multiculturalism among youth from diverse backgrounds in Australia also highlights, the multiplicity of alignments and differentiation among these young people represent "dynamic 'entanglements of ethno-racial difference'" (Harris and Herron 2017. quoted in Johns, Noble and Harris 2017, 252). In their various affiliations, everyday racism and cross-racial friendships indeed exist alongside one another (Harris and Herron 2017). The ways in which young people of diverse backgrounds constitute a sense of themselves with reference to race and ethnicity, however, reflects something more complex than the fact of their increasing exposure and consequent responsiveness to intercultural contexts. In addition, their racialized identities emerge from their responsiveness to the ways in which those intercultural contexts are perceived, managed, and talked about more broadly.

The ways in which young people pursue a sense of belonging and inclusion through both their embracing and denying their own racialization is deeply relevant to the social and political context of Australian multiculturalism. That is, while these young people are constantly exposed to messages dictating where and how they fit in the Australian multicultural context, their identity-making practices effectively figure their own voices into the dialogue, at least on an interpersonal level in their daily lived environments. A significant implication of their identity work, then, is to offer reflection and consideration of how and to what extent the political and broader social framework of Australian multiculturalism fosters plurality and inclusion, as it purports to do.

Nationalism and the Multicultural Promise

Australian multiculturalism is fundamentally related to discourses of national belonging. A formal multicultural framework informs immigration policy and the path to citizenship in the Australian national context. The social and moral framework of multiculturalism, for the young people with whom I worked, emerged through overlapping and sometimes contradictory messages of integration and tolerance. These messages—to which they responded in paradoxical and sometimes oppositional ways—were encountered at their schools and in the broader community spaces through which they traversed in their daily lives.

Through these messages, it was indirectly maintained that young people might seamlessly fit within the mainstream school and community population, as race and ethnic background were of little actual relevance. At the same time, elements of their ethnic background were celebrated under the label of tolerance through festivals and cultural performance. While particular ethnic backgrounds are celebrated in such events, cultural performances are also framed as validating the accomplishments of the host community for their demonstrated tolerance and for their accumulation of a kind of multicultural capital in terms of ethnic food, dance, art, and so forth. (Hage 1998, 117). Despite its explicit aim of inclusion, certain discourses of multiculturalism resulted in an uncomfortable tension in young people's perceptions of belonging to a national space where elements of nationalism are centrally, though silently, linked to multiculturalism.

Multiculturalism is advanced as moving away from nationalism to a more inclusive social and moral framework, but through its articulation and promotion it is certainly not free from formulations of national belonging. Indeed, both nationalism and multiculturalism are premised upon, and protective of, the starting point that the "we," in discussions of how we Australians ought to handle difference, refers to those of white European heritage. This starting point does not change whether "we" express pride, indifference, or intolerance to all of the nonwhite people included in the Australian national space. The project of maintaining this sense of entitlement is present even in articulations of tolerance through which the majority population asserts that yes, the minority population ought to have entitlements and rights as well. When racism is only recognized through its most overt and ugly manifestations, or worse still, when it is altogether denied, we risk side stepping a deep rooted casual racism that can be just as insidious (Wise 2017). That is, what is labeled as racism and what is labeled as tolerance are different ends on a spectrum—inherent to the political and moral framework of multiculturalism—of national belonging (Hage 1998, 2003).

But I want to be careful here not to classify nationalism as an evil, backward, or inherently destructive force. And defining multiculturalism as the progressive antithesis to nationalism is not simply ideologically flawed. Even if it were accurate, such a comparison advances us no further in terms of a more meaningful approach to inclusiveness. Feelings and expressions of national belonging are, for whatever reasons, deeply entrenched across social contexts and local and national space. Moreover, both ethnic majority and ethnic minority populations are equally capable of both nationalist and racist acts and attitudes (as well as those which may be understood as tolerant). It is more productive a goal to understand nationalism than to simply dismiss it; what does it mean to people? How is it constituted? From where does the fear of its loss emerge and how might those suffering from such a fear themselves be integrated into a deeper, more inclusive multiculturalism (Skey 2011)?

In other words, in what ways does the majority population, too, struggle toward a sense of inclusiveness, belonging and a life in which they feel a level of comfort (Hage 1998, 21)? The answers to such questions are beyond the scope of this research. However, they are necessary to ask here, if only to highlight that the culture of fear that so clearly motivates the more abhorrent acts of nationalism is also present in the nicer or more politically correct attempts at inclusion promoted in multicultural policy and discourse (see also Hage 1998, 79). That is, nationalism and multiculturalism are not mutually exclusive, and neither can claim complete moral superiority or inferiority as unequivocally good or bad. Moreover, both evoke discourses of inclusion and discourses of exclusion.

These underlying dynamics, however, should not detract from the fact that, in my experience, the vast majority of professionals, service providers, and community members with whom young people interacted on a regular basis cared profoundly about the degree to which these young people realized their own sense of belonging. Indeed, the schools and other programs young people attended might be described as not only concerned, but quite heavily burdened, with the task of creating such a sense of belonging. My aim here is not to criticize the limits of multiculturalism or its practitioners, or to draw lines of comparison between it and nationalism (or, more alarmingly, racism) to no avail.

Instead, by demonstrating the complex ways in which a small group of young people experience the nuance of multicultural discourse in ethnographic context, I hope to highlight the ways in which it works (see also Clyne and Jupp 2011), but also to flag the need to keep striving where multiculturalism for them appears to have missed the intended mark. Hage (1998, 26) urges "a deeper commitment to a more far reaching multiculturalism" that opens the space for a robust politics of negotiation between equals. In a similar vein, Gutmann (1994) describes Habermas's contribution to her influential edited volume as proposing that the ideal multicultural framework would not only dictate our legal equality, but also foster a shared agreement that "we must also be able to understand ourselves as the authors of the laws that bind us" (ix; see also Habermas 1994).

Such a shift in ownership over the premise of Australian multiculturalism would necessarily require that government policy move beyond an emphasis on tolerance or recognition of cultural difference—a shift from living with or tolerating diversity, to living in diversity (Modood 2016). It would require a move toward an enhanced scope and ability to incorporate the diverse ways in which all people seek for themselves a meaningful life (Hage 2011, 2012). And while multicultural policy must equally validate the plurality of both minority and majority perspectives and pursuits of inclusion, comfort, and belonging, it should also compel a greater acknowledgment of Anglo privilege where racism could be more freely named when observed and experienced (Dunn and Nelson 2011).

However, for a more comprehensive and inclusive multicultural framework, race and racism should not be conflated. While the management of racism is appropriately within the scope of what multicultural policy must confront, the terms in which people express and embrace their own racial and ethnic identity are not. Individuals ought to have freedom to place value on the relevance of race and ethnicity in their own lives; a preference that should not merely underscore or become a requirement for the condemnation of racism.

The identity making practices in which these young people engaged in social context help us to understand multiculturalism in its current form, as it is experienced by those it inherently seeks to address. A more stable sense of belonging among these young people might be approached if, as a starting point, their difference was not at times simultaneously preserved through the celebratory language of tolerance and denied through gestures toward the simplicity of integration. Through depictions of their varied and sometimes seemingly contradictory self-representations, it becomes evident how contestable belonging is for these young people in the spaces where multiculturalism is, for them, enacted. And beyond this, the varied and multiple ways in which these young people represent themselves in engagement with the political, social, and moral framing of their lives reveals a kind of adaptability through which they have a say in defining to whom, to what, or where they belong.

Multiple Belongings: The "So What" of Dynamic Responsiveness

The relevance of the multiplicity with which these young people represent themselves both individually and collectively, then, is twofold. Their capacity for responsiveness and flexibility of identity reveals a strategy of resilience whereby young people may act in both subversion and accordance with the political and moral underpinnings of multiculturalism. The processes of identity making undertaken by these young people provides scope for a responsive engagement with messages inherent to multicultural discourse that both foster and inhibit their sense of belonging. Their oscillating emphasis on hybridized and essentialized elements of their racial and ethnic identity effectively permits these young people, at least partially, to define and address their own sense of belonging or alienation. The identity practices of these young people are equally relevant to an understanding of the social context in which they take place.

It is my contention that by paying attention to those things that young people reference and comment upon in their depictions of who they are—those things to which they are responding in their identity work—we shed light upon, not only their personal preoccupations, but also the things that matter collectively. That we all project a sense of self in response to some element of our social environment is, on the surface, quite obvious. But if we center our analyses of the ways in which people project a sense of self, on what they are either openly or implicitly addressing, we can isolate particular social dynamics. Deconstructing identity in this way engages the perennial anthropological tension between structure and agency, the particular and the universal.

The national story we tell about the importance of multiculturalism is one that seeks to counter the framing lens of inequality, and consequently, the relevance of race and ethnicity. However, the messages used to foster a harmonious multicultural context paradoxically emphasize an imbalance of social and moral entitlements. The premise of multiculturalism is that race does not matter, but the messages of integration and tolerance with which it is framed and executed, show that it does. For these young people, an emphasis on their inherent need for tolerance and integration is felt and interpreted as an indication of inequality related to their ethnic and racial identity. Their identity work seeks to reframe or engage the messages we tell about them in the context of multiculturalism.

In this study, we saw these young people respond to the multicultural ideal of the irrelevance of race by projecting a sense of racial identity and empowerment in their creation of a hip hop song. Through the song, they aligned themselves with the resilience, the resistance and the cool of an essentialized, counterwhite, African American identity. In doing so, they subtly resisted messages that dictate their need for tolerance and urge their integration. Similarly, we saw them reframing the multicultural emphasis on their status as national outsiders in need of inclusion, in their relative disregard of the importance of citizenship and national identity and embracing of a racial difference that instead provided a sense of collective belonging. And on the other hand, as they sometimes described and accounted for their social relationships in their everyday lives through a denial of the relevance of their racial identities, these young people affirmed the multicultural ideal that race does not matter and embraced the benefits of integration.

By detailing minority negotiations of ethnic, racial, and national belonging, I have sought to demonstrate how the political and moral framework of Australian multiculturalism can act, sometimes paradoxically, as an instrument of inclusion or of exclusion. My aim has been to demonstrate how a sense of social belonging might be approached by those who are popularly understood, through broad social policy and moral frameworks, as being somehow outside of the national context, in a process of becoming, and in need of inclusion. By illustrating the complex identity making practices undertaken by young people from refugee backgrounds, I have attempted to show how multiculturalism in the Australian context, and its emergent messages of (national) belonging, is felt and engaged by those it most explicitly seeks to address.

So, what do the responsive, multiple identities of these young people reveal about Australian multiculturalism? Young people appear, at times, to self-essentialize, or self-racialize in response to the ways in which public discourse racializes them. Yes, their emphasis on flexibility, hybridity, and the irrelevance of race can be read as emerging in response to the same dynamic. But what does this mean practically? Of course, their responsiveness to the ways in which they are racialized by others does not mean that their experiences with and interpretations of race and racism are any less real. Does it mean that race should be treated differently in political and social context in order for it not to be so consuming for these young people? Would that work, does it matter, and is their overidentification with race and ethnicity even limiting? These questions are all relevant and better explored with detailed attention to youth engagement with social context. But these questions are not the limit of what youth identity work can reveal.

Interpreting identity through responsiveness highlights that the ways in which we constitute a sense of ourselves considers, and responds in both opposition to and reinforcement of, the ways in which others see us. This information ultimately helps us to understand how broad social messages are perceived—how they work and how they sometimes need to be addressed and adjusted for various purposes, such as fostering a deeper sense of inclusion—and how people may collectively and individually respond to such messages. The identity work of these young people, and how it emerges in response to multicultural context, provides us with a deeper understanding of the complexity of young lives in changing circumstances.

It takes us past the "what" of how they are behaving and interacting with one another and with their broader social environments and provides us with a crucial element of "why." The ways in which a group of young people from refugee backgrounds represent their identities—in the everyday dynamics of friendship making, in the more spectacular dynamics of cultural performance, and in their engagement with the political dynamics through which they are broadly classified in national context—demonstrates the weight of public discourse on personal narratives. Their identity work may thus ultimately be conceptualized as a kind of participation in the politics of belonging to social context.

The interplay between broad social narratives and people's feelings and expressions of who they are and how easily they fit or belong in relation to those narratives, carries grave implications for the effectiveness of inclusion in modern, multiethnic societies. These implications in turn have much to reveal about how people may participate in and affect the social processes that come to frame their lives. Belonging is contestable—it was constantly approached, denied, and manipulated by the young people represented here in their everyday social environments. The limits and possibilities for belonging must therefore be considered in relation to the dynamic ways in which personal identities and discourses that govern broader national spaces respond to one another.

APPENDIX

Key Research Participant Backgrounds

Pseudonym	Country of origin and route to Australia	Time in Australia at start of study	Year at school; age	Primary identified tribal affiliation or ethnic background; language	Other participants identified as relatives or close friends
Aher	Sudan via Kenya	3 years	year 9; 13 years old	Arabic, English	close friends—Omot, Santino, Obama
Alex	Sudan via Kenya	5 years	year 10; 15 years old	Arabic, English	
Aliir	Sudan via Kenya	5 years	year 11; 16 years old	Dinka; Arabic, Dinka, Swahili, English	
Atong	Sudan via Egypt	2 years	year 9; 15 years old	Dinka; Arabic; English	close friends—Lisa and Jenna
Benjamin	Sudan via Egypt	5 years	year 12; 18 years old	Anuak; Arabic	younger brothers—Omar and Santino; younger sister—Lola; cousin—Obama
Brian	Sudan via Kenya	6 years	year 11; 16 years old	Sudanese, Filipino, Spanish	

Catalina	Burma via Tham Hin refugee camp	3 years	year 9; 16 years old	Karen; Thai, Karen, English	younger sister—Jessica; younger brother—Thakin; close friends—Lisa and Paw Wah
Ce Ce	Burma via Tham Hin refugee camp	2 years	year 8; 14 years old	Karen; Thai, Karen, English	cousin—Wah Wah
Cordica	Sudan via Kenya	4 years	year 8; 13 years old	Arabic, English	older sister—Vic; older brother—John; close friends—Elijah, Alex, Sam, Tino, Zaki, Aliir, Nine
David	Sudan via Uganda	4 years	year 10; 15 years old	Nuba; Arabic	
Dombai	Sudan via Egypt	6 years	year 9; 14 years old	Dinka; Dinka, Arabic, English	
Eh Eh	Burma via Tham Hin refugee camp	2 years	year 8; 13 years old	Karen; Thai, Karen, English	close friends—Jessica, Wah Wah and Ce Ce
Elijah	Uganda via Sudan, then Kenya	6 years	year 10; 15 years old	Acholi; Arabic, English	older brother—Sam; close friends—Nine, Tino, Samah, Vic
Gabe	Sudan via Kenya	5 years	year 9; 15 years old	Arabic, English	close friends—Elijah
Jaymaya	migrated from Papua New Guinea	2 years	year 9; 14 years old	Papua New Guinean	close friends—Lisa, Atong and Catalina

(Continued)

Pseudonym	Country of origin and route to Australia	Time in Australia at start of study	Year at school; age	Primary identified tribal affiliation or ethnic background; language	Other participants identified as relatives or close friends
Jenna	Burma via Tham Hin refugee camp	2 years	year 8; 14 years old	Chin	close friends—Lisa and Atong
Jessica	Burma via Tham Hin refugee camp	3 years	year 8; 13 years old	Karen; Thai, Karen, English	older sister—Catalina; younger brother—Thakin; close friends—Wah Wah and Eh Eh
Joseph	Sudan via Egypt	6 years	year 12; 17 years old	Dinka; Arabic, Egyptian Arabic, Dinka, English	cousin—Samah; close friends—Zi and Sam
Lauren	Australia	whole life	year 9; 15 years old	Anglo-Celtic Australian; English	close friends—Vic and Samah; boyfriend—Thomas
Lisa	Burma via Tham Hin refugee camp	2 years	year 9; 14 years old	Burmese; Karen, Burmese, Thai, English	younger brother—Mathew; close friends—Catalina, Jessica, Wah Wah, Eh Eh, Ce Ce, Atong, Jenna, Paw Wah

Name	Origin	Time	Year; age	Languages	Relationships
Lola	Sudan via Egypt	5 years	year 5; 9 years old	Anuak; Arabic	older brothers—Omar, Santino, Benjamin; cousin—Obama
Mathew	Burma via Tham Hin refugee camp	2 years	year 7; 12 years old	Burmese; Karen, Burmese, Thai, English	older sister—Lisa; close friend—Thakin
Nine	Sudan via Kenya	2 years	year 12; 19 years old	Arabic, English	close friends—Zi, Sam, Elijah
Obama	Sudan via Egypt	5 years	year 10; 15 years old	Nuer; Arabic	cousins—Santino, Benjamin, Gabe
Omar	Sudan via Egypt	5 years	year 8; 13 years old	Anuak; Arabic	older brothers—Santino and Benjamin; younger sister—Lola; cousin—Obama
Omot	Sudan via Kenya	2 years	year 9; 13 years old	Arabic, English	close friends—Aher, Santino, Obama
Paw Wah	Burma via Tham Hin refugee camp	2 years	year 9; 14 years old	Karen	close friend—Catalina
Sam	Uganda via Sudan, then Kenya	6 years	year 12; 17 years old	Acholi; Arabic, English	younger brother—Elijah
Samah	Sudan via Kenya	4 years	year 9; 14 years old	Dinka; Arabic, Dinka dialect, English	cousin—Joseph; close friends—Vic and Lauren

(Continued)

Pseudonym	Country of origin and route to Australia	Time in Australia at start of study	Year at school; age	Primary identified tribal affiliation or ethnic background; language	Other participants identified as relatives or close friends
Santino	Sudan via Egypt	5 years	year 10; 15 years old	Anuak; Arabic	older brother—Benjamin; younger brother—Omar; younger sister—Lola; cousin—Obama
Shalla	Burma via Tham Hin refugee camp	2 years	year 7; 12 years old	Karen; Thai, Karen, English	sister—Wah Wah; cousin—Ce Ce
Sunday	Sudan via Kenya	2 years	year 8; 13 years old	Arabic, English	
Thakin	Burma via Tham Hin refugee camp	3 years	year 7; 12 years old	Karen; Thai, Karen, English	older sisters—Jessica and Catalina
Thomas	Sudan via Uganda	4 years	out of school; 20 years old	Nuba; Arabic, Nuba dialect, English	younger sister—Vic; younger brother—John; girlfriend—Lauren
Tino	Sudan via Kenya	6 years	year 10; 16 years old	Arabic, English	close friends—Elijah and Alex

Vic	Sudan via Uganda	4 years	year 12; 18 years old	Nuba; Arabic, Nuba dialect, English	younger brother—John; older brother—Thomas; close friends—Sarah and Lauren
Wah Wah	Burma via Tham Hin refugee camp	2 years	year 8; 14 years old	Karen; Thai, Karen, English	sister—Shalla; cousin—Ce Ce; close friends—Jessica and Eh Eh
Zaki	Sudan via Kenya	3 years	year 11; 16 years old		
Zi	Sierra Leone via Guinea	5 years	year 12; 18 years old		close friends—Nine and Sam

ACKNOWLEDGMENTS

My first thanks go to the young people and their families who have so generously shared of their lives. I thank them for agreeing to act as participants in my research and for graciously allowing me to hang out with them at school, to follow them home, and to tag along with them to various social events throughout the course of my research and beyond. My time with all of you has enriched my life immeasurably. I thank the teachers, administrators and coordinators of the school and after-school programs where I conducted research, for providing me the initial opportunity to work with the young people who are the foundation of this study.

I would like to express gratitude to the University of Queensland (UQ) for support during the research for this book. The research was funded by a University of Queensland Research Scholarship. I am grateful to many members of the UQ faculty and staff for their support and mentorship. In particular, I would like to thank Professor David Trigger for his support of my work and feedback on a number of seminar papers. Dr. Helen Johnson encouraged me to embark upon this research in the first place. I thank her for her useful feedback on initial chapter drafts and for affirming the worthiness of my project in the preliminary stages of research. Ultimate acknowledgment and gratitude must go to my doctoral supervisor, Dr. Sally Babidge, whose support throughout the research and initial writing of this book has been indispensable and who has become the exemplar of superb scholarly craft to which I now aspire. I thank her for providing outstanding doctoral supervision and for her continued support and friendship.

I have presented parts of this research throughout its development at conferences and workshops where I have received feedback for which the book is stronger. Among these, I would like to thank the participants and organizers of the University of Sydney Anthropology Symposium, "Young Lives Changing Times: Perspectives on Social Reproduction," for their generous comments and critique. Dr. Richard Robbins, Distinguished Teaching Professor, at SUNY Plattsburgh organized a review panel of my research which provided me with valuable feedback at a pivotal point. My work has also benefited from feedback at conferences including those held by the American Anthropological Association; as well as "Images of Whiteness: Exploring Critical Issues," hosted by Oxford

University; and "Rethinking Youth Marginalities: Movements, Narratives, and Exchanges," hosted by the AAA Anthropology of Children and Youth Interest Group at Rutgers University.

Jill E. Korbin and E. J. Sobo, editors of the Rutgers Series in Childhood Studies, at Rutgers University Press, provided thoughtful feedback which helped to develop the work from an earlier draft. My two anonymous reviewers provided incisive and penetrating critiques which strengthened my arguments considerably and which I have sought to incorporate here. I also want to thank Kimberly Guinta for her support of my project from the start, and Jasper Chang for his guidance throughout the publishing process.

Portions of this book have appeared in earlier published forms. Chapters 2 and 5 feature, in part, ideas published in the *Journal of Ethnic and Racial Studies:* Moran (2016), "Constructions of Race: Symbolic Ethnic Capital and the Performance of Youth Identity in Multicultural Australia," 39 (4), 708–726. I thank the editors and reviewers of the journal for helping me to further strengthen and develop my arguments.

Many colleagues and mentors have helped in the preparation of this manuscript and have provided critical feedback along the way. I thank them for believing in my work and contributing to its betterment. In particular, I thank Dr. Sarah Webb for her invaluable advice and her willingness to read drafts as well as the manuscript in full, and Dr. Lesley Pruitt for her support, enthusiasm, and shared collegial interests.

I am especially indebted to my family for their patience and encouragement. To my parents, Kathryn and Thomas Moran, thank you for providing the experiences and foundation upon which my interests and capabilities have taken shape and for always being there for me in countless ways as I pursue them. I thank my father also for his careful reading of the book and his astute feedback, for which I am deeply grateful. I lovingly acknowledge my sister, Taryn; my brother-in-law, Creighton; and my nephew, C. E.; you are not only family, you are the dearest of friends. I also express my gratitude to Judith and Ian Marshall for their interest and encouragement throughout this process.

Most of all, I thank my partner, Richard Marshall, for his emotional and intellectual support, as well as his constant willingness to take on additional parenting and domestic responsibilities, without which undertaking this research and seeing it through to completion would not have been possible. Your endless patience and enthusiasm for these efforts that have so absorbed me are beyond expectation. Thank you for reading various pieces and discussing ideas as my project took shape, for your careful reading of the manuscript in its entirety at the end, and for your friendship and good humor always. Finally, to my daughter, Georgia, and my son, William: thank you both for being my constant reminder of the spark and wonder of youth and for providing me with so much joy throughout this process and beyond.

NOTES

CHAPTER 1   FIELDWORK AND RESEARCH FOUNDATIONS

1. See the Appendix, which details background information about the key research participants.
2. The Cronulla riots were a series of race riots and social unrest between white and Lebanese youth in Sydney, Australia. For an in-depth coverage of the Cronulla riots, see Johns, Noble and Harris (2017).

CHAPTER 2   MULTICULTURAL AUSTRALIA AND THE REFUGEE EXPERIENCE

1. Although Burma was officially renamed Myanmar in 1989, my participants, and therefore I, refer to it here as Burma. The majority of refugees currently residing in Australia who identify as Burmese are officially classified as Bamar political refugees.

CHAPTER 4   EVERYDAY IDENTITY

1. This pseudonym is a nickname developed and used by the student's peers. It further reflects the engagement, among these young people, with American cultural symbols.

CHAPTER 5   PERFORMING IDENTITY

1. Arabic word spelled phonetically and translated according to the informant's description.

REFERENCES

Abdullah, Ibrahim. 2005. "'I am a Rebel': Youth, Culture and Violence in Sierra Leone." In *Makers and Breakers: Children and Youth in Postcolonial Africa*. Alicinda Honwana and Filip de Boeck, eds. Pp. 172–187. Trenton, N.J.: African World Press.

Adams, Mathew. 2006. "Hybridizing Habitus and Reflexivity: Towards an Understanding of Contemporary Identity." *Sociology* 40(3): 511–528.

Aidi, Hisham D. 2014. *Rebel Music: Race, Empire and the New Muslim Youth Culture*. New York: Pantheon Books.

Anderson, Benedict. 1991. *Imagined Communities: Reflections on the Origin and Spread of Nationalism*. 2nd edition. London: Verso.

Ang, Ien. 2003. "Together-in-Difference: Beyond Diaspora, into Hybridity." *Asian Studies Review* 27(2): 141–154.

Ang, Ien, Gay Hawkins, and Lamia Dabboussy. 2008. *The SBS Story: The Challenge of Diversity*. Sydney, NSW: University of New South Wales Press.

Appadurai, Arjun. 1996. *Modernity at Large: Cultural Dimensions of Globalization*. Minneapolis: University of Minnesota Press.

Arkin, Kimberly. A. 2009. "Rhinestone Aesthetics and Religious Essence: Looking Jewish in Paris." *American Ethnologist* 36(4): 722–734.

Australian Bureau of Statistics (ABS). 2017. *"2016 Census: Multicultural, Census Reveals a Fast Changing Culturally Diverse Nation."* http://www.abs.gov.au/ausstats/abs@.nsf/lookup /Media%20Release3 (accessed March 16, 2018).

Australian Department of Home Affairs. 2017. *"Multicultural Australia: United, Strong, Successful Australia's Multicultural Statement."* https://www.homeaffairs.gov.au/trav/life /multicultural/multicultural-statement (accessed March 19, 2018).

Australian Department of Immigration and Citizenship (DIAC), n.d.-a. "Citizenship Test." http://www.citizenship.gov.au/learn/cit_test/ (accessed June 18, 2012).

———, n.d.-b. "Australian Citizenship Practice Test." *Australian Government*. http://www .citizenship.gov.au/learn/cit_test/practice/ (accessed June 18, 2012).

———, n.d.-c. "Australian Citizenship Pledge." *Australian Government*. http://www.citizenship .gov.au/ceremonies/pledge/ (accessed June 18, 2012).

———. 2007. "Sudanese Community Profile." *Australian Government*. http://www.immi.gov .au/living-in-australia/delivering-assistance/government-programs/settlement -planning/_pdf/community-profile-sudan.pdf (accessed April 3, 2012).

———. 2011a. "Australia's Humanitarian Program 2012–13 and Beyond." *Australian Government*. http://www.immi.gov.au/about/contracts-tenders-submissions/_pdf/2012-13-humani tarian-program-information-paper.pdf (accessed September 20, 2012).

———. 2011b. *Settlement Outcomes of New Arrivals—Report of Findings: Study for Department of Immigration and Citizenship*. Research report. Ormond, VIC: Australian Survey Research Group.

Australian Government. 2012. "Expert Panel on Asylum Seekers." http://expertpanelonasy
lumseekers.dpmc.gov.au/report (accessed August 13, 2012).

Australian Karen Foundation. *The Karen People.* https://www.australiankarenfoundation.org
.au/karen_people_18.html (accessed October 13, 2018).

Back, Les. 1996. *New Ethnicities and Urban Culture: Racisms and Multiculture in Young Lives.*
London: Routledge.

Badea, Constantina, Jolanda Jetten, Aarto Iyer, and Abdelatif Er-rafiy. 2011. "Negotiating Dual
Identities: The Impact of Group-Based Rejection on Identification and Acculturation."
European Journal of Social Psychology 41(5): 586–595.

Bagnall, Sam. 2010. "Burma's 'Forgotten' Chin People Suffer Abuse." *BBC News*, April 19.
http://news.bbc.co.uk/2/hi/asia-pacific/8626008.stm (accessed September 12, 2012).

Barth, Fredrik, ed. 1969. *Ethnic Groups and Boundaries: The Social Organization of Culture Difference.* Boston: Little, Brown & Company.

Bauman, Zygmunt. 2011. "Migration and Identities in the Globalized World." *Philosophy and
Social Criticism* 37(4): 425–435.

———. 2016. *Strangers at Our Door.* Cambridge: Polity Press.

Benson, Simon, and Rachel Baxendale. 2017. "Citizenship Changes Revealed: Fluent English,
Four Years of Residency, Australian Values." *Australian*, April 20, National Affairs sect.
http://www.theaustralian.com.au/national-affairs/citizenship-changes-revealed
-fluent-english-four-years-of-residency-australian-values/news-story/47a5be9d81ba98
145673cfd65fa44c85 (accessed April 24, 2017).

Bhabha, Homi K. 1994. *The Location of Culture.* London: Routledge.

———. 1996. "Culture's In-Between." In *Questions of Cultural Identity.* Stuart Hall and Paul
du Gay, eds. Pp. 53–60. London: Sage.

———. 2006. "Cultural Diversity and Cultural Differences." In *The Post-Colonial Studies Reader.*
Bill Ashcroft, Gareth Griffiths, and Helen Tiffin, eds. Pp. 155–157. London: Routledge.

Billig, Michael. 1995. *Banal Nationalism.* London: Sage.

Billinger, Michael S. 2007. "Another Look at Ethnicity as a Biological Concept: Moving
Anthropology beyond the Race Concept." *Critique of Anthropology* 27(1): 5–35.

Blainey, Geoffrey. 1984. *All for Australia.* North Ryde: Methuen Haynes.

Bottrell, Dorothy, and Alan France. 2015. "Bourdieurian Cultural Transitions: Young People
Negotiating 'Fields' in Their Pathways into and out of Crime." In *Youth Cultures, Tran-
sitions, and Generations: Bridging the Gap in Youth Research.* Dan Woodman and Andy
Bennett, eds. Pp. 99–112. London: Palgrave Macmillan.

Bourdieu, Pierre. 1977. *Outline of a Theory of Practice.* Richard Nice, trans. Cambridge: Cambridge University Press.

———. 1984. *Distinction: A Social Critique of the Judgment of Taste.* Richard Nice, trans. Cambridge: Harvard University Press.

———. 1986. "The Forms of Capital." In *Handbook of Theory and Research for the Sociology of
Education.* John G. Richardson, ed. Pp. 241–258. New York: Greenwood Press.

———. 1990. *In Other Words: Essays towards a Reflexive Sociology.* Matthew Adamson, trans.
Stanford: Stanford University Press.

———. 2000. *Pascalian Meditations.* Richard Nice, trans. Cambridge: Polity.

Bourdieu, Pierre, and Jean-Claude Passeron. 1990. *Reproduction in Education, Society and Culture.* 2nd edition. Richard Nice, trans. London: Sage.

Bourdieu, Pierre, and Loïc J. D. Wacquant. 1992. *An Invitation to Reflexive Sociology.* Cambridge: Polity Press.

Brisbane City Council. 2018. "One Brisbane Many Cultures—March 2018." https://www
.brisbane.qld.gov.au/community-safety/community-support/multicultural-services
/one-brisbane-many-cultures-march-2018 (accessed May 28, 2018).

Broadbent, Robyn, Marcelle Cacciattolo, and Cathryn Carpenter. 2007. "A Tale of Two Communities: Refugee Relocation in Australia." *Australian Journal of Social Issues* 42(4): 581–601.

Brubaker, Rogers, and Frederick Cooper. 2000. "Beyond 'Identity.'" *Theory and Society* 29(1): 1–47.

Bucholtz, Mary. 2002. "Youth and Cultural Practice." *Annual Review of Anthropology* 31(1): 525–552.

———. 2011. *White Kids: Language, Race and Styles of Youth Identity.* Cambridge: Cambridge University Press.

Butcher, Melissa, and Anita Harris. 2010. "Pedestrian Crossings: Young People and Everyday Multiculturalism." *Journal of Intercultural Studies* 31(5): 449–453.

Butcher, Melissa, and Mandy Thomas. 2006. "Ingenious: Emerging Hybrid Youth Cultures in Western Sydney." In *Global Youth?: Hybrid Identities, Plural Worlds.* Pam Nilan and Carles Feixa, eds. Pp. 53–71. London: Routledge.

Carroll, Tamar W. 2017. "Intersectionality and Identity Politics: Cross-Identity Coalitions for Progressive Social Change." *Signs: Journal of Women in Culture and Society* 42(3): 600–607.

Carruthers, Ashley. 2013. "National Multiculturalism, Transnational Identities." *Journal of Intercultural Studies* 34(2): 214–228.

Castles, Stephen. 2000. "The Future of Australian Citizenship in a Globalizing World." In *Individual Community Nation: Fifty Years of Australian Citizenship.* Kim Rubenstein, ed. Pp. 119–134. Melbourne, VIC: Australian Scholarly Publishing.

Castles, Stephen, Graeme Hugo, and Ellie Vasta. 2013. "Rethinking Migration and Diversity in Australia: Introduction." *Journal of Intercultural Studies* 34(2): 115–121.

Chambers, Deborah. 2013. *Social Media and Personal Relationships: Online Intimacies and Networked Friendship.* London: Palgrave Macmillan.

Chen, Xinyin, Doran C. French, and Barry H. Schneider, eds. 2006. "Culture and Peer Relationships." In *Peer Relationships in Cultural Context.* Pp. 3–23. Cambridge: Cambridge University Press.

Cheney, Kristen E. 2007. *Pillars of the Nation: Child Citizens and Ugandan National Development.* Chicago: University of Chicago Press.

Chhuon, Vichet, and Cynthia Hudley. 2010. "Asian American Ethnic Options: How Cambodian Students Negotiate Ethnic Identities in a U.S. Urban School." *Anthropology & Education Quarterly* 41(4): 341–359.

Chikkatur, Anita. 2012. "Difference Matters: Embodiment of and Discourse on Difference at an Urban Public High School." *Anthropology and Education Quarterly* 43(1): 82–100.

Cho, Sumi, Kimberle Williams Crenshaw and Leslie McCall. 2013. "Toward a Field of Intersectionality Studies: Theory, Applications and Praxis." *Signs: Journal of Women in Culture and Society* 38(4): 785–810.

Clyne, Michael, and James Jupp, eds. 2011. "Epilogue: a Multicultural Future." In *Multiculturalism and Integration a Harmonious Relationship.* Pp. 191–198. Canberra, ACT: Australian National University.

Cohen, Abner. 1974. *Urban Ethnicity.* London: Tavistock.

Cohen, Albert K. 1955. *Delinquent Boys: The Culture of the Gang.* Glencoe, Ill.: Free Press.

Cohen, Roger. 2016. "Broken Men in Paradise: The World's Refugee Crisis Knows No More Sinister Exercise in Cruelty than Australia's Island Prisons." *New York Times*, December 9, opinion sec. https://www.nytimes.com/2016/12/09/opinion/sunday/australia-refugee-prisons-manus-island.html (accessed January 17, 2017).

Collins, Jock. 2013. "Multiculturalism and Immigrant Integration in Australia." *Canadian Ethnic Studies* 45(3): 133–149.

Collins, Jock, Greg Noble, Scott Poynting, and Paul Tabar. 2000. *Kebabs, Kids, Cops and Crime: Youth, Ethnicity and Crime.* Annandale, NSW: Pluto Press.

Community Life Program: Community Development Services. 2002. *Working with Refugees Strategy Brisbane City Council.* http://www.multiculturalaustralia.edu.au/doc/bcc_bris _refugee_strategy.pdf (accessed April 3, 2012).

Correa-Velez, Ignacio, Sandra M. Gifford, and Adrian G. Barnett. 2010. "Longing to Belong: Social Inclusion and Wellbeing among Youth with Refugee Backgrounds in the First Three Years in Melbourne, Australia." *Social Science and Medicine* 71(8): 1399–1408.

Crock, Mary E. 2006. *Seeking Asylum Alone: A Study of Australian Law, Policy and Practice Regarding Unaccompanied and Separated Children.* Annandale, NSW: Themis Press.

Dalsheim, Joyce. 2013. "Theory for Praxis: Peacemaking, Cunning Recognition, and the Constitution of Enmity." *Social Analysis* 57 (2): 59–69.

Dandy, Justine. 2009. "Refugee and Migrant Integration: Examining the Discourse of the Dominant." In *Refugee and Migrant Integration in Developed Nations.* Special issue, *Tamara Journal for Critical Organization Inquiry* 8(1/2): 225–233.

Dao, Andre. 2012. "The Moral Philosophy of the Malaysia Solution." *The Conversation,* June 29, hot topics sec. http://theconversation.edu.au/the-moral-philosophy-of-the-malaysia -solution-7983. (accessed July 31, 2012).

De Boeck, Filip, and Alicinda Honwana, eds. 2005. "Children and Youth in Africa: Agency, Identity and Place." In *Makers and Breakers: Children and Youth in Postcolonial Africa.* Pp. 1–18. Trenton, N.J.: Africa World Press.

Denzin, Norman K., and Y. S. Lincoln. 2003. *Strategies of Qualitative Inquiry.* 2nd edition. London: Sage.

Dimitriadis, Greg. 2009 (2001). *Performing Identity/Performing Culture: Hip Hop as Text, Pedagogy, and Lived Practice.* New York: Peter Lang.

Doherty, Ben. 2016. "UN Official Criticises Australia's Plan for Lifetime Ban on Refugees Who Travel by Sea." *Guardian,* Oct. 31. http://www.theguardian.com/australia-news/2016/nov /01/un-official-criticises-australias-plan-for-lifetime-ban-on-refugees-who-travel-by -sea (accessed January 17, 2017).

Duffield, Mark. 2003. "The Root Causes of Sudan's Civil Wars." *Journal of Refugee Studies* 16(2): 219–221.

Dunn, Kevin, and Jacqueline K. Nelson. 2011. "Challenging the Public Denial of Racism for a Deeper Multiculturalism." *Journal of Intercultural Studies* 32(6): 587–602.

Durham, Deborah. 2004. "Disappearing Youth: Youth as a Social Shifter in Botswana." *American Ethnologist* 31(4): 589–605.

Dyson, Jane. 2010. "Friendship in Practice: Girls' Work in the Indian Himalayas." *American Ethnologist* 37(3): 482–499.

Evans-Pritchard, E. E. 1969. *The Nuer: A Description of the Modes of Livelihood and Political Institutions of a Nilotic People.* Oxford: Oxford University Press.

Fass, Paula S. 2003. "Children and Globalisation." *Journal of Social History* 36(4): 963–981.

———. 2007. *Children of a New World: Society, Culture, and Globalization.* New York: New York University Press.

Fiddian-Qasmiyeh, Elena, Gil Loescher, Katy Long and Nando Sigona, eds. 2014. *The Oxford Handbook of Refugee and Forced Migration Studies.* Oxford: Oxford University Press.

Fine, Michelle. 1994. "Working the Hyphens: Reinventing the Self and Other in Qualitative Research." In *Handbook of Qualitative Research.* N. Denzin and Y. Lincoln, eds. Pp. 70–82. Newbury Park, Calif.: Sage.

Forcier, Natalie I. 2008. "Violence, Crime and the Hip-Hop Identity: Sudanese Youth in Cairo, Egypt." *Pambazuka News,* December 11. http://www.pambazuka.org/en/category/comment /52624/print (accessed September 12, 2012).

Forman, Murray. 2002. *The 'Hood Comes First: Race, Space and Place in Rap and Hip-Hop*. Middletown, Conn.: Wesleyan University Press.

———. 2005. "Straight Outta Mogadishu: Prescribed Identities and Performative Practices among Somali Youth in North American High Schools." In *Youthscapes: The Popular, the National, the Global*. Maria Sunaina and Elisabeth Soep, eds. Pp. 3–22. Philadelphia: University of Pennsylvania Press.

Forrest, James, and Kevin Dunn. 2011. "Attitudes to Diversity: New Perspectives on the Ethnic Geography of Brisbane, Australia." *Australian Geographer* 42(4): 435–453.

France, Alan, Dorothy Bottrell, and Edward Haddon. 2012. "Managing Everyday Life: The Conceptualization and Value of Cultural Capital in Navigating Everyday Life for Working-Class Youth." *Journal of Youth Studies* 16(5): 597–611.

Garner, Steve. 2010. *Racisms: An Introduction*. London: Sage.

Gartrell, Adam. 2012. "PM Hopes Experts will Break Asylum Impasse." *Sydney Morning Herald*, June 28, breaking news national sec. http://news.smh.com.au/breaking-news -national/pm-hopes-experts-will-break-asylum-impasse-20120628-213ik.html (accessed September 12, 2012).

Gatrell, Peter. 2015. *The Making of the Modern Refugee*. Oxford: Oxford University Press.

Gemie, Sharif. 2010. "Re-Defining Refugees: Nations, Borders and Globalizations." *Eurolimes* 9: 28–36.

Gifford, Sandy, Ignacio Correa-Velez, and Robyn Sampson. 2009. *Good Starts for Recently Arrived Youth with Refugee Backgrounds: Promoting Wellbeing in the First Three Years of Settlement in Melbourne, Australia*. Research report. Melbourne, VIC: The La Trobe Refugee Research Center. http://www.latrobe.edu.au/larrc/documents-larrc/reports /report-good-starts.pdf (accessed September 17, 2012).

Gilroy, Paul. 1993. *The Black Atlantic: Modernity and Double Consciousness*. London: Verso.

———. 1997. "Diaspora and the Detours of Identity." In *Identity and Difference*. Kathryn Woodward, ed. Pp. 301–343. London: Sage.

———. 2005. *Postcolonial Melancholia*. New York: Columbia University Press.

Goffman, Erving. 1959. *The Presentation of Self in Everyday Life*. New York: Doubleday.

Goodman, Alan, and Marcy Darnovsky. 2018. "Race, Genetics and a Controversy." *New York Times*, April 2, opinion sect. https://www.nytimes.com/2018/04/02/opinion/genes-race .html (accessed May 2, 2018).

Gow, Greg. 2005. "Rubbing Shoulders in the Global City: Refugees, Citizenship and Multicultural Alliances in Fairfield, Sydney." *Ethnicities* 5(3): 386–405.

Grassby, Albert J. 1973. *A Multi-Cultural Society for the Future*. Canberra, ACT: Australian Government Publishing Service. http://www.multiculturalaustralia.edu.au/doc/grassby_1.pdf

Guerra, Carmel, and Rob White, eds. 1995. "The Making of Ethnic Minority Youth." In *Ethnic Minority Youth in Australia: Challenges & Myths*. Pp. 1–10. Hobart, Tas: National Clearinghouse for Youth Studies.

Guerrero, Alba Lucy, and Tessa Tinkler. 2010. "Refugee and displaced youth negotiating imagined and lived identities in a photography-based educational project in the United States and Colombia." *Anthropology & Education Quarterly* 41(1):55–74.

Gunew, Sneja. 1990. "Denaturalizing Cultural Nationalisms: Multicultural Readings of 'Australia'." In *Nation and Narration*. Homi K. Bhabha, ed. Pp. 99–120. London: Routledge.

———. 1993. "Multicultural Multiplicities: US, Canada, Australia." *Meanjin* 52(3): 447–461.

Gutmann, Amy, ed. 1994. *Multiculturalism: Examining the Politics of Recognition*. Princeton, N.J.: Princeton University Press.

Habermas, Jurgen. 1994. "Struggles for Recognition in the Democratic Constitutional State." Shierry W. Nicholsen, trans. In *Multiculturalism: Examining the Politics of Recognition*. Amy Gutmann, ed. Pp. 107–148. Princeton, N.J.: Princeton University Press.

Hage, Ghassan. 1998. *White Nation: Fantasies of White Supremacy in a Multicultural Society.* Annandale, NSW: Pluto Press.

——, ed. 2002a. "Citizenship and Honourability: Belonging to Australia Today." In *Arab-Australians Today: Citizenship and Belonging.* Pp. 1–15. Melbourne, VIC: Melbourne University Press.

——, ed. 2002b. "The Differential Intensities of Social Reality: Migration, Participation and Guilt." In *Arab-Australians Today: Citizenship and Belonging.* Pp. 192–205. Melbourne, VIC: Melbourne University Press.

——. 2003. *Against Paranoid Nationalism.* Annandale, NSW: Pluto Press.

——. 2011. "Multiculturalism and the Ungovernable Muslim." In *Essays on Muslims and Multiculturalism.* Raimond Gaita, ed. Pp. 155–186. Melbourne, VIC: Text Publishing.

——. 2012. "Critical Anthropological Thought and the Radical Political Imaginary Today." *Critique of Anthropology* 32(2): 285–308.

——. 2018. "Afterword the Ends of Nostalgia: Waiting for the Past-to-Come." In *Ethnographies of Waiting: Doubt, Hope and Uncertainty.* Manpreet K. Janeja and Andreas Bandak, eds. Pp. 203–208. London: Bloomsbury.

Hall, Stuart. 1992. "New Ethnicities." In *'Race,' Culture and Difference.* James Donald and Ali Rattansi, eds. Pp. 252–259. London: Open University.

——. 1993. "Cultural Identity and Diaspora." In *Colonial Discourse and Postcolonial Theory: A Reader.* Patrick Williams and Laura Chrisman, eds. Pp. 392–403. London: Harvester Wheatsheaf.

——. 1996. "Introduction: Who Needs 'Identity'?" In *Questions of Cultural Identity.* Stuart Hall and Paul du Gay. Pp. 1–17. London: Sage.

Hall, Stuart, and Tony Jefferson, eds. 1976. *Resistance through Rituals: Youth Subcultures in Post-War Britain.* London: Hutchinson.

Harasym, Sarah, ed. 1990. *The Post-Colonial Critic: Interviews, Strategies, Dialogues/Gayatri Chakravorty Spivak.* London: Routledge.

Harrell-Bond, Barbara E., and Eftihia Voutira. 1992. "Anthropology and the Study of Refugees." *Anthropology Today* 8(4): 6–10.

Harris, Anita. 2009. "Shifting the Boundaries of Cultural Spaces: Young People and Everyday Multiculturalism." *Social Identities: Journal for the Study of Race, Nation and Culture* 15(2): 187–205.

——. 2013. *Young People and Everyday Multiculturalism.* New York: Routledge.

Harris, Anita, and Melinda Herron. 2017. "Young People and Intercultural Sociality after Cronulla." *Journal of Intercultural Studies* 38(3): 284–300.

Hebdige, Dick. 1979. *Subculture: The Meaning of Style.* London: Methuen.

Heim, Joe, Debbie Truong, and Donna St. George. 2016. "17 Minutes to Memorialize 17 Lives Lost." *Washington Post*, March 10, education. https://www.washingtonpost.com/local/education/17-minutes-to-memorialize-17-lives-lost/2018/03/10/1781c198-2319-11e8-badd-7c9f29a55815_story.html?utm_term=.db5ccabe40f7 (accessed June 21, 2018).

Herron, Melinda. 2018. "A Revised Approach to Racism in Youth Multiculture: The Significance of Schoolyard Conversations about Sex, Dating and Desire." *Journal of Youth Studies* 21(2): 144–160.

Hjorth, Larissa. 2007. "Snapshots of Almost Contact: The Rise of Camera Phone Practices and a Case Study in Seoul, Korea." *Continuum: Journal of Media and Cultural Studies* 21(2): 227–238.

Hollinsworth, David. 2006. *Race and Racism in Australia.* 3rd edition. Melbourne, VIC: Thomas Social Science Press.

Innis, Michelle. 2016. "U.S., in Deal with Australia, Agrees to Take Some Refugees." *New York Times*, Nov 12. http://www.nytimes.com/2016/11/13/world/australia/australia-refugees-united-states.html. (accessed January 17, 2017).

Jackson, Michael. 2002. *The Politics of Storytelling: Violence, Transgression and Intersubjectivity*. University of Copenhagen: Museum Tusculanum Press.

Jakubowicz, Andrew. 1985. "Racism, Multiculturalism and the Immigration Debate in Australia: A Bibliographic Essay." In *SAGE Race Relations Abstracts*. The Institute of Race Relations, London 10(3):1–15.

Jenkins, Richard. 2008. *Social Identity*. 3rd edition. London: Routledge.

Jenks, Chris. 2005. *Childhood*. London: Routledge.

Johns, Amelia, Greg Noble, and Anita Harris. 2017. "After Cronulla: 'Where the Bloody Hell Are We Now?'" *Journal of Intercultural Studies* 38(3): 249–254.

Johnston, Megan. 2011. "Australia Tolerant of Cultural Differences: Study." *Sydney Morning Herald*, February 23, national sec. http://www.smh.com.au/national/australia-tolerant-of-cultural-differences-study-20110223-1b4ib.html (accessed June 5, 2012).

Johnston, Matt, and Paul Maley. 2012. "Asylum Seeker Boat Capsizes North of Christmas Island, as Tempers Flare Between MPs in Parliament." *Herald Sun*, June 27, breaking news sec. http://www.heraldsun.com.au/news/victoria/asylum-seeker-boat-capsizes-north-of-christmas-island-as-tempers-flare-between-mps-in-parliament/story-fn7x8me2-1226409555646 (accessed July 31, 2012).

Joppke, Christian. 2001. "Multicultural Citizenship: A Critique." *European Journal of Sociology* 42(2): 431–447.

Jupp, James. 2000. "British and Non-British Immigrants." In *Individual, Community, Nation: Fifty Years of Australian Citizenship*. Kim Rubenstein, ed. Pp. 92–98. Melbourne, VIC: Australian Scholarly Publishing.

Kapferer, Bruce. 1998. *Legends of People, Myths of State: Violence, Intolerance, and Political Culture in Sri Lanka and Australia*. Bathurst, NSW: Crawford House.

Karen Buddhist Dhamma Dhutta Foundation. *The Karen People*. http://www.karen.org.au/karen_people.htm (accessed October 5, 2011).

Katz, Cindi. 1998. "Disintegrating Developments: Global Economic Restructuring and the Eroding of Ecologies of Youth." In *Cool Places: Geographies of Youth Cultures*. Tracey Skelton and Gill Valentine, eds. Pp. 130–144. London: Routledge.

Kelly, Mary Louise. 2018. "Migrant Children Heard Crying on Tape Are the Voices 'Left Out' of the Conversation." NPR, June 19, *All Things Considered*. https://www.npr.org/2018/06/19/621579091/migrant-children-heard-crying-on-tape-are-the-voices-left-out-conversation (accessed June 21, 2018).

Kymlicka, Will. 2012. *Multiculturalism: Success, Failure, and the Future*. Washington, D.C.: Migration Policy Institute.

Madden, Raymond. 2010. *Being Ethnographic: A Guide to the Theory and Practice of Ethnography*. London: Sage.

Maley, William. 2016. *What Is a Refugee?* New York: Oxford University Press.

Marlowe, Jay M. 2010. "Beyond the Discourse of Trauma: Shifting the Focus on Sudanese Refugees." *Journal of Refugee Studies* 23(2): 183–198.

McIntosh, Peggy. 1990. "White Privilege: Unpacking the Invisible Knapsack." *Independent School* 49 (2): 31–35.

McMaster, Don. 2001. *Asylum Seekers: Australia's Response to Refugees*. Melbourne, VIC: Melbourne University Press.

McMichael, Celia, Caitlin Nunn, Ignacio Correa-Velez, and Sandra M. Gifford. 2017. "Resettlement of Refugee Youth in Australia: Experiences and Outcomes over TIME." *Forced Migration Review* (54): 66–68.

Mead, Margaret. 1928. *Coming of Age in Samoa: A Psychological Study of Primitive Youth for Western Civilization.* New York: William Morrow & Company.

Modood, Tariq. 2004. "Capitals, Ethnic Identity and Educational Qualifications." *Cultural Trends* 13(2): 87–105.

———. 2016. "What Is Multiculturalism and What Can It Learn from Interculturalism?" In *Interculturalism versus Multiculturalism—The Cantle-Modood Debate. Ethnicities* 16(3): 470–493.

Montgomery, Heather. 2009. *An Introduction to Childhood: Anthropological Perspectives on Children's Lives.* Chichester, U.K.: Wiley Blackwell.

Moore, Henrietta L. 2011. *Still Life: Hopes, Desires and Satisfactions.* Cambridge: Polity Press.

Moran, Anthony. 2011. "Multiculturalism as Nation-Building in Australia: Inclusive National Identity and the Embrace of Diversity." *Ethnic and Racial Studies* 34(12): 2153–2172.

Moran, Laura. 2016. "Constructions of Race: Symbolic Ethnic Capital and the Performance of Youth Identity in Multicultural Australia." *Ethnic and Racial Studies* 39(4): 708–726.

Mosselson, Jacqueline R. 2009. "Where am I? Refugee Youth Living in the United States." *Journal of the History of Childhood and Youth* 2(3): 451–469.

Nayak, Anoop. 2003. *Race, Place and Globalization: Youth Cultures in a Changing World.* Oxford: Berg.

———. 2009. "Race, Ethnicity and Young People." In *Children and Young People's Worlds: Developing Frameworks for Integrated Practice.* Heather Montgomery and Mary Kellett, eds. Pp. 91–108. Milton Keynes, U.K.: Open University.

Neal, Sarah, and Carol Vincent. 2013. "Multiculture, Middle Class Competencies and Friendship Practices in Super-Diverse Geographies." *Social and Cultural Geography* 14(8): 909–929.

Ngo, Bic. 2008. "Beyond 'Culture Clash' Understandings of Immigrant Experiences." *Theory into Practice* 47(1): 4–11.

Ngo, Bic. 2010. *Unresolved Identities.* Albany, N.Y.: State University of New York Press.

Noble, Greg. 2009. "Everyday Cosmopolitanism and the Labour of Intercultural Community." In *Everyday Multiculturalism.* Amanda Wise and Selvaraj Velayutham, eds. Pp. 46–65. London: Palgrave Macmillan.

Noble, Greg, Scott Poynting, and Paul Tabar. 1999. "Youth, Ethnicity and the Mapping of Identities: Strategic Essentialism and Strategic Hybridity among Male Arabic-Speaking Youth in South-Western Sydney." *Communal/Plural* 7(1): 29–43.

Noble, Greg, and Paul Tabar. 2002. "On Being Lebanese-Australian: Hybridity, Essentialism and Strategy among Arabic-Speaking Youth." In *Arab-Australians Today: Citizenship and Belonging.* Ghassan Hage, ed. Pp. 128–144. Melbourne, VIC: Melbourne University Press.

Obongo, Dhanojak. 2014. *Clash of Two Cultures: South Sudanese Refugees Living in Australia.* SAALAMATA.

Omi, Michael, and Howard Winant. 2011. "From Racial Formation in the United States." In *Race in an Era of Change.* Heather Dalmage and Barbara K. Rothman, eds. Pp. 3–17. Oxford: Oxford University Press.

Ong, Aihwa. 2003. *Buddha Is Hiding: Refugees, Citizenship and the New America.* Oakland: University of California Press.

Onselen, Peter V. 2012. "An End to the Blame Game." *Australian,* June 26, news features sec. http://www.theaustralian.com.au/news/features/an-end-to-the-blame-game/story -e6frg6z6-1226408324421 (accessed July 31, 2012).

Patterson, Orlando, and Ethan Fosse, eds. 2015. *The Cultural Matrix: Understanding Black Youth.* Cambridge, Mass.: Harvard University Press.

Papastergiadis, Nikos. 1997. "Tracing Hybridity in Theory." In *Debating Cultural Hybridity: Multi-Cultural Identities and the Politics of Anti-Racism.* Pnina Werbner and Tariq Modood, eds. Pp. 257–281. London: Zed Books.

Pieterse, Jan N. 1995. "Globalization as Hybridization." In *Global Modernities.* Mike Featherstone, Scott Lash, and Roland Robertson, eds. Pp. 45–68. London: Sage.

Povinelli, Elizabeth. 2002. *The Cunning of Recognition: Indigenous Alterities and the Making of Australian Multiculturalism.* Durham, N.C.: Duke University Press.

Pruitt, Lesley, Helen Berents, and Gaye Munro. 2018. "Gender and Age in the Construction of Male Youth in the European Migration 'Crisis.'" *Signs: Journal of Women in Culture and Society* 43(3): 787–709.

Queensland Health. 2012. *Burma: Karen, Chin and Rohingya Ethnicities.* Queensland Government. http://www.health.qld.gov.au/multicultural/health_workers/burmese-preg-prof .pdf (accessed September 15, 2012).

Quijada, David A. 2008. "Marginalisation, Identity Formation, and Empowerment: Youth's Struggles for Self and Social Justice." In *Youth Moves: Identities and Education in Global Perspective.* Nadine Dolby and Fazal Rizvi, eds. Pp. 207–220. London: Routledge.

Rajaram, Prem K. 2002. "Humanitarianism and Representation of the Refugee." *Journal of Refugee Studies* 15(3): 247–264.

Refugee Council of Australia. 2016a. *Australia's Refugee and Humanitarian Program Statistics.* Department of Immigration and Border Protection (DIPB) (2016) Annual Report p. 70. http://www.refugeecouncil.org.au/getfacts/statistics/aust/australias-refugee -humanitarian-program-2/html. (accessed January 17, 2017).

Refugee Council of Australia. 2016b. *Refugee Needs and Trends: A Statistical Snapshot.* http:// www.refugeecouncil.org.au/ourwork/refugee-needs-trends-statistical-snapshot-2 /html. (accessed January 17, 2017).

Reich, David. 2018. *Who We Are and How We Got Here: Ancient DNA and the New Science of the Human Past.* New York: Pantheon.

Reynolds, Tracey. 2010. "Editorial Introduction: Young People, Social Capital and Ethnic Identity." In Young People, Social Capital and Ethnic Identity. Special issue, *Ethnic and Racial Studies* 33(5): 749–760.

Rios-Rojas, Anne. 2011. "Beyond Delinquent Citizenships: Immigrant Youth's (Re)Visions of Citizenship and Belonging in a Globalized World." *Harvard Educational Review* 81(1): 64–94.

Shah, Bindi, Claire Dwyer, and Tariq Modood. 2010. "Explaining Educational Achievement and Career Aspirations Among Young British Pakistanis: Mobilizing 'Ethnic Captial'?" *Sociology* 44(6): 1109–1127.

Shakespeare-Finch, Jane, and Kylie Wickham. 2010. "Adaptation of Sudanese Refugees in an Australian Context: Investigating Helps and Hindrances." *International Migration* 48(1): 23–46.

Sherwood, Harriet, and Shiv Malik. 2014. "Image of Syrian Boy in the Desert Triggers Sympathy—and then Backlash." *Guardian*, February 18. https://www.theguardian.com /world/2014/feb/18/image-syrian-boy-desert-un-refugees-tweet (accessed June 21, 2018).

Simmons, Charlana, Cameron Lewis, and Joanne Larson. 2011. "Narrating Identities: Schools as Touchstones of Endemic Marginalisation." *Anthropology and Education Quarterly* 42(2): 121–133.

Skey, Michael. 2011. *National Belonging and Everyday Life: The Significance of Nationhood in an Uncertain World.* New York: Palgrave Macmillan.

Skrbis, Zlatko, Loretta Baldassar, and Scott Poynting. 2007. "Introduction—Negotiating Belonging: Migration and Generations." In Negotiating Belonging: Migration and Generations. Special issue, *Journal of Intercultural Studies* 28(3): 261–269.

Song, Miri. 2003. *Choosing Ethnic Identity*. Cambridge: Polity Press.

Spivak, Gayatri C. 1988. "Can the Subaltern Speak?" In *Marxism and the Interpretation of Culture*. Cary Nelson and Lawrence Grossberg, eds. Pp. 271–316. Urbana: University of Illinois Press.

———. 1990. *The Post-Colonial Critic: Interviews, Strategies, Dialogues/Gayatri Chakravorty Spivak*, Sarah Harasym, ed. London: Routledge.

STARTTS: NSW Service for the Treatment and Rehabilitation of Torture and Trauma Survivors. 2007. *Oldest Burmese Group: the Karen Community Seeks Australian Haven*. http://www.startts.org.au/default.aspx?id=343 (accessed September 12, 2012).

Tabar, Paul, Greg Noble, and Scott Poynting. 2010. *On Being Lebanese in Australia: Identity, Racism and the Ethnic Field*. Beirut: Institute for Migration Studies and Lebanese American University Press.

Taub, Amanda. 2016. "Behind 2016's Turmoil, a Crisis of White Identity." *New York Times*, November 1. http://www.nytimes.com/2016/11/02/world/americas/brexit-donald-trump-whites.html?_r=0 (accessed November 15, 2016).

Taylor, Charles. 1994. "The Politics of Recognition." In *Multiculturalism: Examining the Politics of Recognition*. Amy Gutmann, ed. Pp. 25–74. Princeton, N.J.: Princeton University Press.

Tharoor, Ishaan. 2016. "A Picture of a Syrian Boy Goes Viral, but the War Goes On." *Washington Post*, August 19, world views. https://www.washingtonpost.com/news/worldviews/wp/2016/08/19/a-picture-of-a-syrian-boy-goes-viral-but-the-war-goes-on/?noredirect=on&utm_term=.716459273002 (accessed June 21, 2018).

Thomas, Paul. 2011. *Youth, Multiculturalism and Social Cohesion*. London: Palgrave Macmillan.

Thompson, Jeremy. 2011. "High Court Scuttles Malaysia Swap Deal." *ABC News*, September 6. http://www.abc.net.au/news/2011-08-31/high-court-rules-on-asylum-seeker-challenge/2864218?&utm_source=amnesty-org-au (accessed October 10, 2011).

Tsolidis, Georgina, and Vikki Pollard. 2009. "Being a 'Wog' in Melbourne: Young People's Self-Fashioning through Discourses of Racism." *Discourse: Studies in the Cultural Politics of Education* 30(4): 427–442.

Turner, Victor. 1995. *The Ritual Process: Structure and Antistructure*. Piscataway, N.J.: Transaction Publishers.

UNESCO. "What Do We Mean by 'Youth'?" In *Learning to Live Together*. United Nations, 2017. http://www.unesco.org/new/en/social-and-human-sciences/themes/youth/youth-definition/ (accessed March 7, 2018)

UNHCR. *Convention and Protocol Relating to the Status of Refugees*. UNHCR: The UN Refugee Agency. http://www.unhcr.org/3b66c2aa10.html (accessed February 29, 2012).

UNICEF. "Childhood Defined." In *Childhood under Threat: The State of the World's Children 2005*. UNICEF, 2004. http://www.unicef.org/sowc05/english/childhooddefined.html (accessed March 7, 2018).

"UN Rights Chief Slams Racist Australia." (2011), *Sydney Morning Herald*, May 26, world sec. http://smh.com.au/world/un-rights-chief-slams-racist-australia-20110526-1f4yy.html#ixzz1NPMlt9i7 (accessed October 5, 2011).

Valentine, Gill, Tracey Skelton, and Deborah Chambers. 1998. "Cool Places: An Introduction to Youth and Youth Cultures." In *Cool Places: Geographies of Youth Cultures*. Tracey Skelton and Gill Valentine, eds. Pp. 1–32. London: Routledge.

Van Meijl, Toon. 2006. "Multiple Identifications and the Dialogical Self: Urban Maori Youngsters and the Cultural Renaissance." *Journal of the Royal Anthropological Institute* 12(4): 917–933.

Vasek, Lanai. 2011. "Immigration Minister Dismisses Detention Concerns." *The Australian*, January 11, the nation sec. http://www.theaustralian.com.au/news/nation/immigration -minister-dismisses-detention-concerns/story-e6frg6nf-1225985239908 (accessed August 1, 2012).

Warren, Andrew, and Rob Evitt. 2010. "Indigenous Hip-Hop: Overcoming Marginality, Encountering Constraints." In Creativity in 'Peripheral Places': Redefining the Creative Industries. Special Issue, *Australian Geographer* 41(1): 141–158.

Webster, Mark. 2017. "Changes to Australian Citizenship-Guide for Applicants." *Acacia Immigration Australia*, April 24. https://www.acacia-au.com/changes-to-australian-citizen ship-guide-for-applicants.php (accessed April 24, 2017).

Weller, Susie. 2010. "Young People's Social Capital: Complex Identities, Dynamic Networks." In Young People, Social Capital and Ethnic Identity. Special issue, *Ethnic and Racial Studies* 33(5): 872–888.

Werbner, Pnina. 1997a. "Essentialising Esssentialism, Essentialising Silence: Ambivalence and Multiplicity in the Constructions of Racism and Ethnicity." In *Debating Cultural Hybridity: Multi-Cultural Identities and the Politics of Anti-Racism*. Pp. 226–254. Pnina Werbner and Tariq Modood, eds. London: Zed Books.

———. 1997b. "Introduction: the Dialectics of Cultural Hybridity." In *Debating Cultural Hybridity: Multi-Cultural Identities and the Politics of Anti-Racism*. Pp. 1–26. Pnina Werbner and Tariq Modood, eds. London: Zed Books.

———. 2013. "Everyday Multiculturalism: Theorizing the Difference between 'Intersectionality' and 'Multiple Identities.'" *Ethnicities* 14 (4): 401–419.

Whyte, Chelsea. 2018. "Children Seized at US Border Will Face Lasting Health Effects." *New Scientist*, June 20. https://www.newscientist.com/article/2172120-children-seized-at-us -border-will-face-lasting-health-effects/ (accessed June 21, 2018).

Willis, Paul E. 1977. *Learning to Labour: How Working Class Kids Get Working Class Jobs*. Farnborough, U.K.: Saxon House.

Wise, Amanda. 2017. "The Long Reach of the Riots: Denying Racism, Forgetting Cronulla." *Journal of Intercultural Studies* 38(3): 255–270.

Wise, Amanda, and Selvaraj Velayutham. 2009. *Everyday Multiculturalism*, edited by Amanda Wise and Slevaraj Velayutham. London: Palgrave Macmillan.

———. 2013. "Conviviality in Everyday Multiculturalism: Some Brief Comparisons Between Singapore and Sydney." *European Journal of Cultural Studies* 17(4): 406–430.

Wulff, Helena. 1995a. "Inter-Racial Friendship: Consuming Youth Styles, Ethnicity and Teenage Femininity in South London." In *Youth Cultures: A Cross-Cultural Perspective*. Vered Amit-Talai and Helena Wulff, eds. Pp. 63–80. London: Routledge.

———. 1995b. "Introducing Youth Culture in its Own Right: The State of the Art and New Possibilities." In *Youth Cultures: A Cross-Cultural Perspective*. Vered Amit-Talai and Helena Wulff, eds. Pp. 1–18. London: Routledge.

Young, Robert. 2006. "The Cultural Politics of Hybridity." In *The Post-Colonial Studies Reader*. 2nd edition. Bill Ashcroft, Gareth Griffiths, and Helen Tiffin, eds. Pp. 158–162. London: Routledge.

Zappala, Gianni, and Stephen Castles. 1999. "Citizenship and Immigration in Australia." *Georgetown Immigration Law Journal* 13(2): 273–316.

INDEX

ABOUT THE AUTHOR

LAURA MORAN is a cultural anthropologist whose current research explores issues of youth identity, the refugee experience, and multiculturalism. She received her Ph.D. from the University of Queensland, holds a master's degree from Oxford University, and lives in the United States.

Available titles in the Rutgers Series in Childhood Studies:

Michelle Ann Abate, *Raising Your Kids Right: Children's Literature and American Political Conservatism*

Michael Bourdillon, Deborah Levison, William Myers, and Ben White, *Rights and Wrongs of Children's Work*

Jane A. Siegel, *Disrupted Childhoods: Children of Women in Prison*

Valerie Leiter, *Their Time Has Come: Youth with Disabilities on the Cusp of Adulthood*

Edward W. Morris, *Learning the Hard Way: Masculinity, Place, and the Gender Gap in Education*

Erin N. Winkler, *Learning Race, Learning Place: Shaping Racial Identities and Ideas in African American Childhoods*

Jenny Huberman, *Ambivalent Encounters: Childhood, Tourism, and Social Change in Banaras, India*

Walter Hamilton, *Children of the Occupation: Japan's Untold Story*

Jon M. Wolseth, *Life on the Malecón: Children and Youth on the Streets of Santo Domingo*

Lisa M. Nunn, *Defining Student Success: The Role of School and Culture*

Vikki S. Katz, *Kids in the Middle: How Children of Immigrants Negotiate Community Interactions for Their Families*

Bambi L. Chapin, *Childhood in a Sri Lankan Village: Shaping Hierarchy and Desire*

David M. Rosen, *Child Soldiers in the Western Imagination: From Patriots to Victims*

Marianne Modica, *Race among Friends: Exploring Race at a Suburban School*

Elzbieta M. Gozdziak, *Trafficked Children and Youth in the United States: Reimagining Survivors*

Pamela Robertson Wojcik, *Fantasies of Neglect: Imagining the Urban Child in American Film and Fiction*

Maria Kromidas, *City Kids: Transforming Racial Baggage*

Ingred A. Nelson, *Why Afterschool Matters*

Jean Marie Hunleth, *Children as Caregivers: The Global Fight against Tuberculosis and HIV in Zambia*

Abby Hardgrove, *Life after Guns: Reciprocity and Respect among Young Men in Liberia*

Michelle J. Bellino, *Youth in Postwar Guatemala: Education and Civic Identity in Transition*

Vera Lopez, *Complicated Lives: Girls, Parents, Drugs, and Juvenile Justice*

Rachel E. Dunifon, *You've Always Been There for Me: Understanding the Lives of Grandchildren Raised by Grandparents*

Cindy Dell Clark, *All Together Now: American Holiday Symbolism among Children and Adults*

Laura Moran, *Belonging and Becoming in a Multicultural World: Refugee Youth and the Pursuit of Identity*